24402
£110.0

452

Furniture at Temple Newsam House and Lotherton Hall

Christopher Gilbert

A catalogue of the Leeds collection
In two volumes

Volume II

Published jointly by the National Art-Collections Fund
and the Leeds Art Collections Fund
1978

©Copyright Christopher Gilbert 1978

Published jointly by the National Art-Collections
Fund and the Leeds Art Collections Fund

Made and printed in Great Britain by
Lund Humphries, Bradford and London
Designed by Godfrey Meekin

ISBN 0 9503334 1 7

CONTENTS
of Volumes I and II

Author's Acknowledgements   6

Preface and List of Guarantors   7

Explanations   8

Introduction. The formation of the collection   11

The Catalogue

  Part One   English furniture (Alphabetical sequence by category)   17
                  Sub-groups:
                      Furniture by Gillows from Parlington   375
                      Ormolu   384
                      Papier-mâché bedroom suite   388
                      The Salt furniture by Marsh and Jones   394
                      Furniture from the Victorian Chapel at Temple Newsam   408
                      Unregistered furniture (Lotherton Chapel and Aberford Almshouses)   412

  Part Two   Continental furniture   417
                      Dutch and Flemish   419
                      French   430
                      Germanic   443
                      Italian   448
                      Portuguese   460

  Part Three Colonial and Oriental furniture   461
                      Cape Colony   463
                      Peruvian   463
                      Chinese   481
                      Japanese   488
                      Indian (Ceylon)   489
                      Java   491
                      Korean   494

  Part Four   Documentary material   497
                      Manuscript designs   499
                      The Pratt collection of furniture trade catalogues and ephemera   503

Index   513

PORTFOLIO STANDS

307 PORTFOLIO STAND
Probably by Gillows, Lancaster
*c.*1820
Mahogany

The H-pattern underframe supports two tapering uprights headed by a cross-bar mounted with a pair of hinged trellis-work flaps which can be raised or lowered by means of an adjustable horse on each side connecting with ratchets on the base runners; the mechanism, operated by a turned bar handle, permits the flaps to fall down to any degree until both become level. The runners terminate in large reeded brass shoes set with swivel castors.
H.109 (43); W.69 (27); D.79 (31).

A portfolio stand of precisely this pattern appears in Gillows' *Estimate Sketch Book* (344/100, p.3037) under 29 Feb. 1820. Since the model was available from stock an attribution to Gillows is acceptable.

The decorative castors are closely similar to examples in a hardware pattern book at the V. & A. (M.60g) of *c.*1815–20.

PROV: Agnes and Norman Lupton Bequest 1953.
[13.392/53]

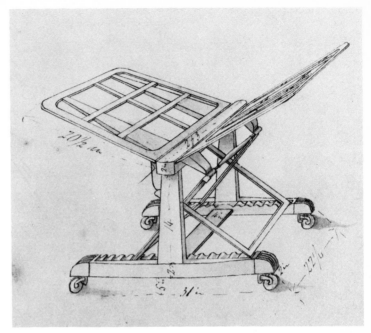

307

307

SCONCES AND GIRANDOLES

308 PAIR OF SCONCES
*c.*1700
Pine

Each is in the form of an enriched baluster with gadrooned shoulders, the upper part carved in high relief with a putto head between paired wings surmounted by a peacock displayed, the middle stage is decorated with a sunk panel edged by open strapwork and the lower part terminates in a foliate pendant; a single candle-branch of scrolled design with acanthus ornament springs from the base of each baluster, the arms being secured by pin-hinges; circular brass drip-pans and nozzles; the gilt surface is embellished with stipple, cross-hatched and diaper patterns.
H.61 (24).

PROV: Given by Mrs A. Cooke in memory of her husband, Alf Cooke and her son Lt. Alfred Cooke, R.A. 1965.
[3.3/65]

309 PAIR OF SCONCES
*c.*1730
Lime

Of carved and gilt scroll design enriched with scales, the upper terminals styled as satyr-heads suspending bunched oak festoons and swags; the bases centre on lion-masks backed by shells, richly ornamented with scrolled acanthus fronds, husks and laurel wreaths held in the lions' jaws which

308

are fitted with ormolu candle-branches having leaf rosette drip-pans and foliate sockets.
H.86 (34); W.56 (22).

The sconces display affinities with the work of James Richards who succeeded Grinling Gibbons as Master Carver to the Crown in 1721 – he ornamented the Royal Barge which William Kent designed for the Prince of Wales in 1732 (*Burlington*, Aug. 1970, pp.488–92, esp. fig.5).

A carved and gilt limewood sconce of virtually identical design was given to the Metropolitan Museum, New York by J. Pierpont Morgan in 1906 and there are eight closely similar examples at Grimsthorpe Castle, Lincs. (illustrated by C. Latham, *In English Homes*, 1904, p.64). This set is fitted with four candle-branches and the oak pendants do not fall in bunches. In view of the possible connection with James

Richards it may be significant that several owners of Grimsthorpe Castle were Lords Chamberlain, an office which entitled the holder to annex, as a perquisite, any surplus furnishing on the monarch's death. Benjamin Goodison has been mentioned in the past as a possible author.

LIT: M. Jourdain and F. Rose, *English Furniture, The Georgian Period*, 1953, p.167, fig.133; *Antique Collector*, April 1953, p.63, repr.

EXH: London, Royal Academy, *English Taste in the 18th Century*, Winter 1955/6 (10).

PROV: Ronald A. Lee (Antiques); bought 1953.   [5/53]

310 PAIR OF GIRANDOLES
*c.*1750
Attributed to Matthias Lock, London
Gilt pine

The fantastic composition is skilfully worked around an inner structure of rococo scrolls and curved brackets to create a flamboyantly asymmetrical, yet delicately balanced system of ornament; the design features a hound pursuing a stag in a setting of lush bullrushes and foliage garlanded with fruit and flowers; the framework supports six spiralling candle-branches enriched with leaves terminating in circular pans with brass liners and sockets of later date; finely tooled, burnished and textured surface. The bullrushes have gilt-iron stalks and the candlearms are reinforced with internal iron rods.
H.211 (83); W.152 (60).

The theme of a dog pursuing game is introduced into several of Matthias Lock's designs; his drawing for a girandole (V. & A., Lock collection, No.2550, see P. Ward-Jackson, *English Furniture Designs of the 18th Century*, 1958, fig.58) features hounds chasing a stag. An article in *Apollo* (q.v.) traces the source of this motif to contemporary engravings by Hubert Gravelot and J. B. Oudry portraying hounds hunting amid bullrushes; the subject also occurs on a table in the manner of Lock sold at Christie's, 16 April 1970, lot 105, repr.

LIT: F. Lenygon, *Decoration in England 1640–1760*, 1914, pl.34; *Apollo*, July 1938, p.14, repr; *D.E.F.*, III, p.52, fig.22; R. Edwards and M. Jourdain, *Georgian Cabinet-Makers*, 1955, fig.73; A. Coleridge, *Chippendale Furniture*, pl.114; C. G. Gilbert, 'The Temple Newsam Suite of early-Georgian Gilt Furniture', *Connoisseur*, Feb. 1968, pp.84–8, fig.5; *Apollo*, Aug. 1969, pp.145–6, fig.24.

EXH: Temple Newsam, *Pictures and Furniture*, 1938 (237).

PROV: Commissioned by Henry Ingram, 7th Viscount Irwin, for the Long Gallery at Temple Newsam; recorded in the

310 (Dust Jacket illustration Vol. I)

1808 inventory '10th Room Picture Gallery First Floor – 2 very large Gerandoles with hunting ornaments with six branches each'; given by the Earl of Halifax 1922.

[1922/F21]

311 PAIR OF GIRANDOLES

*c.*1755
Gilt pine

The shaped reflector plates are set in elaborately carved and tooled frames of scroll design styled with fanciful rococo ornament supported at each side by a gnarled leafy branch inhabited by birds and surmounted by a pelican finial; a narrow ledge below resting on asymmetric scrolls and decorated with fronds, rockwork and falling water, the candle-

branches are now missing. Pine backboards, mirror glass renewed.
H.82 (32½); W.43 (17).

Although genuine enough and of attractive design, the frames are of disappointing quality.

PROV: H. C. Foot (Antiques); bought 1946.   [10.1 & 2/46]

312 SET OF FOUR SCONCES

*c.*1760
Pine

Each is in the form of an eagle displayed, rising from a sea of asymmetric scrolls, flame borders and rococo sprays, gripping, in its beak, a twisted branch embellished with leaf scales and florets, terminating in a brass socket. Carved and gilt pine, the spiralling stems have stiff wire cores bound with felt and an outer gesso shell; the brass nozzles are modern.
H.53 (21).

The set consists of two pairs, each with inward-turned eagle heads; one is definitely of higher quality.

EXH: *Temple Newsam Heirlooms*, 1972 (29).

311

312

PROV: Recorded in the Temple Newsam inventory of 1808 '5th Room 1st Floor – 2 carved and gilt Eagle Gerandoles' and '9th Room Lady Irwin's Dressing room first floor – 2 carved and Gilt Eagle Brackets'; the Temple Newsam sale (Robinson, Fisher & Harding) 26–31 July 1922, lots 410 & 793; Dr. Arthur Robinson of Ilkley; given by Mrs M. B. Cresswell 1963. [3/63]

313 PAIR OF SCONCES
Late 18th century
Cut-glass

Each with three S-scroll cable twist branches springing from metal sockets embraced by a fluted cup, the central arm rising to an apex; the scalloped drip-pans are hung with faceted lustres and the framework is elaborately festooned with wired bead chains and short prismatic drops; attached to the wall by a tubular arm into which the central pendant screws; dished cut-glass back plate.
H.38 (15); W.61 (24).

PROV: Charles Thornton (Antiques) York; bought 1948.
[2/48]

TWO PAIRS OF SCONCES, brass
Supplied by G. F. Bodley, 1877
Under Cat. Nos.530, 531

SCREENS

314 FIRE SCREEN
*c.*1760
Mahogany; pine

The tripod legs are vigorously carved with acanthus fronds headed by anthemion motifs and terminate in rosette whorls; the turned shaft is raised on a bulbous base pierced in the gothic taste and ornamented with husks, leaf-tongues and foliate collars, the pole is capped by a wrythen finial. The panel of *petit-point* wool needlework portrays lovers in a pastoral landscape within a rococo cartouche; mahogany surround; pine support backed by old flock paper, brass ring fitments with steel springs, iron joint-tie underneath,
H.142 (56).

The finial and pole are replacements, one whorl foot has been renewed and the screen may not belong to the stand.

EXH: Temple Newsam, *Thomas Chippendale*, 1951 (87).

PROV: Alfred Jowett; W. Waddingham (Antiques); bought 1957. [11/57]

313

314

315 FIRE SCREEN
c.1765
Mahogany; pine

The splayed tripod legs carved with paired fronds terminate in volute feet; the pole has an elaborately turned bulbous base and urn finial; the panel of *gros* and *petit-point* floral needlework executed in coloured wools and silk is mounted on a pine support framed by a ribbon and rosette moulding; originally backed with green silk; brass ring and screw fitments.
H.147 (58).

The column appears to have been added to the tripod and the screen is probably married to the stand.

PROV: J. J. Wolff (Antiques); bequeathed by Frank Savery 1966.   [1.5/66]

316 PAIR OF POLE SCREENS
c.1790
Mahogany

The swept tripod legs ending in stump feet support a small triangular platform through which the turned, vase-shaped standard is screwed; the adjustable oval screens each frame a panel of cut-paperwork backed by navy-blue paper mounted on white silk; one depicts a basket among garlands, the other exhibits a bird and vase of flowers. The decorative finials and base stretchers are missing.
H.127 (50).

PROV: J. & W. Tweed (Antiques) Bradford; bought 1948.   [4./48]

316

317 HORSE FIRE SCREEN
c.1790–95
Mahogany; rosewood, box

The upright frame, with a serpentine crest rail and cross stretcher, is fitted with a sliding panel held in position by steel springs set into the grooved posts. The stand and slender splayed legs ending in spade toes are of solid mahogany outlined with box corner strings and the wide stretcher is faced with rosewood; the legs are reinforced underneath with original brass spines; lifting knob missing. The screen panel is covered on both sides with a brocaded silk dress fabric dating from *c*.1765–70; the pattern of floral bouquets and and blue meanders suggests French work.
H.89 (35); W.54 (21½).

Originally offered as one of a pair; impressed underneath 'II' and inscribed with the stock number '3399'.

PROV: Lenygon & Morant, Ltd; given by Frank H. Fulford 1939.   [9.42/39]

317

318 FIRE SCREEN (converted into a tripod table)
*c.*1795–1800
Beech; pine

The octagonal screen panel, japanned with an oriental garden scene, has been fitted with cross braces, a catch, and hinged block into which the pillar is socketed, creating a small tip-up table; screw holes on the back show where the ring attachments were fixed. The stand, designed with swept tripod legs ending in blocked toes and a central acorn pendant, supports an amputated hexagonal column, the upper section of which has been renewed; the tripod and shaft are decorated in gold on a black ground with formal husk and rosette patterns in outlined panels.
H.84 (33).

PROV: Frank H. Fulford, Headingley Castle, Leeds; bequeathed by Sir George Martin 1976. [51.30/76]

318

319 SIX-FOLD SCREEN
*c.*1800
Leather, pine

Each panel is mounted on a simple pine framework and edged with a gilt-leather binding secured by brass nails. The leaves are surfaced with a moiré pattern grain and painted in oil colours with rustic farmyard scenes, portraying from left to right: a spaniel; ducks; a guinea fowl; turkey; hen and chicks and a parrot. The leather has been extensively patched and re-backed with canvas; the iron hinges are stamped 'BALDWIN'.
H.213 (84); L335 (132).

PROV: The Gascoigne family; probably the screen recorded in the entrance hall in the Parlington inventory of 1843; Parlington Hall sale (Hollis & Webb, Leeds) 24–29 July 1905, lot 675 (bought in); the Gascoigne gift 1968.
[7.159/68]

BALDWIN

320 PAIR OF POLE SCREENS
By Jennens and Bettridge, Birmingham
*c.*1855
Rosewood and papier-mâché

Each pole, capped by a gadrooned and spired finial, supports a shaped papier-mâché panel framed by a scrolling border patterned with gilt chinoiserie and rococo revival motifs on a black japanned ground; the tripod stands of double-scroll design carved with fronds and incised gilt lines are mounted on triangular bases with volute feet; each tripod centres on a baluster shaft into which the pole section screws; the screen panels display chromo-lithographic pictures of festive peasant girls in idealized landscapes, each is signed 'Jennens & Bettridge' and the brass ring fitments are impressed 'J & B / PATENT / *'.
H.155 (61).

PROV: Bequeathed by Mrs D. U. McGrigor Phillips 1967.
[24.1/67]

321 FOUR-FOLD SCREEN
By E. H. Kahn & Co, London
*c.*1910
Leather; pine

The four painted and gilt-leather panels are mounted on a simple pine framework, each leaf has a serpentine top rail and is edged with gilt-leather binding secured by brass nails. The folds are decorated in oil colours and gold with a series

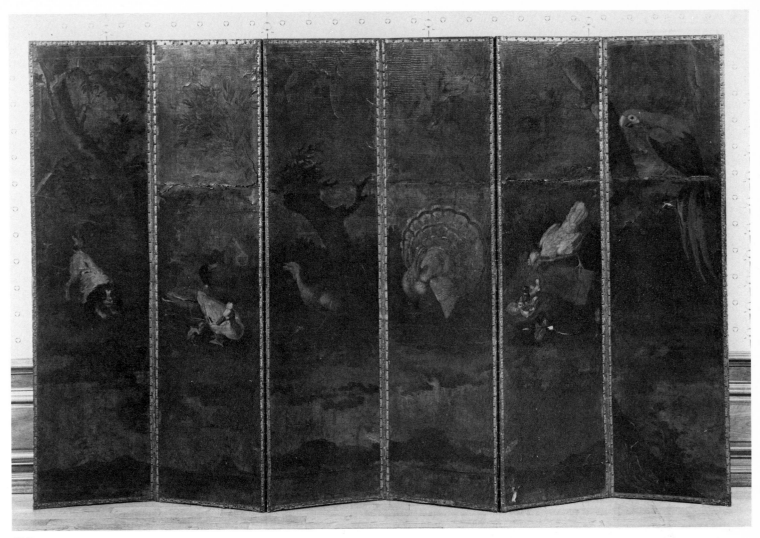

319

of shaped panels bordered by fronds and floral festoons; the large central reserves, headed by curtain drapes, portray idealized rustic scenes with shepherds and shepherdesses, musicians and children; the upper row enclose pastoral landscapes, while the lower panels contain exotic fruit. H.183 (72); W.213 (84).

An ivoret tablet fixed to the back frame is inscribed 'F. W. GREENWOOD & SONS / ART DEALERS & FURNISHERS / 24, STONEGATE YORK'. Artistic leather screens of similar character were made in large numbers around 1900 and marketed under such names as 'Watteau', 'Lancret', 'Fragonard' or 'Boucher' depending on the source of the decorations. E. H. Kahn & Co Ltd of London illustrated this model in their trade catalogue titled *Examples of French Furniture from Louis XIII, XIV, XV, XVI and Empire Periods*, nd. (*c*.1910) p.34, No.K.278 – described as '6 ft. fourfold hand-painted leather screen "Springtime" £20.5.0'. There is a copy of this catalogue in the Pratt collection (32.10/72).

PROV: Given by Lady Martin 1956.   [23/56]

321

SETTEES AND DAY-BEDS
Couches, Sofas, Settles

322–323 DAY-BED AND SOFA
Probably by Philip Guibert, London
*c.*1700–05
Beech, painted black with gilt carvings

Rectangular upholstered backs framed by gadrooned mouldings with scrolled foliate ear-pieces; the day-bed is surmounted by a single and the sofa a triple cresting of scrolled design richly styled with florets, curling fronds and husks on a trellised ground, each centres on a cartouche bearing the cipher 'D.C.L.' with a ducal coronet above; the curved arms, ornamented with gadrooned borders and snail-head terminals, rest on inverted vase-shaped supports; the rectangular seats are raised on eight fluted and tapered legs with square gadrooned shoulders and bases united by a series of nulled oval stretchers supporting low platforms; turned rear legs; bun feet cut at a later date for castors. The backs, squabs, arms and seat rails are stuffed and covered with contemporary floral and arabesque pattern Genoese cut-velvet in crimson, green and cinnamon on a dark-cream satin ground, edged with tasselled fringes. The sofa has two wedge-shaped bolsters and five square cushions (three for the backs and one at either end) the day-bed has two pillows; later green plush behind the backs. Both have been re-railed. P.Macquoid, writing in 1905 (q.v.) referred to the 'long squabs supported on a foundation of cords and sacking', they now rest on fabric stretched over the frame; comparison with photographs reproduced in *The Age of Walnut*, pls.73 & 4 indicate that breadths of material have been re-arranged, evidently when new seat rails were inserted and the fringes either shortened or replaced with piping. These disturbances have unfortunately disfigured the sumptuous countenance of the upholstery.
Sofa: H.110 (43½); W.208 (82); D.71 (28).
Day-bed: H.110 (43½); L.152 (60); W.71 (28).

The monogram 'D.C.L.' proves that the pieces were made after 1694, for Thomas Osborne was not created Duke of Leeds until May 1694, the other letters proclaim his alternative titles Earl of Danby and Marquess of Carmarthen. The Duke built a magnificent palace at Kiveton, Yorkshire between 1697–1705 and these luxurious pieces were presumably intended for that house, the rooms being described in 1724 as 'richly furnished with Damask & Velvet' (*Country Life*, 8 Feb. 1973, p.336). The Duke of Leeds' papers, deposited at the Y.A.S. include a personal account book 1702–15 (D.D.5/39) recording a small but significant entry under 9 Nov. 1703 'Pay'd Gilbert, ye joyner by my Lady Duches's order 2/-'. This craftsman can be plausibly identified as Philip Guibert who, in 1697–8, equipped Windsor Castle and Kensington Palace with opulent furniture. In 1697 he

320

322

supplied 'a couch of carved walnutree, the headboard carved with his Ma'ties cyphers and ornaments belonging to it' for £6, and in the same year 'a fine black soffa of a new fashion, filled up with fine hair, and its cushion filled up with downe, the frieze and cheeks all molded and fringed' for £16. In 1699 he was owed £1,695.5.3 for furnishing his Majesty's bed chamber and dining-room at Windsor and other lodgings. (*D.E.F.*, II, p.251). Guibert (who also spelt his name 'Gibbard' and 'Gilbert') was evidently a prominent upholsterer and the striking analogies between the japanned sofa and couch made for William III and the Duke of Leeds' suite strongly suggest common authorship, there can have been few workshops in London capable of producing such resplendent furniture.

A pictorial equivalent of the day-bed is to be found in a volume titled *Oeuvres Du St D. Marot*, 2nd ed., Amsterdam, 1712, fol.14, where it is portrayed standing in the corner of a room *en suite* with stools having vase-shaped legs connected by hoop stretchers. Daniel Marot, architect and designer, was employed by William III in Holland and England; he could

well have designed the furniture Guibert supplied to the royal palaces.

A velvet of identical pattern covers a chair reproduced by F. Lenygon, *Furniture in England 1660–1760*, 1914, p.33, fig.26. Items from two other late Stuart suites with contemporary cut-velvet upholstery in the Duke of Leeds' collection are illustrated by Macquoid (q.v.). William Thomas owns a gilt mirror frame with a cresting (incorporating the Duke of Leeds' cipher and coronet) of virtually identical pattern to the crestings on this suite.

LIT (only important references are cited):
P. Macquoid, *The Age of Walnut*, 1905, pp.74–9, figs.73 & 4; *Country Life*, 14 July 1906, pp.60–3; 29 May 1920, p.720; 8 Feb. 1973, p.336; C. Latham, *In English Homes*, II, 1907, pp.88–9, repr; *L.A.C.*, No.12 (1950), pp.3–5, repr.; *D.E.F.*, II, p.141 & pl. vii (colour) and III, p.78 & pl. iv (colour); P. Thornton, *Baroque and Rococo Silks*, 1965, pl.107; J. Cornforth & J. Fowler, *English Decoration in the 18th Century*, 1974, p.167, fig.163.

323

323

324

EXH: London, 25 Park Lane, *The Age of Walnut*, 1932 (459) – sofa; London, Royal Academy, *British Art*, 1934 (1514) – sofa; Temple Newsam, *Furniture Upholstery*, 1973 (4) – sofa.

PROV: The 1st Duke of Leeds who owned and furnished grand houses at Wimbledon, Surrey, and Kiveton, York-shire; recorded in an inventory of Hornby Castle, Yorks dated 1839 (Y.A.S. DD5 Box XII) 'Great Hall – 429A Japaned & Gilt Antique Sofa with squab and two bolsters and six pillows covered with embossed Genoa velvet fringed. 330 A Japaned and Gilt Duchesse Chaise Lounge; pillow stuffed and covered en suite'; sold by the Duke of Leeds at Christie's, 10 June 1920, lots 115 & 116; Sir Philip Sassoon; Mrs Hannah Gubbay; Lord Wilton; Frank Partridge & Sons; given by Sir Henry Price 1950.

[11.1 & 2/50]

324 PAIR OF SETTEES
By James Moore, the Younger, to a design by William Kent.
1731
Mahogany; oak, pine

The rectangular backs, composed of three framed panels with leaf and dart mouldings, are surmounted by heavy scrolled pediments enriched with fluting, Vitruvian scrolls and a central shell; the solid wood seats have fluted rails with a pierced apron formed of paired scrolls and acanthus sprays joined by an oak swag; square panelled legs and arms of console design carved with stylized foliage and husks; the front legs lightly stippled. Mahogany with faced oak rails, glue blocks and three under braces of pine; the back treated with a dark wash.
H.129 (51); W.211 (83); D.59 (23).

324

Between 1725 and 1730 Sir John Dutton initiated a general repair and partial refurnishing of his property at Sherborne, Gloucestershire. An account book amongst the Sherborne muniments (G.R.O., D.678, Acc.1790) records under 29 Oct. 1728 'To Mr Kent for his trouble making Plans for me at my Lodge & House £31', proving that the fashionable architect-designer William Kent was concerned with these improvements. Other payments, entered on 2 Nov. 1731, relate to furniture for bedrooms, the drawing room, hall and 'ye Lodge', a two storied building erected in the park about 1650 as a palatial banqueting house. Several items for the Lodge were supplied by James Moore, the Younger, including 'To Mr Moore for 2 Mahogany Settees for ye Dining Room at ye Lodge Carved £30'; these are referred to in an inventory dated 17 April 1740 (D.678/FAM.598) and are evidently the pair now at Temple Newsam. They are based on a design by William Kent published in John Vardy's *Some Designs of Mr Inigo Jones and Mr William Kent*, 1744, pl.42 and it is interesting to recall that between 1723 and 25 James Moore's father had executed Kent's designs for furniture in 'the new apartment at Kensington Palace'. Moore also made '4

Mahogany Stools Carved, for ye Dining Room at ye Lodge £20' which match the settees and were obviously designed by the same hand. One stool and an allied hall chair are reproduced in *Burlington* (q.v.).

Hall settees related to the same design are recorded at Devonshire House (O. Brackett, *Encyclopedia of English Furniture*, 1927, p.165, repr.); Raynham Hall (*Country Life*, 14 Nov. 1925, p.783, repr.) and Houghton Hall (*Country Life Annual*, 1963, p.29, repr.) all houses where William Kent was responsible for internal decorations and remodelling. There is also a set of four at Boughton.

LIT: C. G. Gilbert, 'James Moore, the Younger, and William Kent at Sherborne House', *Burlington*, March 1969, pp. 148–9, figs.51–4; G. Wills, *English Furniture 1550–1760*, 1971, p.157, repr.

PROV: By descent from Sir John Dutton of Sherborne House, Gloucestershire to Lord Sherborne; bought from Leonard Knight, Ltd 1943.   [12/43]

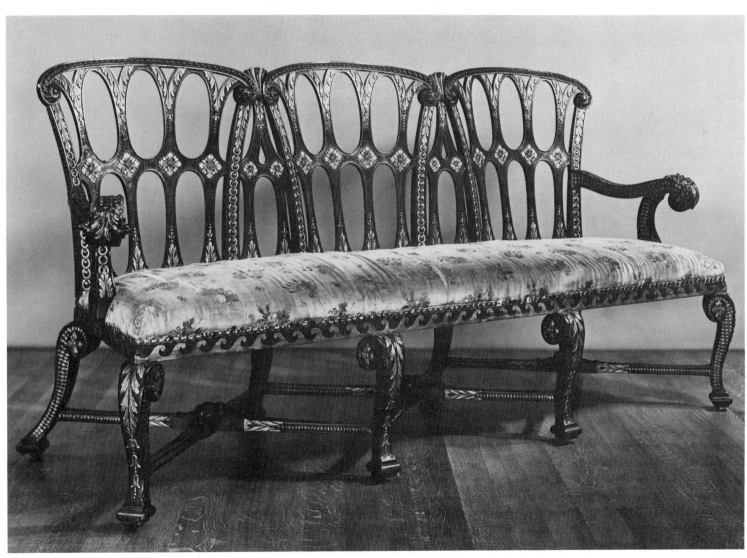

325 SETTEE
c.1735–40
Mahogany, parcel gilt; beech, oak

Of triple chair-back design with gadrooned top rails and scrolled shoulders, the slightly curved backs are pierced with ovals having foliate borders, leaf rosettes at the intersections and chain ornament on the stiles; the arms, terminating in lions'-masks, the scrolled legs and X-shaped stretchers are enriched with scales, acanthus fronds, husks and bosses on a textured ground; the rails are carved with Vitruvian scrolls and the seat is upholstered in cream Chinese silk painted with detached flower sprays; brass nails, castors and tie bars. Mahogany, the inner seat frame and braces beech and oak. The upholstery is contemporary but not original to the settee. H.104 (41); W.202 (79½); D.61 (24).

From a suite consisting of two settees and twelve chairs, the companion settee is now in the V. & A. (W.8–1964) and the chairs were sold at Christie's, 11 Nov. 1971, lot 96. The unusual form suggests this suite may have been designed by an architect.

LIT: O. Brackett, *Encyclopedia of English Furniture*, 1927, p.163, repr; *L.A.C.*, No.55 (1964) p.3. fig.2; *Burlington*, May 1965, p.285 & fig.94; *Furniture History*, I (1965) p.58, pl. x; H. Hayward (ed.) *World Furniture*, 1966, p.129, fig.471 (wrongly credited).

EXH: London, Burlington House, Winter 1927/8 (31).

PROV: Francis North, 1st Earl of Guildford, Wroxton Abbey, Oxfordshire; sold in the 1920s to Rice & Christy, Ltd; Sir John Ward; Christie's, 22 Nov. 1962, lot 42; R. L. Harrington Ltd; J. A. Lewis & Son; bought with the aid of a government grant 1964.   [9/64]

326 SETTEE
c.1745–50
Mahogany; beech, oak

Of triple chair-back form, the hooped uprights enclose slightly hollowed open splats of shell design with interlaced

straps connected to gadrooned shoes; scrolled, outward-curving arms with swept supports raised on six cabriole legs with fronded knees terminating in claw and ball feet at the front, plain with club feet at the rear; the arms and back are embellished in low relief with rococo foliage, husks, C-scrolls and flamework decoration; upholstered seat stuffed over the rails and covered in modern cut-velvet, replacing earlier leather secured with brass nails. Mahogany with beech rails and oak corner struts, the back laminated and veneered. H.96 (38); W.160 (63); D.53 (21).

The pair to this settee was acquired separately by an American collector. They once formed part of a large set, including six chairs, bought from Hotspur, Ltd by G. S. Boston and sold at Sotheby's on 27 June 1974, lot 8, repr. Many virtually identical suites of high quality shell-back seat furniture are known; some differ in the design of the legs, others are parcel-gilt. Three pairs were sold at Sotheby's, 3 June 1977, lots 102–4. The number of extant suites and the existence of modern copies makes them difficult to provenance, but the lot ticket 197 on the underframe of this settee may one day prove helpful.

R. W. Symonds (q.v.) noted examples stamped with the initials 'TT' and 'BR' under a crown which could be significant, for Giles Grendey permitted his journeymen to initial their work and there is at Stourhead a set of standard shell-pattern chairs which may relate to payments to Grendey, including £64 for chairs in 1746. They are in any case all likely to be the product of one large workshop.

LIT: *Apollo*, Nov. 1954, p.275, repr; R. W. Symonds, 'The Chair with a Shell Back', *Antique Collector*, Oct. 1956, pp.177–82, fig.9; *L.A.C.*, No.65 (1969), p.4. fig.2; *L.A.C.*, No.72 (1973), p.30.

PROV: Cecil Millar (Antiques); Hotspur, Ltd; Major Farley; Hotspur, Ltd; bought with the aid of a government grant 1969. [6/69]

327

FOUR SETTEES, gilt and needlework
By James Pascall, London, 1746
Under Cat. No.45 (illustrated)

DAY-BED, gilt and needlework
By James Pascall, London, 1746
Under Cat. No.45 (illustrated)

327 SETTLE
1756
Oak

The back is divided into four upright and three oblong fielded panels, the lower row carved with a formal design of leaved tulips, the upper bearing scrolled stems and foliage centering on vestigial masks; the top rail, decorated with lunettes, is initialled and dated 'H 1756 S', the medial rail is inscribed 'DEUS VIDET Q.N.T.N.L. TAYTA MEAETA' and the stiles bear guilloche enrichment; the back posts are carved at the base with a diapered strapwork pattern and above the arms with a tall frond headed by scrolled ears and corner crestings. Undulating arms on short turned supports; the box seat with a hinged lid, is fronted by three oblong panels embellished with stems supporting palmettes framed by a top rail with scrolling arabesques and tulip heads, guilloche stiles and a fluted bottom rail, plain fielded end panels, board base.
H.140 (55); W.185 (73); D.53 (21).

The settle has a renewed seatboard fitted with butterfly-hinges, the corner lugs are later additions and three of the legs have restored base sections. A blocked mortice slot in the lower back rail and unaligned pegs on the corner posts show that the back panels and seat have been slightly lowered, but the piece should definitely not be condemned as fraudulent. Confirmation of the late date is provided by the diapered strapwork patterns below the arms which are derived from the incised enrichment found on early Georgian gesso furniture, while the traditional ornament displays a degenerate, stereotyped character typical of retarded examples of this style. Settles, too, were among the very last furniture types to express traditional Carolean carving. The regional content is consistent with a north country origin.

The abbreviations 'Q.N.T.N.L' in the Latin and Greek text can be expanded to read 'quae natura tuae nocte latent' and the whole roughly translated as 'God sees those thoughts that lie hid in your soul at night' (Psalm 139). A late seventeenth century settle at Cannon Hall, Barnsley, bears the same text.

LIT: *Burlington,* June 1970, p.399, fig.70.

PROV: At Lotherton in 1905 and recorded in the 1930s inventory as '1 Large Oak Seat'; the Gascoigne gift 1968.
[7.143/68]

328

328 SOFA
*c.*1765
Mahogany; oak

The contoured back and high scroll-over arms are of solid upholstered design and the seat is stuffed over the front rail; the three cabriole forelegs enriched with flamework cabochon motifs on the angular knees and knurled feet are headed by fronded brackets and terminate in leather castors; the three plain rear supports end in stump feet. Oak seat rails united by dipped cross braces, modern corner blocks and upholstery.
H.101 (40); W.201 (79); D.70 (27½).

PROV: Given by Charles Brotherton, Kirkham Abbey, Yorkshire 1939.
[11/39]

SOFA, gilt and tapestry
By Fell and Turton, London, 1771
Under Cat. No. 46 (illustrated)

328

329

329 SOFA
c.1785
Mahogany; oak, beech

The upholstered serpentine back with rounded corners is framed by a fluted surround leading into padded arms with scroll elbows and curvilinear channelled supports; the serpentine seat rail and four straight turned front legs headed by disc paterae are similarly fluted; stump rear legs, the middle pair now missing. Mahogany, backed by an oak seat rail, dipped cross rails and beech corner braces. Recovered in modern brocaded silk.
H.94 (37); W.185 (73); D.71 (28).

PROV: Bought by Sam Wilson from Burgess Hill, Maddox Street, London and entered in his notebook on 9 November 1912 'An old Adam period settee covered in red crimson silk £63'; the Sam Wilson Bequest 1925.   [S.W.224]

330 COUCH
Probably by B. Evans, London
c.1825
Mahogany; ash

Raised on sabre legs with plate castors at the head and turned tapering legs ending in socket castors at the foot; one scrolled arm connected to the back by a padded rest; stuffed-over seat and solid upholstered back covered in a late Victorian chintz printed in reds, blues, greens, yellows and sepia with a design of lanterns, exotic birds and insects, baskets of fruit and floral boughs in the Chinese taste. Elm rails and dipped medial brace.
H.89 (35); L.125 (49); W.53 (21).

Probably supplied with the bed (Cat. No.5) and originally upholstered *en suite* with the hangings and window curtains. A pencilled inscription on the underframe 'Jn Page, Upholsterer, York Dec'r 7th 1880' presumably dates the chintz. For evidence of authorship see Cat. No.5.

330

PROV: By descent from Timothy Hutton of Clifton Castle, Yorkshire to Mrs J. Curzon-Herrick who gave it to Leeds 1963. [23.2/63]

331 SOFA
*c.*1830
Mahogany; beech

Of rectangular design with a solid upholstered back and arms to which fragments of the original glazed cotton cover, roller printed with an arabesque pattern in dark blue on a pale blue ground adhere. The arms are faced with reeded lotus columns capped by circular rosettes and the heavily reeded inverted cone-shaped legs ending in socket castors, are headed by square florets connected by a reeded front rail. Beech carcase with two dipped cross braces, the seat frame united to the end rails by large counter-sunk bolts. The seat would originally have supported a squab with roll bolsters and cushions at each end.
H.94 (37); W.213 (84); D.74 (29).

331

The form and enrichment is closely related to a design in J. C. Loudon's *Encyclopedia of Cottage, Farm and Villa Architecture and Furniture*, 1833, p.1059, fig.1918. The glazed cotton is strikingly similar to some samples of blue printed fabric pasted into Gillows' *Decorators and Upholstery Estimate Book 1817–24* used to cover couches and sofas (Westminster City Library Archives Dept. 344/142, pp.183–6).

PROV: Given by Mrs Blanche Leigh 1937. [1937/F1]

332 SOFA
Mid 19th century
Walnut

The solid upholstered back is framed by a shaped and moulded surround decorated with an acanthus band; the serpentine-fronted seat with rounded ends is stuffed over the rails and outlined by a hollow moulding while the open padded arms enriched with fronds have curving supports and scroll elbows; the four cabriole legs carved in the rococo taste with shells, cabochon motifs and foliage, rest on volute feet. The tapestry back woven in coloured wools on a drab ground centres on a vase of garden flowers surrounded by leafy floral borders, the sprung seat represents a bunch of flowers bordered by garlands.
H.99 (39); W.135 (53); D.61 (24).

PROV: Bought from the Harding Fund 1943. [28/43]

PAIR OF SETTLES, oak
By Atkinson & Barker, Leeds, 1846
Under Cat. No.538 (illustrated)

333 SETTEE
By E. H. Kahn & Co, London
*c.*1900–10
Mahogany; beech

The rectangular padded back and sprung seat are framed by panelled members faced with formalized acanthus fronds, olive sprays and rosettes in cast brass. The arms are supported by seated sphinx figures modelled in brass and the forelegs are designed as monopods mounted with winged lions'-heads and paw feet. The sabre back legs, roll-over top rail and general styling reflect the 'Empire' taste. Covered in pink brocaded silk with a machined trellis pattern.
H.99 (39); W.122 (48); D.54 (21½).

This settee originally formed part of a salon suite of early twentieth century reproduction 'Empire' furniture. An advertisement placed in the *Connoisseur*, Nov. 1903, by George Lawson, 165 High Street, Tunbridge Wells, illustrates a matching armchair from a set comprising 'Settee, Two Arm Chairs, Two small ditto, Table and Clock on pedestal.' An identical suite (pair of armchairs, pair of single chairs and a settee) was sold by Christie's, 9 Dec. 1976, lot 146, repr. The

332

maker was E. H. Kahn & Co, Wholesale Furniture Manufacturer with premises in Charlotte Street and St Andrew's Street, London. One of their trade catalogues titled *Designs of English and French Artistic, Furniture, c.*1908, p.239 shows a closely similar range of seat and cabinet furniture 'in mahogany with ormolu mounts, upholstered in silk tapestry' (Nos. R.996–R.1000).

PROV: Bequeathed by Charles Brotherton, Kirkham Abbey, Yorkshire 1949.   [14.1/49]

334 PAIR OF SOFAS
Probably by Liberty & Co, London
*c.*1905
Oak; beech

In the William and Mary style; of double chair-back design with high wings, scroll-over arms, shaped and valanced seat rails upholstered in pink cotton damask and silk braid, sprung seats each with two squab cushions; short turned and blocked legs with fluted bulbous supports on 'Spanish' feet, the three front legs united by paired scrolls carved with foliage and centering on a vase motif, are connected to the rear legs by turned stretchers; inner frame beech.
H.142 (56); W.137 (54); D. 71 (28).

En suite with a 'reproduction' triple chair-back sofa advertised in a Liberty & Co *Furniture Catalogue* (no.89), of *c.*1905.

LIT: F. Moss, *Pilgrimages to Old Homes*, V, 1910, p.319; repr. (view of the Great Hall).

EXH: *Temple Newsam Heirlooms*, 1972 (40).

333

PROV: Temple Newsam; the Temple Newsam sale (Robinson Fisher & Harding) 26–31 July 1922, lots 1180 & 1181; Colonel F. R. T. Gascoigne, Lotherton Hall; the Gascoigne gift 1968.   [7.137/68]

335 SETTEE
Various dates
Mahogany; pine

The open back, designed as a row of seven Corinthian style pilasters supported on a lattice-work cross tie, is headed by a straight top rail with upward scrolling ends; the chamfered back posts, crest rail, seat frame and L-section front legs are pierced by long slits alternating with carved chinoiserie details; the side and central stretchers are decorated with open lattice panels and S-scrolls, fretted spandrels; the curved arms rest on plain moulded supports. Pine slip seat. Three of the spandrels, the central stretcher and the right-hand arm support have been renewed; the seat frame, originally braced by three cross bars now has a single medial strut and modern corner blocks.
H.100 (39½); W.132 (52); D.49 (19½).

The rather disjointed assembly of decorative elements strongly suggests this settee is a picturesque fake combining old components and new members.

PROV: Dr. Chadwick; Agnes and Norman Lupton Bequest 1953.   [13.378/53]

334

335

SIDEBOARDS AND SIDEBOARD TABLES

336 SIDEBOARD TABLE
*c.*1750
Mahogany; pine, oak

The rectangular top with a reeded edge bordered by box-wood strings is a later replacement; the ends are fitted with extension slides and the frieze contains one long and two narrow drawers with a small corner pot-cupboard on the right-hand side; the front and sides are carved with laurel swags suspended from rings; there are two pairs of scrolled supports at the front headed by fluted blocks, the upper scrolls decorated with fronds and the panelled shafts with scales and money moulding, the back legs carved on one side; volute feet on tablets; original cast-brass drop handles in the rococo taste with oak-pattern rosettes. Pine carcase faced with mahogany, the front rails and drawer linings are of oak, solid mahogany top, slides and legs.
H.87 (34½); W.183 (72); D.86 (34).

There is a virtually identical table at Newby Hall, York-shire, another of similar design from Stanmer House is illustrated by C. Musgrave, *Adam and Hepplewhite Furniture*, 1966, pl.13, a third survives at Euston Hall; G. Jetley advertized an example in *Apollo*, Sept 1947, p.vii and Malletts had a pair formerly at Chiddingstone Castle, Kent, in stock, *Apollo*, March 1945, p. xi. Since the companion examples all bear marble tops it is probable that this table originally supported a slab; the present wooden top dates from the early nineteenth century.

PROV: By descent from the Earls of Lindsey of Uffington House, Lincolnshire to Lady Muriel Barclay-Harvey; bought 1953.   [12.6/53]

337 SIDEBOARD TABLE
Attributed to John Cobb, London
*c.*1767
Mahogany; pine

Plain rectangular top, the frieze carved with hollowed Vitruvian scrolls and corner-leaf motifs; straight term legs with sunk panels containing acanthus and husk pendants; block feet with carved details, open scrolled brackets. Solid mahogany top with veneered edge bedded on pine sleepers, pine corner blocks, medial stretcher and rails faced with mahogany; solid legs. Formerly fitted with a rear brass gallery (not an original feature).
H.89 (35); W.168 (66); D.82 (32½).

A contemporary card tacked to the medial stretcher is inscribed 'For / Sr Geo: Strickland / at Boynton / Yorkshire'.

336

The attribution to John Cobb derives from a series of entries in the pocket account book of Sir George Strickland recording payments to this firm between 1754 and 1773, the largest disbursements being '4 May 1767 a bill to Mr Cobb £251.17.0' and '24 Sept. 1773 a bill to Mr Cobb £49.14.6'; small sums were also paid to Chippendale and Gillows during the same period. The furnishings were probably ordered for an extension to the north front completed about 1770. See Cat. No.347 for details of the companion sideboard pedestal and cellaret. There is an almost identical sideboard table at the National Gallery of Victoria, Melbourne, Australia. Both express, through their carefully studied proportions, restrained decoration and fine craftsmanship, qualities which foreigners particularly admired in English furniture at the time.

LIT: *L.A.C.*, No.14 (1950–1) p.4, repr.

PROV: By descent from Sir George Strickland, 5th Baronet of Boynton to the Rev J. E. Strickland; purchased at the Boynton Hall sale (Henry Spencer, Retford) 21–23 Nov. 1950, lot 290. [42.2/50]

337

337

338 SIDEBOARD
*c.*1790
Mahogany; satinwood, pine, oak, box

Semi-circular top with a frieze tablet and concave centre supported on six Marlbro' legs; veneered mahogany front crossbanded and panelled with satinwood; the legs inlaid with strings and fan medallions; provided with a plain central drawer flanked on the left by a cellaret drawer (gutted) and on the right by a cupboard containing a shallow cutlery drawer, shelved corner cupboards at each end; the wine and cutlery drawers secured by locks, the doors fitted underneath with flush bolts, handles replaced. The top and frieze veneered on to a foundation of pine blocks, back, base and shelves also pine; inner boards, doors and drawer fronts oak; solid mahogany legs.
H.87 (34½); W.244 (96); D.80 (31½).

At this date sideboards were often provided with a gallery formed of brass rods which extended across the back as a prop for displaying plates (see Cat. No.340); this example undoubtedly once had such a structure for, although a strip has been cut off the back, ring scars indicate the position of the posts.

This sideboard is related to, but not directly based on, a composite design by Thomas Shearer in *The Cabinet-Makers' London Book of Prices*, 1788, pl.5. Variously shaped cellaret sideboards fitted with convenient drawers and cupboards proved extremely popular during the late eighteenth century. This piece displays comparatively few decorative refinements and is of only medium provincial quality.

LIT: *Connoisseur*, June 1956, p.10, fig.4; *L.A.C.*, 32–3 (1956), p.27 repr.; C. G. Gilbert, *L.G. & R.F.*, 1972, p.32, repr.

PROV: John Ambler of Killinghall, Yorkshire whose father bought the sideboard prior to 1914; given by Lady Martin through the L.A.C.F. in 1955.   [20.1/55]

339 SIDEBOARD
*c.*1800
Mahogany; pine, oak, satinwood, sycamore, ebony, box

Rectangular, with an elliptical middle containing a shallow drawer with deep drawers on either side; one is fitted as a cellaret with a lift-out box partitioned for nine bottles and three fixed wells behind, the other incorporates a small cutlery drawer; raised on six turned legs ending in peg feet.

338

339

The front is divided by stiles inset with green-stained cockle-shell medallions and decorative stringing, the central drawer bears an octagonal satinwood panel with chequered border; crossbanded top, ivory keyhole surrounds and modern cast-brass ring handles replacing turned wooden knobs. Pine carcase veneered with mahogany, oak drawers and bearers, shaded and stained sycamore inlay, ebony and boxwood strings.
H.95 (37½); W.183 (72); D.76 (30).

A sheet of writing paper bearing the address 'Linden-thorpe, Howland Rd, Leeds' and the following inscription is pasted inside the central drawer 'This Sheraton sideboard was purchased by Dr Hawkyard about 1910. It was presented to the great grandmother of the seller by the Lady St Vincent of that day on her marriage. June 11/24'.

PROV: Said to have been a wedding present from Martha, wife of John, 1st Earl St Vincent (d.1816) to her maid, whose great grand-daughter sold it to Dr Arthur Hawkyard; given by the Misses H. and M. Hawkyard 1956.
[32.1/56]

340 SIDEBOARD
c.1800–5
Mahogany; oak, pine

The unusually deep top with ovolo corners is outlined by a chequered herringbone band between ebony, box and green-stained strings; a ledge at the back, faced as six dummy drawers, has two hinged lids which open to reveal twelve bottle-wells and supports a rear-structure of brass rails and posts headed by urn finials; the frieze drawer, centering on a tablet is flanked by shelved cupboards. The six square tapered legs resting on spade feet and the spandrels are

outlined with string panels. Oak and pine carcase, original lion's-mask ring handles.
W.160 (63); D.84 (33).

This type of sideboard, incorporating a bottle-well beneath a shelf at the back, is a distinctive Scottish design. One of the leading Glasgow firms of the time was Messrs. Cleland and Patterson, an instructive engraving of their wareroom in Trongate was published in *Glasgow Delineated*, 1812.

PROV: By descent from the McGregor family of Glasgow to Dr William McGregor of Leeds; his widow bequeathed the sideboard to Dr D'Arcy Hann who gave it to Leeds 1952.
[10/52]

341 RUNNING SIDEBOARD
Early 19th century
Mahogany; Oak

Three tiers of open shelves bordered on three sides by low galleries and supported at each corner by columns resting on turned feet fitted with high brass socket castors. Oak rails veneered with mahogany.
H.110 (43½); W.125 (49); D.64 (25).

Running sideboards, later known as dinner-wagons, were introduced during the early nineteenth century. George Smith in 1826 stated 'Their use is for the purpose of bringing the dinner at once from the hall into the dining room . . . and likewise for receiving and carrying away such dishes and plates as have been used' and J. C. Loudon writing in 1833 explained that they were 'usually placed in large dining rooms, for the convenience of holding the dessert, the plate, the glasses and other articles in use, while the top of the principal sideboard is covered with articles for display'. Although not recorded in the Temple Newsam inventory of 1808 this is undoubtedly an early example.

340

341

LIT: *Country Life*, 8 Oct. 1904, p.528, repr.

EXH: *Temple Newsam Heirlooms*, 1972 (33).

PROV: The Ingrams of Temple Newsam; bought at the Temple Newsam sale (Robinson, Fisher & Harding) 26–31 July 1922, lot 113.   [1922/F.27]

342 PAIR OF SIDEBOARD TABLES
*c.*1820
Mahogany; pine, ebony

Square top with ovolo corners and crossbanded border between ebony strings, the frieze rails carved with panels of overlaid bay leaves centering on a crossed ribbon, raised on six turned reeded legs headed by ebony insets. Pine top and underframe faced with mahogany, the leg joints incised with Roman numerals I-XII.
H.76 (30); W.158 (62½); D.91 (36).

A photograph of the dining room at Temple Newsam in *Country Life*, 8 Oct. 1904, p.528 shows the corner of a dining table *en suite* with the sideboards.
The London Cabinet Makers' Union Book of Prices (1811, 1824 and 1836), pl. i, illustrates the design and method of framing pier table tops; this pair of sideboards corresponds exactly to plan E. In *The Cabinet Dictionary*, 1803, p.305, Sheraton observes 'The most fashionable sideboards at present are those without cellerets, or any kind of drawer, having massy ornamented legs, and moulded frames'.

EXH: *Temple Newsam Heirlooms*, 1972 (35).

PROV: The Ingrams of Temple Newsam; bought at the Temple Newsam sale (Robinson, Fisher & Harding) 26–31 July 1922, lots 1128 & 1129.   [1922/F.26]

343 SIDEBOARD
By Messrs Norman & Burt, Burgess Hill, Sussex to the design of C. E. Kempe.
1894
Oak

The plinth stage, containing three cupboards with drawers above, supports a rear structure of open and arcaded shelves carved with renaissance ornament, the upper ledge is backed by a screen of linenfold and rose-carved panels topped by a crocheted cornice; of pegged construction with occasional concealed screws. Wrought iron handles and

342

escutcheons with pierced gothic patterns supplied by Thomas Elsley; three and four lever patent locks, the key stamped 'ELSLEY'S GT PORTLAND ST LONDON'. H.371 (146); W.246 (97); D.91 (36).

This sideboard is built into a coved alcove in the dining room at Temple Newsam which, with other interiors, was remodelled in the Elizabethan style by the Hon Mrs E. C. Meynell Ingram under the direction of C. E. Kempe in 1894. The structure was made at the workshops of Norman & Burt, a firm specializing in ecclesiastical and country house commissions. The foreman joiners on this contract were P. J. Court and W. Vine. Several sheets of annotated drawings at large of ornamental details signed 'C. E. Kempe, 28 Nottingham Place' survive at the firm's offices.

C. E. Kempe (1834–1907) worked for G. F. Bodley and with the Morris circle, he eventually founded his own firm and took his nephew W. E. Tower into partnership. Thomas Elsley is recorded in London directories from 1870 until the mid 1930s, the entry for 1895 states 'Elsley, Thomas, art metal worker, 32, Great Portland Street, wholesale cabinet and builders' ironmonger, architectural and decorative metal worker, patentee of the Era mortice lock . . . church furnisher, Smith and stove manufacturer; works, 19, Little Portland Street.'

343

LIT: C. G. Gilbert, 'C. E. Kempe's Staircase and Interiors at Temple Newsam 1894', *L.A.C.*, No.65 (1969), pp.6–11, fig.5.

PROV: Bought as an integral feature of the house 1922.

[1922/F42]

344 SIDEBOARD
1910
Mahogany

The rectangular canted top edged with a ribbon and rosette moulding rests on heavily carved console supports and plain back stays; the elaborate frieze of waved foliate design centering on a large shell set between volutes with a floral apron below, contains two shallow drawers; the panelled consoles are styled with acanthus fronds, money moulding and garlands; enriched side friezes; low platform base. H.96 (38); W.183 (72); D.69 (27).

PROV: Sam Wilson recorded this purchase in July 1910 'A Console Table with fine carving & specially selected mahogany £120'. It was bought from Herbert E. Wheeler, 55, Victoria Street, Westminster – a firm of house decorators and furnishers to whom Sam Wilson paid £1745 for redesigning his dining room at Rutland Lodge, Leeds in

346

345

344

1910. Their charges included £9.15.0 for 'Removing base to Dining room table (console) & putting mahogany platform'; the Sam Wilson Bequest 1925. [S.W.234]

345 SIDEBOARD TABLE
Restyled by Litchfield & Co, London
c.1910
Mahogany; pine

Serpentine fronted; the top is edged with a chain-pattern and the frieze, styled with fluting and oval paterae, centres on a tablet depicting a festooned classical vase; square tapered legs, the visible sides panelled and enriched with husks suspended from tied ribbons; block feet. Pine underframe and medial brace. The frieze has been refaced and embellished at a later date but the carving of the top and legs appears to be original.
H.90 (35½); W.137 (54); D.61 (24).

PROV: This table was bought on 9 Feb. 1910 from Litchfield & Co, Bruton Street, London being recorded in Sam Wilson's notebook as 'An Adams mahogany side table £75.0.0'. This firm of decorators and cabinet makers displayed 'Antiques, Works of Art and Reproductions' in their galleries (advert. *Connoisseur* Sept. 1912) and were typical of many Edwardian dealers who rebuilt and 'beautified' old furniture; the Sam Wilson Bequest 1925.
[S.W.218]

346 SIDEBOARD (DRESSER)
By Heal & Sons, London
Early 20th century
Oak; pine, walnut

Of rectangular design, the back and sides extended to form a low gallery around three sides of the top; fronted by two short above one long drawer with a cupboard enclosed by double doors below. The doors, each formed of three tongue and groove jointed planks backed by batons, are latched by a turn-buckle; arched front stretcher rail. Stained oak with a panelled pine back and baseboard, the drawers have walnut sides and pine bottoms, turned oak knobs. The top rail is impressed behind '297'.
H.99 (39); W.122 (48); D.44 (17½).

No drawings for this oak dresser (model 501) survive, but it was certainly designed by Ambrose Heal. It is first recorded in the firm's 1906 stockbook and illustrated in their *Country Cottage* furniture booklet of 1907. Model 501 was still being made in 1933, but in that year was superseded by a revised version C1090 with different handles, feet and stretcher rail. The stamped No.297 is probably the job number.

PROV: John A. Ellis, Fernleigh, Workington, Cumbria; W. Waters; bought from the Lotherton Endowment Fund 1975. [29/75]

SIDEBOARD-PEDESTALS AND URNS

347 SIDEBOARD-PEDESTAL AND URN
Attributed to John Cobb, London
c.1767
Mahogany; oak, pine

The wrythen, lead-lined vase and cover fitted with a pewter cock, rests on a pedestal of square pillar form ornamented on three sides with a gadrooned border and Vitruvian scrolls; the top drawer contains an open lead-lined box and the lower drawer is divided into six leaded bottle-wells; the central compartment serves as a pot-cupboard having a perforated back; the front is styled as three drawers with astragal panels and brass ring handles (the central pull operates the door catch); the bottom drawer is fitted with a lock and travels on a metal roller set under the front edge. The vase has an inner shell of oak faced with mahogany; the pedestal is mahogany with a veneered pine top, dustboards and base; the drawers have oak bottoms and mahogany sides with pine backboards and bottle divisions.
H.173 (68).

The attribution to John Cobb derives from a series of payments in Sir George Strickland's pocket account book (see Cat. No.337).

Sideboard pedestals were normally supplied in pairs, but no record of the companion has been traced. The stand is *en suite* with the sideboard (Cat. No.337) and an unpublished photograph of the dining room at Boynton Hall shows the matching wine cooler decorated with a band of Vitruvian scrolls; it is of octagonal form with brass bands, a lid, straight term legs and scroll brackets.

LIT: *L.A.C.*, No.14 (1950–1), p.2, repr.

PROV: By descent from Sir George Strickland, 5th Baronet of Boynton to the Rev J. E. Strickland; purchased at the Boynton Hall sale (Henry Spencer, Retford) 21–23 Nov. 1950, lot 74. [42.1/50]

348 PAIR OF SIDEBOARD-PEDESTALS AND URNS
c.1770
Mahogany; oak, pine

The bucket-shaped urns and covers bear carved mouldings and bands of overlapping leaves and are mounted with ormolu husk festoons, paterae and hoops in the neo-classical

347

348

taste; the circular covers rise to inverted leaf-cup finials and are flanked by ormolu scroll handles; square chamfered pedestals, the gadrooned shoulders enriched with anthemion corner mounts and leaf borders; the arcaded panel doors are mounted with ormolu beading, spandrel ornaments, fan paterae and caduceus ornaments. The urns are lead-lined, one being fitted with a conduit (now missing) to discharge water into a lead-lined drawer in the pedestal with a shelf below, the other stand is lined with tin and contains two cast-iron plate racks; the plate-warmer opens by pressing a side-catch, the other pedestal is secured by a lock (replaced) and opens on a steel spring fixed inside the door. Solid mahogany urns of coopered construction, the stems and covers turned; mahogany pedestals with veneered fronts, oak backs and bases, inner structures oak and pine. Incised Roman numerals on carcase I-VIII; impressed location numbers on mounts and hinges. H.183 (72).

There is no apparent reason why the caduceus emblem should figure on dining room furniture. It is defined in Sheraton's *Cabinet Dictionary*, 1803, p.121, as 'A rod entwined at one end by two serpents, in the form of two semi-circles. It was the attribute of Mercury, and was given him, as the story goes, by Apollo, in return for the lyre. This caduceus had also a pair of wings. This rod, according to poetical fiction, is said to perform wonders, as laying men asleep, and even raising the dead. By the two serpents, is represented prudence or wisdom; and by the wings, diligence. When the caduceus is found upon medals, it is a common emblem of peace, prosperity, and good conduct.'

During the 1770s sideboard pedestals and urns became a standard feature of well-appointed dining rooms. Hepple-white's *Guide* contains six designs, dated 1787, for 'Pedestals and Vases' with the following note 'One pedestal serves as a plate-warmer, being provided with racks and a stand for a heater; and is lined with strong tin; the other pedestal is used as a pot-cupboard. The vases may be used to hold water for the use of the butler, or iced water for drinking.' The custom of washing glasses during dinner is cited in George Smith's *Household Furniture*, 1808, p.17.

LIT: *Country Life*, 26 Feb. 1943, p.411 and 22 Sept. 1944, p.519; *Apollo*, Oct. 1943, p.107, repr.; *Connoisseur*, Nov. 1965, p.158, repr.; C. G. Gilbert, *L.G. & R.F.*, 1972, p.27, repr.

PROV: The Earls of Cadogan, Culford Hall, Suffolk; the Culford Hall sale (Messrs George Trollope & Sons) 24–28 Sept. 1934; Frank Partridge & Sons; Colonel Norman Colville, Penheale Manor, Cornwall; Frank Partridge & Sons; bought by the L.A.C.F. with the aid of a contribution from the vendors in memory of Claude A. Partridge 1959.   [L.A.C.F./F.8]

SPINNING-WHEELS

349 SPINNING-WHEEL
By John Planta, Fulneck, nr. Leeds
*c.*1798–1802
Mahogany; oak, box, rosewood, ivory

Rectangular platform with underdrawer, supported on splayed legs joined by cross stretchers centering on an urn-finial, the framework embellished with rosewood cross banding and box strings; the foot treadle operates a brass rimmed single thread wheel, having flyer lead and automatic bobbin traverse with screw tensioning brake device; the mechanical apparatus built up of mahogany, brass and ivory components, an articulated arm supports the turned distaff and the drawer is released by a spring catch. Solid mahogany framework apart from the veneered oak platform;

349

internal joints incised with Roman numerals; one leg repaired with a brass strip, the distaff probably replaced. H. to top of wheel 94 (37).

The drawer, which has been lined with blue paper, contains a printed label 'Made by JOHN PLANTA, / AT / FULNECK, near LEEDS'. Planta's label has been recorded on more than a dozen spinning-wheels of almost identical design although of differing quality; all were intended for spinning flax, the spool dimensions being inadequate for wool yarn. Planta's models incorporated an important technical invention perfected by John Antes of Fulneck in 1793; an example formerly owned by G. E. Blake retained a leaflet in the drawer titled 'Directions / for using / Mr Antes Improved Line-wheel / with sliding Bobbins / Made by Mr John Planta at / Fulneck, near Leeds'. Two upright wheels bearing Planta's label have been reported.

John Planta's parents were members of the Moravian Mission to the Heathens in Jamaica where he was born in 1764; he later emigrated to England and was received into the Moravian community at Fulneck in 1798. No furniture other than spinning-wheels are known to bear his label although records at Fulneck reveal that he made various small articles such as bellows, fire screens, tea-caddies, work boxes and writing tables for members of the community. He died in about 1825.

LIT: C. G. Gilbert, 'John Planta of Fulneck, Yorkshire', *Furniture History*, IV (1970) pp.40–2, pls.25b & 27a; F. Davis, *A Picture History of Furniture*, 1958, pl.347; *Collector's Guide*, Jan. 1971, p.69, repr.; C. G. Gilbert, *L.G.&R.F.*, 1972, p.5, repr.

EXH: Leeds Art Gallery, *English Furniture*, 1930 (92); Temple Newsam, *Yorkshire Furniture*, 1974 (5).

PROV: The spinning-wheel is shown in a portrait of Mrs William Rhodes painted by John Russell in 1802; she lived at Armley House, Leeds with her married daughter Elizabeth Gott and left it to her daughter Abigail; it subsequently passed to her niece Caroline Abigail Mac-Braire and by descent to Frank Gott of Weetwood Garth whose widow bequeathed it to Leeds 1941.   [7.22/41]

349

350 SPINNING-WHEEL (Irish)
By James McCreery & Son, Belfast
c.1891
Birch; mahogany, oak, bog oak

A low Irish wheel for spinning flax, with bobbin lead and separate pulley for driving the spindle and bobbin. The tilted platform, encircled by a shamrock trail and ebonized bead, is raised on three turned legs centering on a black faceted collar with brass studs; the treadle, designed in the shape of an Irish harp is ornamented with shamrocks and tubular brass 'strings'. The mahogany driving wheel with turned spokes, is supported by baluster standards; the flyer and horizontal bobbin mechanism, set between elaborately turned uprights, is fitted with a tension adjustment device worked by a screw handle projecting from the end; the distaff pole is embellished with a small carved bog oak cross and a tower; the cross bar below the spindle bears a brass plaque of the Royal Arms. All the components can be dismantled. Birch, with a mahogany treadle, distaff and wheel, oak hub, applied bog oak carvings.
H.119 (47); W.79 (31); D.33 (13).

350

PROV: Presented to Miss Jessie Lennox on her retirement as Matron of the Belfast Children's Hospital in 1891; given by Mrs K. Turberville 1967. [3.53/67]

350

STANDS AND PEDESTALS

Candle, Tea-Kettle, Urn, What-Nots, Various

351 PAIR OF CANDLESTANDS
*c.*1700–05
Gilt pine and oak

The circular gadrooned tops are supported on tall stems which rest upon open scrolled tripods with gadrooned feet; the columns rise in three stages, the lower, vase-shaped sections being surmounted by tapered triangular pillars with knopped shoulders headed by flared plinths; the stands are styled with raised borders, richly carved acanthus foliage, shells, husks, flowers and formal scroll work with a variety of incised patterns on the gesso surfaces.
H.153 (60½).

In the style of John Pelletier who supplied somewhat similar candle-stands to Hampton Court between 1699 and 1701.

LIT: *L.A.C.*, Nos.32–3 (1955–6), p.31, repr.; *Connoisseur*, June 1956, p.10, fig.2.

PROV: Alexander Keiller, Avebury Manor, Wilts; Sotheby's 21 Jan 1955, lot 174; W. Waddingham (Antiques); bought with the aid of a government grant 1955. [15/55]

The wheel is accompanied by a glass tablet faced with a photograph of the elderly Queen Victoria seated at her spinning-wheel and backed by a trade label 'From JAMES M'CREERY & SON / CARVERS IN IRISH BOG OAK / Spinning Wheel Manufacturers, &c / PATRONIZED BY HER MAJESTY THE QUEEN / The Lord Lieutenant of Ireland / The Presidents of France and U.S.A., &c'.

James McCreery & Son appear in the Belfast trade directories between 1880 and 1920. The directory of 1887 gives their address as 93 & 95 Thorndyke Street and prints an advertisement recording the names of celebrated patrons and a list of prize medal awards.

From
JAMES M'CREERY & SON,
CARVERS IN IRISH BOG OAK,
Spinning Wheel Manufacturers, &c.

PATRONIZED BY HER MAJESTY THE QUEEN.
THE LORD LIEUTENANT OF IRELAND.
THE PRESIDENTS OF FRANCE and U.S.A., &c.

350

352 CANDLESTAND
Early 18th century
Gilt pine and oak

The circular gadrooned top is raised on a triangular pillar divided by ledges into three sections and supported at the base by a high scrolled tripod with paw feet; the tapered lower column, pierced by slits and headed by *lambrequin* motifs, is surmounted by three clustered scrolls of open design enriched with shells and the vase-shaped plinth above is carved with fronds; the whole stand is richly styled with a system of raised borders, acanthus foliage, husks, scrolls and incised patterns on the gesso ground.
H.158 (62½).

PROV: Bought from S. Afia (Antiques) 1944. [16/44]

351

352

353 SET OF FOUR CANDLESTANDS

Probably by James Pascall, London
*c.*1746
Gilt pine; walnut

The shaped triangular platforms are supported on vigorously carved columns with consoles fronted by sculptured female busts with flowing tresses, large shell-like headdresses and terminating below in fanned skirts; the stems are festooned with floral garlands, sheathed in tall rushes and lavishly embellished with leafy scrolls, frills and other rococo motifs; the asymmetrical tripod bases composed of richly layered swirling fronds and wave formations, rest on volute feet. Each stand differs slightly from its companions. Carved in pine on an inner foundation of walnut, the surface detail is executed in the gesso layer; much original gilding survives.
H.126 (49½).

From a set of eight candlestands, the four companions were sold by Mallett & Son to a German collector (*Connoisseur*, June 1961, p.61, repr.). The Gallery at Temple Newsam was furnished by Henry, 7th Viscount Irwin in 1745–6 and a payment in the accounts dated 7 Aug. 1746 to 'James Pascall, London 4 Tables, 2 Settees, etc. £364' was almost certainly for supplying the great needlework and gilt suite (Cat. No.45); a pair of console tables (Cat. No.450) and a pair of side tables (Lenygon, pl.211). The decorative styling of these torchères is so closely allied to carved ornament on the tables as to leave no doubt of their common origin. The female figure-heads relate interestingly to the female terms on a pair of chimneypieces after one of William Kent's designs erected in the Gallery in 1740.

LIT: F. Lenygon, *Furniture in England 1660–1760*, 1914, pl.284; F. Moss, *Pilgrimages to Old Homes*, V, 1910, p.320, repr.; C. G. Gilbert, 'The Temple Newsam Suite of Early-Georgian Gilt Furniture', *Connoisseur*, Feb. 1968, pp.84–8, fig.8; *Connoisseur Year Book*, 1951, p.101, pl. vi.

PROV: Recorded in the Temple Newsam inventory of 1808 '10th Room Picture Gallery First Floor – 8 large carved and gilt candle stands with heads and 8 covers to ditto lined with serge'; removed to Hickleton Hall, Yorkshire in 1922 and sold by Lord Halifax at the Hickleton sale (Hollis & Webb, Leeds) 18–22 March 1947, lots 191–194; W. Waddingham (Antiques); Walter P. Chrysler, Jnr., Warrington, Virginia; Chrysler sale (Parke-Bernet, New York) 29–30 April, 1960, lot 383; Needham (Antiques); Leonard Knight Ltd; John Fowler (Antiques); The Hon Michael Astor, Bruern, Oxford; bought with the aid of a government grant 1976.   [18/76]

354 PAIR OF CANDLESTANDS

*c.*1755–60
Gilt pine and beech

The circular dished tops of turned beech are supported on open triangular shafts formed of clustered scrolls rising in three stages, carved with fronds, shells and garlands; the tripod bases, centering on rococo flamework stumps capped by flowers are similarly styled.
H.107 (42½).

EXH: Temple Newsam, *Pictures and Furniture*, 1938 (244–5).

PROV: Charles Lumb & Sons; Robert Reid, Moor Park, Harrogate; bought 1941.   [13.1/41]

354

353

353 Photographed in its original setting, the Long Gallery, at Temple Newsam House.

355

355 CANDLESTAND
Designed by Thomas Johnson
*c.*1758
Pine

The lobed top is supported on an irregular shaft of clustered columns entwined by a pair of dolphins mounted on an intermediate triangular base of piled rockwork; the open tripod stand of fronded scrolls rises in two stages, the whole structure being lavishly carved in the rococo taste with C-scrolls, flame borders, ridgework, acanthus and grotto formations; the shaft is headed by a pierced bracket fitted with two contorted branches – one single, the other divided – with foliate ormolu nozzles; the stand is partly stained to resemble mahogany and partly painted stone colour. The

branches have an iron core cased in brown composition embellished with stumps and carved pine leaves.
H.157 (62).

This candlestand is from a set of four originally at Hagley Hall, Worcestershire – two are now at the Philadelphia Museum of Art (50–83–3,–4) and one is in the V. & A. (W.9–1950). They correspond closely to a design dated 1756 by Thomas Johnson in *150 New Designs* (1758) pl.13 and freely adapted in the third edition of Chippendale's *Director*, pl. cxiv. There formerly existed at Hagley other carved pieces based on Johnson's designs, Oliver Brackett records having seen the relevant bills (*Thomas Chippendale*, p.53) but they were destroyed by fire in 1925. The candlestands were probably made as well as designed by Thomas Johnson who owned a workshop in the Soho district of London.

LIT (only the more important references are cited): *Country Life*, 16 Jan. 1926, p.85, fig.7; *Apollo*, Jan. 1950, pp.8–10, fig. iv; *L.A.C.*, No.13 (1950), p.8 and No.38 (1957) pp.19–21, repr.; H. Hayward, *Thomas Johnson and English Rococo*, 1964, pp.39–40, pl.39; A. Coleridge, *Chippendale Furniture*, 1968, pp.61–2, fig.107; H. Honour, *Cabinet Makers and Furniture Designers*, 1969, p.120, repr. (colour); G. Wills, *English Furniture 1760–1900*, 1971, p.75, repr.

PROV: By descent from George, 1st Lord Lyttelton of Hagley Hall, Worcestershire to Viscount Cobham; Sotheby's, 17 March 1950, lot 134; bought with the aid of a government grant 1950.   [15/50]

356 PAIR OF CANDLESTANDS
*c.*1760
Mahogany

The frond-carved tripod stands resting on scroll toes support tapered openwork shafts of triangular design with scroll terminals and simple gothic piercing, the shaped platforms are surrounded by fretted galleries.
H.117 (46).

EXH: Temple Newsam, *Thomas Chippendale*, 1951 (100).

PROV: W. Waddingham (Antiques); David Dunstan Schofield Bequest 1962.   [18.27/62]

357 PAIR OF CANDELABRA STANDS
*c.*1770–5
Pine

Of classical tripod form standing on a concave triangular base, the slender ram-headed uprights have lion's-paw feet and the central richly carved and reeded shaft is raised on a small plinth ornamented with goat-heads; the upper stage features three eagles displayed, standing on rocks backed by oak leaf festoons with pairs of entwined serpents and floral swags below; the standard supports a fluted lamp-shaped

355

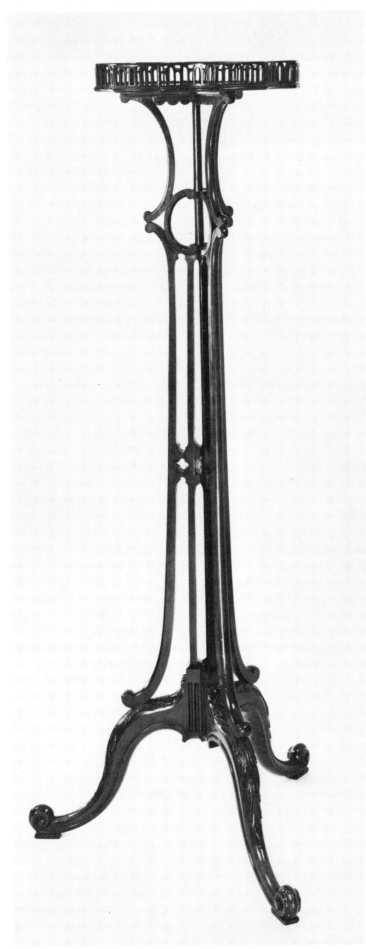

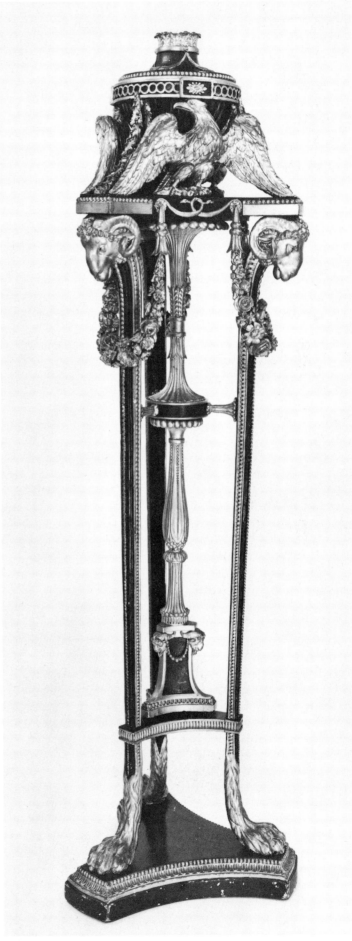

356

357

holder socketed to receive a candelabrum. The whole structure is painted black and gilt. Incised numerals I–III under each base.
H.153 (60½).

The emblems are entirely appropriate to a torchère for, as R. Wittkower demonstrates in 'Eagle & Serpent: A Study in the Migration of Symbols', *Warburg Journal*, II (1938–9), pp.392–425, the eagle is the bird of light and the serpent symbolizes darkness; the emblems therefore represent the triumph of light over the realms of darkness.

LIT: *L.A.C.*, No.22 (1953), pp.2–3, repr.

PROV: By descent from the Earls of Lindsey of Uffington House, Lincolnshire to Lady Muriel Barclay-Harvey (having been saved from the great fire at Uffington in 1904); purchased 1953.   [12.4/53]

358

358 TEA-KETTLE STAND
*c.*1755
Mahogany

Circular dished top raised on a spiral-turned column; the baluster base is ornamented with acanthus leaves, rings and a ribbon and rosette collar; the tripod legs are carved with rococo fronds and terminate in lion's-paw feet.
H.54 (21½); Diam. 53 (14¼).

EXH: Temple Newsam, *Thomas Chippendale*, 1951 (102).

PROV: David Dunstan Schofield Bequest 1962.   [18.19/62]

359 URN STAND
*c.*1760
Mahogany; oak

The square platform is enclosed by a spindle gallery and edged with an escalloped border; the top rests on channelled double-scroll legs united at the break by a flat, pierced cross stretcher centering on a wrythen urn-finial; inward scrolling feet with leaf toes. Mahogany, with oak rails and glue blocks.
H.64 (25); W.33 (13); D.33 (13).

LIT: *Country Life*, 7 Oct. 1933, p.365, fig.7; *D.E.F.*, III, p.157, fig.7; E. T. Joy, *Chippendale*, 1971, p.8, repr.; G. Wills, *English Furniture 1760–1900*, 1971, p.55, fig.42.

EXH: London, Grafton Galleries, *Art Treasures* (B.A.D.A.) 1928 (153).

PROV: Fred Skull, Bassetsbury Manor, Bucks; Christie's 23 April 1952, lot 265; Mallett & Son; Stair & Co; W. Waddingham (Antiques); David Dunstan Schofield Bequest 1962.   [18.17/62]

360 TEA-KETTLE STAND
*c.*1760–65
Mahogany

The octagonal tray-top with a wavy gallery, is set on a fluted column rising from a bulbous gadrooned base; the tripod stand enriched with an egg and dart collar, has splayed moulded legs carved with husk chains headed by shell motifs between opposed C-scrolls and incised panels in the gothic taste; volute feet on pads. The top is a replacement.
H.74 (29); Diam. 30 (11¾).

PROV: J. J. Wolff (Antiques); bequeathed by Frank Savery 1966.   [1.14/66]

359

360

361

361 TEA-KETTLE STAND
*c.*1785
Mahogany, sycamore

The circular, slightly dished top with beaded rim and a slide, is raised on a baluster-turned column embellished with beading, fluting and leaf collars; the triangular base ornamented with inset pen-work roundels and fluting is set on plain tripod legs with pointed toes. Two of the legs have been renewed.
H.67 (26½); Diam. 30 (12).

LIT: *L.A.C.*, No.19 (1952) p.12, repr.

EXH: Temple Newsam, *L.A.C.F. Members Exhibition*, 1952 (220).

PROV: David Dunstan Schofield Bequest 1962.   [18.23/62]

362 URN STAND
*c.*1790 (modified later)
Mahogany; box, elm

The oval top, bordered by a wavy three-ply gallery, is fitted with a slide to set the tea-pot on; the serpentine frieze and square tapered legs are outlined with box corner strings; laminated elm carcase. The legs, which are old but not original to the piece, were once united by an X-member; foot blocks added.
H.71 (28).

PROV: Christie's, 26 Jan 1956, lot 98; bequeathed by Sir George Martin 1976.   [51.16/76]

363 PAIR OF PEDESTALS
*c.*1730
Mahogany; pine, oak

In the form of tapered columns with block capitals and panelled sides supporting applied carved and gilt ornaments; the shafts are fronted by double shells and leaf pendants, and each side is decorated with a long fronded scroll; the capitals

are enhanced with a central foliate rosette and three classical leaf-drops on each side; gilt acanthus moulding below the platform; square base. Mahogany with gilt pine carvings and an oak backboard.
H.122 (48).

A related pair, formerly at Canons Ashby and identical to one depicted in Gainsborough's portrait of Viscountess Ligonier, is owned by John Hunt, Dublin; F. Lenygon, *Furniture in England 1660–1760*, pl.275 illustrates an example with similar carved enrichment, apparently designed by William Kent for Rousham.

PROV: Lady Cunard, Neville Holt, Leicestershire; M. Harris & Sons; bought 1942. [30/42]

364 PAIR OF PEDESTALS
Probably *c*.1775
Mahogany; satinwood

In the form of tapered columns with hexagonal capitals and feet, the bases enriched with a fluted band between guilloche and acanthus mouldings; the ribbed pillar is ornamented with alternating chains of husks and beads featuring acanthus clasps and anthemion terminals; the capitals are divided by acanthus fronds into six paired panels delicately carved with classical urns, oval paterae and formal scrolled foliage, the motifs being festooned with husks and neo-classical detail; the platform has a gadrooned border surrounding a satin-wood panel.
H.116 (45½)

The age of these pedestals has been the subject of much debate. Their inclusion in the *D.E.F.* was for many years accepted as evidence of accredited status, but a failure to trace their provenance beyond 1900, the obvious addition of a fluted capping, the exhibitionist character of the carving and use of dark stain fuelled suspicions they were made for an 'Adam style' Edwardian interior. However, the carving and construction are now believed on excellent authority to be consistent with eighteenth century work, and although lingering doubts remain they deserve, on balance, to be catalogued as of the period.

LIT: *D.E.F.*, III, p.160, fig.7; *Apollo*, Oct. 1943, p.107, repr.

PROV: Acquired about 1900 by A. C. W. Dunn Gardner and bequeathed to his grand-daughter Mrs H. C. Leader of Denston Hall, Suffolk who sold them in 1940 to S. Woolstin (Antiques), Cambridge; Frank Partridge & Sons; bought 1944. [19/44]

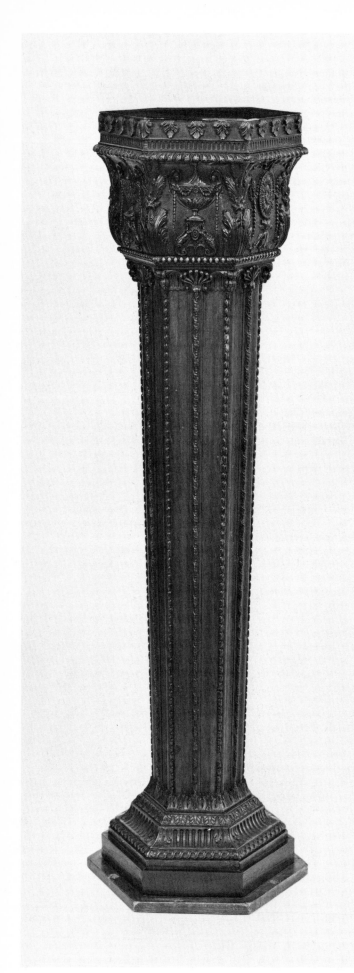

365 PEDESTAL
*c.*1880
Mahogany; walnut, pollard elm, satinwood, pine

Rectangular and tapering; faced in front as an Ionic pilaster with a panel of pollard elm framed by a broad mahogany border and headed by a circular ormolu medallion of a garlanded female figure between Ionic shoulder mounts; the frieze is ornamented around three sides with cast floral swags, pendant torches and corner paterae, with an inlaid dentil cornice above; the shaft and splayed base are richly styled with ormolu mouldings; the top is of serpentine marble; pine carcase. The original medallion was stolen and has been replaced by a replica cast from one of the matching pedestals at the V. & A.
H.112 (44).

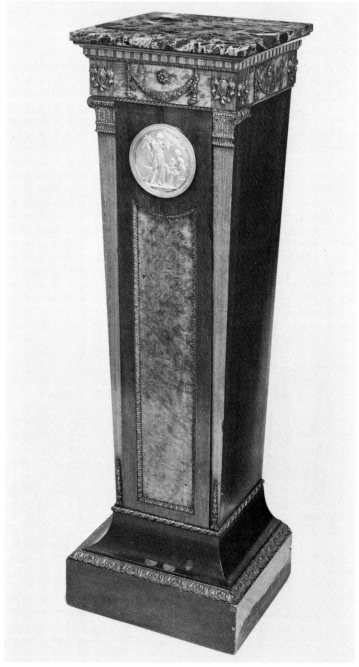

364

365

Many pedestals of virtually identical design were made, usually in pairs; some are set with Wedgwood plaques, others have vase-pattern corner mounts or ebony facings but all six recorded pairs are of matching form. Examples have been noted at the V. & A. (No.59 & A–1917); the Lady Lever Art Gallery (No.H.209); at Euston Hall; in the Gersh collection, New York; in the trade, *e.g. Apollo*, July 1939, p. iv, repr.; and in the sale room, Sotheby Belgravia, 13 Nov. 1974, lot 158. A closely similar Louis XVI style pedestal is illustrated in an anonymous furniture pattern book (design No.224) formerly owned by Marsh, Jones & Cribb of Leeds, now in the V. & A. Library. One design in this volume is dated 1877.

PROV: Bought by Sam Wilson from Thomas Sutton (Antiques) Eastbourne in Nov. 1907 for £50; the Sam Wilson Bequest 1925.　　　　　　　[S.W.336]

366 PEDESTAL
By Gillow & Co, Lancaster
1907
Walnut; satinwood, mahogany, pine

The circular column is divided by fluted pilasters into three sunk panels inlaid with husk chains suspended from tied ribbons; the carved capitals, mounted with cast brass Ionic scrolls linked by swags, support a cornice inlaid with a key pattern, ringed by brass mouldings and set with three cherub-head mounts; the base is enriched with three fan paterae and raised on squat lion's-paw legs of cast brass, serpentine marble capping slab. Veneered on to a pine foundation.
H.118 (46½).

PROV: Bought by Sam Wilson from Gillow & Co in 1907 for the drawing room at Rutland Lodge, Leeds and entered in his notebook under July 1907 '1 Inlaid Marqueterie Pedestal £25'; the Sam Wilson Bequest 1925. [S.W.335]

367 PAIR OF PEDESTALS
*c.*1910
Walnut

The fluted columns are headed by egg and dart collars with a reeded band tied by crossed ribbons at the base; the spreading feet ringed by acanthus mouldings are set on low plinth blocks.
H.106 (42).

PROV: Acquired by Sam Wilson for Rutland Lodge, Leeds to display bronze statuettes; the Sam Wilson Bequest 1925.　　　　　　　[S.W.333]

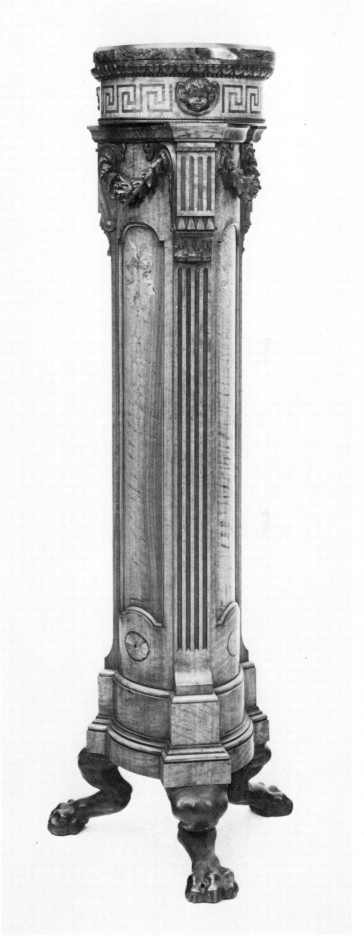

366

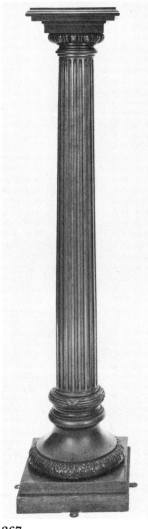

367

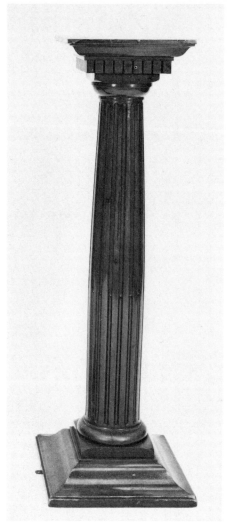

368

368 PAIR OF PEDESTALS
By Marsh, Jones and Cribb, Leeds
1913
Mahogany

The square tops designed with a dentil cornice are set on fluted columns styled with cabling and a bold *entasis* profile; the turned shafts are raised on square splayed bases.
H.91 (36).

PROV: Bought by Sam Wilson for Rutland Lodge, Leeds; in Feb. 1913 he paid Marsh Jones & Cribb £15.10.0 for the pair which were commissioned to display a pair of bronze statuettes by Sir Alfred Gilbert; the Sam Wilson Bequest 1925.　　　　　　　　　　　　　　[S.W.334]

369 PAIR OF PEDESTALS
Early 20th century
Walnut; pine, mahogany

In the form of square tapered columns raised on plinth blocks, the shafts are carved on each side with shallow cabled flutes headed by cup hollows with tablets above; the inner structures are of pine and mahogany.
H.122 (48).

PROV: Bought 1942.　　　　　　　　　　　[29.1&2/42]

PORTFOLIO STAND, mahogany
By Gillows, Lancaster, *c*.1820
Under Cat. No.307 (illustrated)

TOWEL HORSE, papier-mâché
Birmingham, *c*.1851
Under Cat. No.521 (illustrated)

WHAT-NOT, papier-mâché
Birmingham, *c*.1851
Under Cat. No. 519 (illustrated)

STOOLS

370 STOOL
17th century, perhaps third quarter
Oak

The rectangular moulded top is raised on splayed block turned legs of slightly bulbous cup and cover form, each carved with a pair of ribbed acanthus fronds; the rails are decorated with stylized floral lunettes and spandrel ornaments with stamped enrichment and a moulded lower edge; channelled stretchers, turned feet, pegged construction.
H.59 (23); W.47 (18¼); D.26 (10½).

One stretcher renewed, local restoration to the top and base blocks of one leg.

PROV: S. W. Wolsey (Antiques); Hamilton Smith; P. H. Gillingham (Antiques); bought 1972.　　　　[25/72]

370

371 STOOL
17th century, probably second half
Oak

The rectangular moulded top is raised on four well splayed block turned legs of Tuscan column form with ringed tops and necked bases united by moulded rails and plain stretchers; pegged construction.
H.54 (21½); W.49 (19¼); D.34 (13½).

PROV: Maxwell Joseph; Christie's, 19 Dec. 1969, lot 145; bought from the Oxley Bequest Fund 1969.　　[29/69]

371

372 SET OF SIX STOOLS
c.1700
Gilt pine; beech, oak

There are two long and four short stools of oblong design, stuffed over the rails and covered in red velvet secured by gimp; the bold lion's-paw legs are fronded at the knees and edged with fur; the base stretchers, enriched with ribbon twist, form rectangular frames with moulded inner borders, the front and side panels being filled with an elaborate openwork system of scrolling acanthus stems and flowers (of slightly variant design) centering on a palmette; the rear stretcher and backs are plain. Carved pine with beech legs and oak rails, composition corner fronds, pegged construction; formerly covered in red leather with traces of red velvet underneath.
H.46 (18); W.48 (19); L.74 (29) and 122 (48).

Window stools of this design are not common; there is a comparable set at Drumlanrig Castle, Scotland, (*Country*

372

Life, 8 Sept. 1960, p.58) and another at Hardwick Hall (P. Macquoid, *Age of Walnut*, 1905, p.68, fig,63). They bear an interesting stylistic relationship to the pierced foliate balustrades of some late seventeenth century staircases.

LIT: *Country Life*, 13 Jan. 1912, p.58, repr.

PROV: Lord Ebury, Moor Park, Herts; Dower House Antiques; bought 1956.   [15/56]

373 STOOL
*c.*1730–40
Walnut; oak, pine

Of rectangular form with veneered, slightly shaped rails and a corner moulding around the top; the cabriole legs, carved with a shell and leaf-drop motif, terminate in club feet; the pine slip seat is upholstered in contemporary wool needlework worked in tent-stitch with a colourful design of a parrot surrounded by garden flowers on a yellow ground. H.44 (17½); W.61 (24); D.51 (20).

The seat rail bears a Newcastle-upon-Tyne furniture depository label inscribed 'Langstaff'?

EXH: Temple Newsam, *Thomas Chippendale*, 1951 (101).

PROV: David Dunstan Schofield Bequest 1962.   [18.26/62]

373

374

374 CLOSE STOOL
*c.*1755
Walnut; oak

The rectangular seat has plain rails supported on enriched cabriole legs ending in fronded volutes; there are deep, elaborately shaped aprons on four sides, those at the front and ends being carved with a lively rococo design of leafy C-scrolls and flame borders merging with acanthus foliage and strap patterns on the legs; plain rear apron. The loose seat covered in blue damask is a modern replacement, plugged slots prove the former seat was hinged and an early red-flock lining paper indicates the depth (6 in.) of the original internal box compartment which held a pan. Oak corner blocks. Many close stools were similarly modified when water closets came into general use.
H.43 (17); W.53 (21); D.39 (15½).

LIT: *Connoisseur*, Dec. 1960, p. xx, repr.; *Burlington*, July 1966, p.373, fig.52.

PROV: Paul Smith (Antiques) Ludlow; J. E. Bulmer; Hotspur, Ltd; bought 1966.   [3/66]

375 STOOL
After a design by C. H. Tatham
*c.*1800
Marbled beech; mahogany

The massive rectangular legs, designed as tapering fluted columns, are headed by detached roundels enclosing florets and terminate in block feet; the seat is carved to simulate fringed drapery falling over the sides in folds and all visible surfaces are painted to simulate yellow Siena marble with

375

purple and grey mottling. The original finish was found beneath a later coat of white paint with gilt details. Beech with a mahogany seat board.
H.46 (18); W.62 (24½); D.47 (18½).

The design is taken from an etching in C. H. Tatham's *Ancient Ornamental Architecture Drawn from Originals in Rome*, 1799, pl.46. The plate, dated 1798, is titled 'Antique Seats of white marble from Originals at Rome' and, apart from a base board and slightly different floret motif, it provides an exact source for the stool as executed, including the simulated marble finish. A pair to this stool was acquired by the V. & A. (W.2–1975).

LIT: *Antique Collector*, Dec. 1962, p.236, repr.; *Country Life*, 30 Jan. 1975, p.257, fig.6.

PROV: By descent from Sir Richard Neave (d.1814) of Dagenham Park, Essex to Lady Arundel Neave; Mrs C. G.

Lancaster, Hasley Court, Oxfordshire; Christie's, 12 Dec. 1974, lot 32 (one of a pair); Ronald A. Lee (Antiques); bought from the Harding Fund 1975. [2/75]

376 STOOL
By Morel and Seddon to the design of A. W. N. Pugin (the Younger)
1827–8
Oak

The squared legs and seat rails are of pollard oak faced with gothic panels and headed by sunk quatrefoils centering on florets; each side is designed as an equilateral arch formed by deep spandrels carved with seaweed and ripple leaf foliage in the style of about 1300; block moulded feet. The drop seat has been recovered in an antique green pressed velvet designed by G. F. Bodley in 1877 for the private chapel at Temple Newsam (Cat. No.484). The seat rail is branded 'WINDSOR CASTLE ROOM 186' with a crown between 'VR', the date '1866' and a second impressed crown.
H.36 (14½); W.43 (17); D.43 (17).

From a set of twenty-eight stools listed in Morel's Estimate for Furnishing the Gallery at Windsor Castle '28 window seats of oak, ornamented to correspond with the banquets, stuffed and covered in suit'. Deliveries were made on 4 Oct. 1827 and later, each frame cost £25 and on 28 Feb. 1828 twenty-six seats were supplied each costing £3.1.6. Two of the stools are visible in a lithograph of the Gallery at Windsor by Joseph Nash, published in 1848. The brand mark shows that when the inventory of 1866 was taken this example stood in the Beaufette Room – an octagonal ante-room in the

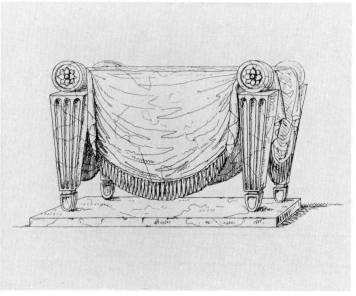

375

Brunswick Tower. Several of the stools remaining at Windsor preserve their original wool tapestry covers woven with a neo-classical pattern of a central rosette surrounded by a band of Vitruvian scroll work and a stylized outer ring of alternating anthemion and acanthus leaves detailed in cream and gold on a scarlet ground. A number of stools have been dispersed: Robert Mopherson owns one and Christopher Gibbs had another in stock in 1972. In his notes for an uncompleted autobiography, the younger Pugin stated that the designs he made for Windsor Castle included 'the Long Gallery' and that he supervised the making of the furniture in Morel and Seddon's workshop in Aldersgate Street.

LIT: D. Linstrum, 'Pugin Furniture at Lotherton', *L.A.C.*, No.70 (1972) pp.26–9, figs.2 & 3; G. de Bellaigue and P. Kirkham, 'George IV and the Furnishing of Windsor Castle', *Furniture History*, VIII (1972) pp.16 & 27, pl.10a (the authors cite the full archive references for the quotations above).

PROV: Ordered by George IV for the Gallery at Windsor Castle; Christopher Gibbs, Ltd; bought 1971.   [15/71]

WINDSOR CASTLF V⊕R ROOM 186 1866

²/₅th actual size

377

377 STOOL

By Josiah Wedgwood & Sons, Stoke on Trent
1875
Earthenware, decorated with coloured glazes

Of square form, the pottery body moulded and coloured to simulate carved wood and upholstery; the brown cruciform pattern frame is enriched with guilloche, fluting and naturalistic reliefs; the royal blue seat and drapes are set with gold buttons, braid and tasselled cords while the inside, corner lappetes and bun feet are covered with brown glaze, pink touches. Impressed 'WEDGWOOD' (twice) and the date code 'HID' for 1875.
H.46 (18); W.33 (13); D.33 (13).

This stool, marketed as a garden seat, was available in various hues priced in 1875 at 63/–; it does not feature in the firm's catalogues but there are two coloured drawings of this model in the Majolica Pattern Book in the Wedgwood archive at Barlaston. One is inscribed '1740 Garden Seat, Cushion in green with orange Buttons, inside all mixed brown finished in one oven fire'; the other, numbered M 1739, is similarly inscribed.

Wooden stools of comparable design are rare, but the prototype is illustrated in *Verscheyden Schrynwerk* published by P. Vredeman de Vries in 1630, pl.16.

LIT: *Collector's Guide*, Jan. 1971, p.67, repr.

PROV: Sylvia Head (Antiques); bought 1969.   [24/69]

377

378 PAIR OF STOOLS
By Liberty & Co, London
*c.*1900
Oak, beech, mahogany

Hollow, D-shaped seats on three splayed legs with pointed toes and revealed joints tightened by wedges; oak seats, one raised on mahogany legs, the other has one oak and two beech legs; coated with dark stain.
H.35 (14); W.35 (14); D.28 (11).

A small white enamel plaque inscribed 'LIBERTY & Co / LONDON' is screwed beneath one of the seats which also bears the impressed name 'J. WRIGHT' – presumably the craftsman who made this stool and possibly an employee of B. North & Sons or William Birch Ltd, High Wycombe, who executed large orders for Liberty's who did not own their own furniture workshops. North's *Furniture Catalogue*, 1915 illustrates an almost identical stool, p.60, No.3016. The stool is very closely modelled on an ancient Egyptian original in the British Museum (No.2481) and was marketed as the 'Thebes' stool featuring in Liberty's *Yule-tide Gift Catalogues* between *c.*1905 and 1912 under the section 'Artistic Furniture'. Models were advertised in mahogany or oak, priced 17/6d. It is an excellent example of Liberty's inexpensive trendy furniture, successfully blending utility with the curvilinear impulses of the Art Nouveau style. An identical specimen was bought in Paris by the Trondheim Museum, Norway, from S. Bing's fashionable 'Maison de l'Art Nouveau' in 1896. Another example bearing the Registration Number 16674 proves that this design was registered by Liberty's in 1884. Relevant documentation at the Patent Office includes a neat sketch of the stool and a plan of the seat.

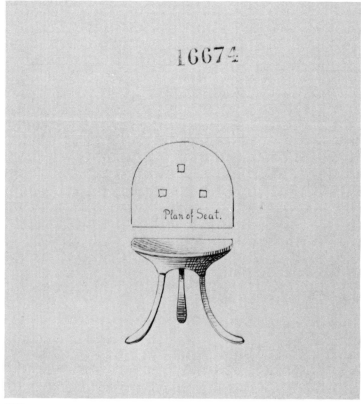

378

LIT: *Collectors Guide*, Jan. 1971, p.66, repr.; C. G. Gilbert, 'A "Thebes" Stool by Liberty & Co *c.*1900', *Burlington*, Dec. 1971, p.741, fig.53.

PROV: Ordered by Major and Mrs Robert Dunbar Sinclair-Wemyss, Wedderburn Castle, Berwickshire, Scotland, from a trade advertisement about 1900; the stools served in the drawing room as seats for their daughters to whom they passed by descent; purchased from Mrs N. Barstow and Mrs J. E. Arbuthnot 1970. [18/70]

378

SWAGS

379 PAIR OF SWAGS
Late 17th century
Oak; pine

Straight, asymmetric pendants of massed fruit and foliage falling from tied ribbons and terminating in bows with festoons of drapery and diminishing husks below. Carved in oak on a pine foundation, the ribbons, drapery and local restoration executed in pine.
H.168 (66).

These swags are two from a set of four found in the stables at Temple Newsam and reused to decorate the South East room which was remodelled as a library in the early Georgian style by Lenygon and Morant in 1912 after designs by Freeman Smith to whom the other pair was given. They flanked the large book recess prior to being removed and stripped of green paint in 1938.

PROV: Temple Newsam; given by the Earl of Halifax 1922.
[1922/F49]

380 PAIR OF SWAGS
*c.*1730
Lime

Two asymmetric pendants of carved fruit, flowers and foliage falling in three clusters from openwork bows with intertwining stems and twisted ribbons.
H.178 (70) and 180 (71).

These swags were painted and installed over the chimney-piece in the South East room when it was remodelled as a library in the early Georgian style by Lenygon and Morant in 1912. The green paint was stripped in 1938.

PROV: Temple Newsam; given by the Earl of Halifax 1922.
[1922/F16]

381 PAIR OF SWAGS
By W. G. Rogers, London
*c.*1850
Fruitwood

Two asymmetrical festoons of clustered flowers, fruit and foliage suspended from laurel sprays; each pendant is carved in two sections reinforced by a metal back strip; the ornament includes fir-cones, ears of wheat, apples, plums, cherries, strawberries, pods, nuts and various blooms.
H.137 (54).

Impressed on the back 'W. G. ROGERS' (one swag is stamped twice). W. G. Rogers (1792–1875) and his son were the leading figures in the Victorian carving revival. The father was an expert on Grinling Gibbons and restored many of his carvings; his own creations, which are of the highest quality, often pass for seventeenth century work. In a pamphlet titled *A List of Carvings and other Works of Art collected by W. G. Rogers*, 1854, Nos.37, 42, 43, 44, & 45 are 'drops of fruit and flowers'.

LIT: *Country Life*, 27 Dec. 1946, p.1264, repr. and 7 Feb. 1947, p.339; G. W. Beard, *Georgian Craftsmen*, 1966, p.181.

PROV: Bought from F. W. Greenwood & Son, York 1943.
[10/43]

W G ROGERS

380

381

382

curving stilts supported on a stepped rack, the top can thus be adjusted at different heights and angles. The drop-front pulls forward on divided legs to reveal a sloping, cloth-covered slide with dished finger grips and a partitioned well below; a small tray divided for writing materials swings out from the side. The table has a simply moulded top with holes to receive a bar rest, straight chamfered legs and deep rails. The fall-front is released by brass press studs, the ornate key escutcheon, loop handle and lock are not original. Built of solid mahogany with internal oak structures, a mahogany drawer and some repairs in beech.
H.71 (28) rising to 157 (62); W.99 (39); D.66 (26) extended 114 (45).

Tables of this design could be used in either a sitting or standing position and were often used in libraries. This model is scaled to take the largest double-elephant size drawing paper or folios.

PROV: Beevers & Shaw (Antiques), Huddersfield; given by Mrs Margaret Newton in memory of her husband 1965.
[16/65]

TABLES, ARTISTS'

382 ARTIST'S TABLE
*c.*1765
Mahogany; oak, beech

The rectangular double-rising top has two folding leaves; the upper flap is backed by a horse engaging a ratchet on the underframe which can itself be elevated by means of two

TABLES, CARD AND GAMES

383 CARD TABLE
*c.*1715
Laburnum and walnut; pine, beech, mahogany

383

PROV: Frank Partridge & Sons; Colonel N. R. Colville, Penheale Manor, Cornwall; private collection; Phillips of Hitchen; bought from the Lady Martin Bequest Fund 1969.   [14/69]

384 CARD TABLE
*c.*1730
Mahogany

Shaped folding top supported when open by both rear legs which swing outwards on oak hinges; the apron contains a drawer grooved for inserting partitions; cabriole legs on club feet. Front edge of the drawer neatly incised with initials 'I.A' (presumably the original owner). Oak carcase, the curved front and sides veneered with mahogany, pine drawer linings with dovetailed joints. Stamped brass drawer handle renewed. The top is abnormally thin for a card table because it has not been dished with counter wells.
H.71 (28); W.61 (24); D.34 (13½).

EXH: Leeds Art Gallery, *English Furniture*, 1930 (22).

PROV: David Dunstan Schofield Bequest 1962.   [18.18/62]

Rectangular folding top with circular corners dished for candlesticks and oval counter wells, the flap is supported when open by one rear leg which pivots on a beech hinge; the top is veneered in quartered laburnum with a narrow border of chequered strings, the beech fly-rail is crudely painted with black stripes to simulate the vivid figure of the veneered frieze; raised on straight walnut legs headed by lappets ending in club feet; the top is covered with modern green velvet bordered by a silver galoon. Pine carcase, beech fly and outer back rails, mahogany counter wells probably renewed.
H.74 (29); W.86 (34); D.43 (17).

LIT: *D.E.F.*, III, p.196, pl.12.

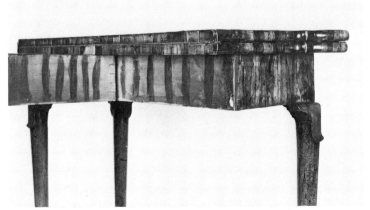

383

384

385

385 CARD TABLE
*c.*1740
Mahogany; oak, beech

Rectangular folding top lined with baize, the square corner lugs dished for candlesticks, one rear leg swings out to support the flap; the front cabrioles, carved on the knees with acanthus sprays, end in claw and ball feet, plain rear cabrioles on pad feet; the inner back rail was formerly fitted with a small drawer for cards. Solid mahogany top and legs, the frieze veneered onto oak, beech fly and back rails reinforced at a later date.
H.73 (28¾); W.84 (33); D.41 (16¼).

PROV: Agnes and Norman Lupton Bequest 1953.
[13.375/53]

386 CARD TABLE
*c.*1745 (modified)
Mahogany; oak

The square fold-over top with lugged corners is supported when open on a concertina underframe grooved for a sliding board; the cabriole front legs, carved with dart and acanthus volute ornaments, end in claw and ball feet; straight turned rear legs headed by lappets with pad feet; the frieze folds on iron hinges stamped 'H. TIBATS'.
H.72 (28½); W.91 (36); D.44 (17½).

Concertina-action card tables were always made with matching legs; the simply styled back pair on this table are modern. Edwardian dealers often cannibalized antique furniture to make up new stock; in this case the original back legs were probably built into another card table, but they were replaced by an incongrous set reproducing the style of an earlier period. A note on hinges signed by Tibats appeared in *Furniture History*, II (1966), pp.44–5.

H TIBATS

PROV: The acquisition is recorded in Sam Wilson's notebook under 25 Nov. 1907 'Fine Old Chippendale Card Table with claw & ball feet. Thomas Sutton, Eastbourne £22'; the Sam Wilson Bequest 1925.   [S.W.229]

387 CARD TABLE
*c.*1780
Mahogany; oak, pine, beech

Serpentine folding top lined with green baize, the fluted frieze and rounded peninsular corners carved with oval paterae; raised on four straight chamfered legs of shaped section headed by small leafy brackets; one rear leg, secured by a wooden catch, swings out to support the hinged flap. The upper leaf is veneered on to a pine panel framed in mahogany, lower leaf pine with oak side rails and a mahogany surround; laminated oak frieze and corner blocks faced with mahogany; veneered beech gate and back bars.
H.74 (29); W.86 (34); D.43 (17).

LIT: C. G. Gilbert, *L.G. & R.F.*, 1972, p.29, repr.

EXH: Temple Newsam, *Thomas Chippendale*, 1951 (99).

PROV: H. B. L. Hughes; the David Dunstan Schofield Bequest 1962.   [18.24/62]

387

388 PAIR OF CARD TABLES
*c.*1795
Satinwood; mahogany, pine, beech

Circular folding top lined with original green baize, both rear legs swing out on beech fly-rails to support the flap; the top and frieze veneered with satinwood, mahogany crossbanding and compound strings in light and dark wood; square tapered legs standing proud of the frieze, spade feet. Pine top and frame with mahogany facing bars along the hinge line; hollow moulding under front edge for finger grip; laminated frieze, medial brace. The fly hinges of one table repaired.
H.74 (29); W.91 (36); D.45 (17¾).

PROV: Agnes and Norman Lupton Bequest 1953.

[13.371/53]

389

An approximate date is established by a closely similar card table made by George Oakley in 1810 illustrated *D.E.F.,* III, p.202, fig.42.

PROV: Mrs D. U. McGrigor Phillips; given by her niece Miss Ludmila Mlada 1968.   [6.6/68]

388

389 CARD TABLE
*c.*1810–15
Rosewood; mahogany, beech, pine

The folding D-shaped top surfaced with baize is made to swivel round, the open flap being supported on the underframe; the panelled frieze centres on a tablet faced with a marquetry design of paired anthemion and arabesque motifs executed in brass; the top is raised on four hipped splay legs ending in cast lion's-paw feet with friction-roller castors. The legs, base block, frieze and top are outlined with brass strings. The top and rails are of pine with beech cross bars, rosewood columns, a beech platform and mahogany legs.
H.74 (29); W.91 (36); D.46 (18).

The underside bears an old railway freight label 'London Brighton and South Coast / Victoria to / Chichester'.

390 COMBINATION GAMES AND WORK TABLE
By Jenks and Holt, Cheapside, London
*c.*1878
Walnut; sycamore, amboyna, oak, pine, box

390

The folding swivel top, inlaid with a chess board and two amboyna medallions opens to form a baize-lined games table with counter wells at each corner and two peg-boards marked 10–900 in the veneered border; the table is fronted by a partitioned long drawer lined with sycamore between pairs of short drawers and the kneehole is fitted with a sliding box well for mending or needlework, veneered in walnut and with the original green patterned lining paper; the ornamental turned and fluted legs screw into the corner blocks and end in socket castors with pottery rollers impressed 'C & C PATENT' (for Cope & Collinson). Pine and oak carcase with a mahogany top, veneered in figured walnut with box and sycamore inlay; walnut legs and drawers.
H.71 (28); W.76 (30); D.44 (17½) open 89 (35).

The peg-boards are headed by marquetry arabesques incorporating a standard diamond-shape patent registration mark. The Patent Office records show this design was registered on 16 Feb. 1872 by Jenks & Holt, 55 Bread Street, Cheapside, London E.C. (Ref. B.T. 44/6). The accompanying drawing (B.T.43/58) represents the top and front view

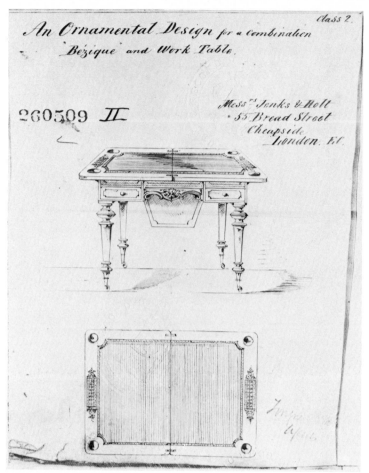

390

of an almost identical table captioned 'An Ornamental Design for a combination Bezique and Work Table 260509'. One of the small drawers bears a paper label inscribed in ink 'No. 3422/7/-/- / J & H / 8/11/78' indicating that the model was still available to retailers six years after the design had been registered and cost £7. Southport Museum has an identical (ebonized) table (7A/60).

PROV: Austins of Peckham; bought 1968.   [29/68]

391 CARD TABLE
*c.*1900
Mahogany; beech

Of boldly serpentine form with block corners and a vine-trail frieze moulding; the cabriole legs ending in square claw and ball feet are carved at the front with a full acanthus frond, the rear pair have demi-fronds and the fifth leg which swings out on a beech rail to support the hinged flap when open is plain.
H.72 (28½); W.86 (34); D.43 (17).

The flat carving, a general lack of wear and structural oddities indicate this is a reproduction table. The form is closely related to a distinctive group of period card tables made in New York and it is interesting to speculate on the

390

391

origin of the model that served as a source for this copy since several furniture historians believe that the New York design derived from English prototypes.

EXH: Temple Newsam, *Thomas Chippendale*, 1951 (121).

PROV: Bought by Sam Wilson from L. Ramus of Eastbourne and recorded in his notebook on 19 Nov. 1907 'Serpentine Chippendale card table with five legs, claw and ball feet £55'; the Sam Wilson Bequest 1925. [S.W.216]

392 CARD TABLE
*c.*1910
Satinwood; rosewood, pine, oak

The D-shaped top and frieze are veneered in satinwood outlined with crossbanded rosewood borders between strings; the square tapering legs are headed by inset rosewood panels and edged with ebony corner strings, the two rear supports swing out on veneered oak rails to support the baize-covered flap; pine carcase.
H.79 (31); W.91 (36); D.44 (17½).

The vivid veneers, modern type of hinge, fly-rails faced with satinwood and unorthodox construction indicate this table is an Edwardian creation. The frieze, instead of being laminated, is built-up of large curved corner blocks joined by short sections of rail.

PROV: Recorded in Sam Wilson's notebook '13 March 1913 To Old Sheraton Card Table £20 (London Curio Club Ltd)'; the Sam Wilson Bequest 1925. [S.W.228]

393 CARD TABLE
Partly 18th century
Mahogany; oak, pine, beech

Rectangular, with tower corners and straight mantled front legs ending in pad feet; the top has two folding leaves supported when open on a hinged rear leg fitted with a pivoted lug to adjust the height; the upper flap is plain; the lower deck, lined with baize, contains counter wells and the rounded corners are dished for candles, the frieze is fronted by a drawer.
H.75 (29½); W.85 (33½); D.39 (15½).

A 'made up' piece with many new structural elements and much restored veneer, the mahogany stained to simulate rosewood and french polished.

PROV: Bequeathed by Sir George Martin 1976. [51.22/76]

393

TABLES, CENTRE

Garden, Library, Loo, etc

394 LOO TABLE
*c.*1820
Rosewood; oak, mahogany

Octagonal tip-up top veneered with Brazilian rosewood on an oak foundation, the crossbanded border inlaid with floral motifs in brass, applied brass beading on frieze rail, the underside painted to simulate rosewood; octagonal column support with turned gilt base and lotus-pattern foot mount

394

resting on a triangular stepped plinth inlaid with brass anthemia; the castor plates, stamped 'YATES & HAMPER', secured to mahogany blocks masked by rich ormolu mounts in the Empire style, the side rosettes made to unscrew; the brass tip-up fitment with handle release (extension rod missing) operates two spring catches.
H.74 (29); Diam.140 (55).

Loo tables, designed for the card game formerly known as lanterloo, were generally placed in drawing rooms; they feature in many contemporary pattern books and J. C. Loudon, who illustrated two models in 1833, observed 'they may be executed in rosewood or any other rare and handsome foreign wood'.

PROV: Purchased by Mr and Mrs R. Farmerey at a country house sale near Skipwith, East Yorkshire about 1899; given by Mrs Farmerey 1959.   [7/59]

395 LIBRARY CENTRE TABLE (Jacket illustration Vol. 2)
By Edward H. Baldock, London
1840
Ebony; tulipwood, kingwood, mahogany, pine, cedar, chestnut, various stained and shaded woods, ivory, pearl-shell, copper, brass

The octagonal revolving top, fitted with four frieze drawers, rests on a massive concave-sided central support raised on four splayed inward-scrolling feet. The top is surfaced with green leather outlined by tooled and gilt lilies and centres on a lobed marquetry panel representing flowers and a butterfly. The shaped border is inset with opposed pairs of floral sprays and clusters of fruit alternating with eight oriental scenes framed by rococo cartouches. The pictorial subjects, executed in coloured woods with brass, copper, ivory and pearl-shell elements are, in rotation:
1. A cow leaping over a prostrate chinaman.
2. A chinaman fishing, another climbing a date palm.
3. A winged serpent threatening a man wading a river bearing on his head a child in a circular dish.

395

4. A mandarin and a monkey by a roadside playing a horn and a trumpet.
5. A chinaman gathering herbs in a landscape with a palace.
6. A man with a spear fending off a crocodile, an elephant in the background.
7. A man in a castle tower throwing a life-line to a mariner whose ship has been struck by lightening.
8. A chinaman with a crossbow and dog in a landscape with a running leopard.

The shaped frieze containing two long and two short drawers is decorated with alternating versions of a branched rococo stem bearing shell-like spurs backed by different floral sprays. The central support, veneered in ebony and cross-banded in tulipwood, is faced with four bouquets each framed by an asymmetrical cartouche, while the feet are enriched with a rococo meander and floral trails in various woods; the top rotates on hardwood sliders; concealed brass castors. Mahogany top with chestnut rails and cedar drawer linings, the base is of pine with mahogany inner structures.
H.76 (30); Diam.152 (60).

E. H. Baldock was a fashionable London art dealer, furniture maker and restorer who traded from Hanway Street between 1805 and his retirement in 1843. Various commissions executed for the royal family and members of the nobility were investigated in an important two-part article by Geoffrey de Bellaigue 'Edward Holmes Baldock', *Connoisseur*, Aug. 1975, pp.290–99 and Sept. 1975 pp.18–25. Between May 1840 and Feb. 1841 the Duke of Buccleuch purchased goods to the value of £1,035.8.0 from Baldock for Dalkeith Palace, Bowhill and Drumlanrig Castle, Scotland. This

395

library table was invoiced by 'E. H. Baldock, Chinaman to Her Majesty, Hanway Street, Oxford Street, London' on 30 Sept. 1840 'A beautiful Octagon Ebony Table with pictures in each side – Flowers in centre. Intervals lined in Green Leather. Gold borders, 5 ft diam'r £85'.

The form of the table may well have been inspired by a design in Richard Bridgens' *Furniture with Candelabra*, 1838 for a 'Marqueterie Centre Table' which has a closely similar pedestal support. There is also a manuscript design amongst the Buccleuch papers at Drumlanrig inscribed 'No. 3 Amboyna wood ground with coloured flowers' for a comparable table. The chinoiserie vignettes were probably copied from an engraved source as yet unidentified, since a writing table branded 'EHB' in the Buccleuch collection is decorated with fanciful pictorial cartouches taken from a series of dwarfs published by Jacques Callot in 1616.

A number of marquetry centre tables possessing a striking family resemblance to this example are known: the group includes another model from the Buccleuch collection (Christie's, 1 April 1971, lot 33, repr.); a specimen at Charlecote Park where the owner George Lucy certainly had dealings with Baldock; while a third, at the Duke of Norfolk's Yorkshire home, Carlton Towers, corresponds almost exactly to the version now at Leeds and furthermore is stamped on one of the drawers 'EDWARDS & ROBERTS' – a high class Victorian firm of cabinet makers and dealers with premises in Oxford Street. There is also one at Penrhyn Castle, Wales. A virtually identical model from the Earl of Stair's collection (now at the V & A) is inlaid with cartouches of similar chinoiserie character.

LIT: *L.A.C.*, No.68 (1971), p.4, repr.; G. de Bellaigue, 'Edward Holmes Baldock', *Connoisseur*, Sept. 1975, p.19, fig.4.

PROV: Purchased by the 5th Duke of Buccleuch for Dalkeith Palace, Midlothian, Scotland; by descent to the 8th Duke; sold Christie's, 1 April 1971, lot 34; H. Blairman & Sons; bought with the aid of a government grant 1971.   [14/71]

396 CENTRE TABLE
*c.*1825
Rosewood; mahogany

The specimen marble top is recessed in a circular frame with a gadrooned corner moulding and supported on a central shaft profiled as a gadrooned cup; the platform base of inward-curving triangular design has a beaded edge and scroll feet with fronded brackets concealing swivel castors. The top is inset with a concentric radiating pattern composed of 140 segments of coloured marbles centering on a malachite medallion and ringed by a band of green serpentine. The framework is of rosewood veneered on to a mahogany foundation with a solid rosewood pillar.
H.76 (30); Diam.90 (35½).

Specimen marble tables were known during the Regency period as 'Dejune tables' and intended, according to George Smith (1808) for 'Ladies Boudoirs or Morning Breakfast

396

Rooms'. The colourful mosaic tops were imported from Italy, sometimes with a diagram and key identifying the marbles. See C. G. Gilbert, 'A Specimen Marble Table', *Connoisseur*, Oct. 1973, pp.78–81. Two similar circular rosewood slab frames illustrated in Gillows Estimate Sketch Books, 17 Aug. and 22 Nov. 1824 (Westminster City Libraries, 344/101/p. 3364 and 3385) give a useful indication of the likely date.

PROV: Sylvia Head (Antiques); bought 1970.   [7/70]

397 CENTRE TABLE
*c.*1845
Slate; mahogany, pine

The circular top, formed of a single slab of purple slate, has a moulded edge and a shallow painted pine frieze with gilt enrichments; the slate is painted a purplish-brown and decorated with a gaily coloured composition centering on a large floral bouquet surrounded by a garland of morning glory and a lavish outer border of gilt rococo fronds inhabited by exotic birds; the tip-up top, backed by a mahogany panel, is supported on a tapered hexagonal column set on an inward-curving triangular platform base; the pillar and base are faced with slate tablets ornamented with floral sprays and gilt foliage; the boldly carved and bronzed mahogany lion's-paw feet conceal castors; brass tip-up release mechanism, the central pillar incorporates an iron stem.
H.79 (31); Diam.106 (42).

397

The underside bears a label inscribed 'A large Slate Table / A Gift to Alick / from his mother / Jane Stewart / Sept. 15th 1900'.

PROV: Richard Allen of Ramsgate (d.1864), by descent to his daughter Jane Stewart and her son Alexander Patrick Stewart (d.1951) who left it to his cousin Mrs Joan Gilbert-Barney, from whom it was bought 1971.　　　　　[13/71]

398 CENTRE TABLE
Designed by William Burges
*c.*1867
Pine; walnut

The rectangular marble top, set in a walnut surround, is raised on trestle end-supports connected by a rail secured with wedges. The frame is painted in gold and black with medieval motifs in the Moorish taste on a scarlet ground.

The pine trestles, profiled as pillars with splayed bases, are each decorated on both sides with leafy capitals and the elaborately shaped edges are enriched with scale, chevron, rosette, quatrefoil and floral patterns, while the crossbar is stencilled with stylized ball flowers and florets; the feet conceal pottery castors. The marble top is inset with panels of late seventeenth century *pietra dura* bordered by brown onyx, serpentine, Siena and other decorative marbles intersected by black bands. The central tablet features a parrot in a fruit tree and the four small panels portray birds with exotic plumage. The underframe is impressed 'II'; the castors are stamped 'THE / PATENT / CB& ?' and a label under the top is inscribed 'Minshall 29/5/39 Bentalls Furniture Depository'.
H.74 (29); W.137 (54); D.81 (32).

A companion table, now owned by Birmingham Art Gallery (M 134.7), is of identical design except the feet are

398

profiled with double-steps and the top incorporates *pietra dura* panels of a fountain and butterflies. The tables belong to a coherent group of red-painted furniture designed by Burges in 1867 for his Buckingham Street house comprising: a bed, washstand, dressing table, bookcase, bedside table, the pair of centre tables now at Leeds and Birmingham and a third, slightly smaller version. This repertoire is discussed by C. Handley-Read, 'Notes on William Burges's Painted Furniture', *Burlington*, Nov. 1963, pp.496–509.

There are two working drawings for this table in the R.I.B.A. collection: Arc.IV/XVII (no.101) executed in pencil, ink and yellow wash shows the side and end elevations, a profile of the trestle supports and various mouldings, it gives dimensions and is inscribed 'See Photographs: Own Furniture, Pl.13. A table with porphry top which was evidently executed to this design.' Arc. IV/XXXV/I (no.106) portrays the table in pencil and red wash with measurements and inscriptions 'Alabaster table' and 'Bird table'.

It is not known for certain who was responsible for crafting the table but it is significant that entries in Burges's Estimate Book 1875–81 (V. & A. reserve case JJ 40) relating to work performed for Lord Bute, reveal that Burke & Co of London and Paris frequently supplied marble and Walden of Covent Garden, London was employed for furniture. J. Crook supports attributions to these tradesmen.

LIT: R. P. Pullan, *The House of William Burges*, 1885, No.40; *Country Life*, 9 Sept. 1971, p.609, fig.4; Christie's, *Review of the Year 1970/71*, pp.336–7, repr.; *L.A.C.*, No.70 (1972), p.3, fig.1.

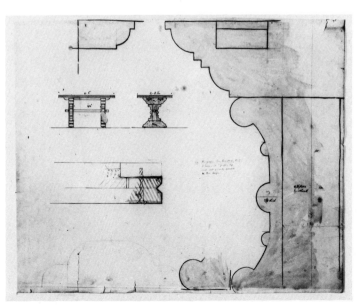

398

398

PROV: William Burges, 15, Buckingham Street, London and then Tower House, Melbury Road, London; Colonel T. H. Minshall; Tower House sale (Chesterton & Sons) 16 Oct. 1933, lot 120 (withdrawn); sold Christie's, 8 July 1971, lot 100; Phillips & Harris; bought with the aid of the N.A.C.F. 1971.   [32/71]

398

399 LIBRARY CENTRE TABLE
*c.*1890
Mahogany

Rectangular top with canted corners inset with a panel of leathercloth; raised on four cabriole legs coated in dark stain and enriched with vigorously executed acanthus leaves and interlacing C-scrolls, on bold claw and ball feet.
H.76 (30); W.183 (72); D.137 (54).

This ample, richly carved table is a product of the Victorian 'Chippendale Revival'; it could well have been acquired for the room which served as a library following Mrs Meynell Ingram's conversion of the Georgian library at Temple Newsam into a chapel in 1877. Since the table features in a photograph of the Great Hall published in 1910 it must pre-date the library created in 1912.

LIT: F. Moss, *Pilgrimages to Old Homes*, V, 1910, p.319, repr.

PROV: The Hon. Mrs E. C. Meynell Ingram; bought at the Temple Newsam sale (Robinson, Fisher & Harding) 26–31 July 1922, lot 1151.   [1922/F.22(a)]

399

400 GARDEN TABLE
Probably made by A. W. Simpson of Kendal to the design of C. F. A. Voysey
*c.*1898
Oak

The square boarded top with plain frieze rails, is supported on four massive splayed staves set angle-wise to the corners; the low stretchers carry a plank platform. The top is tied by pegged joints and a curved underbrace. Originally polished light brown.
H.67 (26½); W.76 (30); D.76 (30).

Arthur W. Simpson, described in a trade leaflet dated 1894 as 'Wood Carver and Designer, Finkle Street, Kendal' was regularly employed by Voysey from 1896 onwards to execute his furniture designs and there is a strong tradition that they collaborated in furnishing Moor Crag, Windermere, built by

Voysey between 1898 and 1900. It could, however, be the work of a Mr Gibbs of Stavely, nr. Kendal, who at the time specialized in good quality garden furniture.

PROV: J. W. Buckley, Moor Crag; his daughter, Mrs H. I. L. Speller; bequeathed to Miss D. M. Dixon; bought from the Lotherton Endowment Fund 1976.   [23.1/76]

401 CENTRE TABLE
*c.*1900
Beech, mahogany

Of rectangular design with four cabriole legs entirely decorated with gilt gesso work on a punched ground. The top is enriched with a formal, interlacing strapwork system enclosing fronds and centering on a foliate medallion; the border contains a husk meander with corner shells. The frieze, styled with a scrolling *lambrequin* pattern, is ornamented on each long side with a grotesque mask and the legs, embellished with acanthus foliage and stylized shells, end in knurled feet; originally fitted with castors.
H.74 (29); W.110 (43½); D.64 (25).

PROV: Lord Moynihan, Carr Manor, Leeds; Carr Manor sale (Hollis & Webb, Leeds) 30 Nov.–3 Dec. 1937, lot 643; bequeathed by Sir George Martin 1976.   [51.18/76]

401

402 LIBRARY CENTRE TABLE
Perhaps by Lenygon and Morant, London
*c.*1912
Mahogany

Of similar but not identical design to Cat. No.399; the top surround is crossbanded, the longer frieze on each side is ornamented with a carved shell between acanthus fronds and the claw and ball cabriole legs are embellished with a different decorative scheme.
H.76 (30); W.183 (72); D. 137 (54).

400

Possibly supplied by Lenygon and Morant of London who, in 1912, were commissioned to remodel the South East room at Temple Newsam as a library in the early Georgian style. The shells between paired acanthus fronds on the frieze are closely allied to the central motif of the Edwardian chimneypiece. The mean proportions, flat, rather academic carving on the legs and lack-lustre surfaces suggest this table is younger than its companion (Cat. No.399).

EXH: *Temple Newsam Heirlooms*, 1972 (39).

PROV: Purchased at the Temple Newsam sale .(Robinson, Fisher & Harding) 26–31 July 1922, lot 1150.

[1922/F.22(b)]

403 CENTRE TABLE
20th century fake
Walnut; mahogany, oak

The rectangular Florentine marble top is supported on four walnut cabriole legs each carved with a fronded fan centering on a scaled plume with leaf-drops below and scrolled brackets; the blocked corners and oak frieze are veneered in mahogany.
H.74 (29); W.91 (36); D.61 (24).

The marble slab replaces a wooden top and the rails are not original, indicating that this piece has probably been built from four card table legs.

PROV: Bequeathed by Frank Savery 1966. [1.8/66]

TABLES, OCCASIONAL

China, Coffee, Tea, etc

404 TEA TABLE
18th century, third quarter
Mahogany

The circular scalloped tip-up top with a 'pie-crust' edge is set on a cage with Doric corner columns supported by a fluted and cabled pillar with enriched mouldings; the spreading tripod legs, carved with leaf tongues and claw and ball feet, formerly terminated in castors. Although the cross batons and spring catch have been re-orientated this table appears to be intact.
H.76 (30); Diam.82 (32½).

PROV: Bought at a sale in Horsforth, near Leeds, about 1913; bequeathed by Sir George Martin 1976.   [51.28/76]

404

405 TEA TABLE
18th century, third quarter
Mahogany

Circular tray-top with a 'pie-crust' edge, made to tilt and revolve; fitted with a 'bird-cage' below and supported on a

405

turned pillar and tripod base, the baluster shaft spirally fluted and the frond-carved legs end in talon and ball feet.
H.71 (28); Diam.67 (26½).

Although this table has been stripped and repolished it is a period piece.

PROV: Given by Samuel Smith of Newcastle-upon-Tyne 1940.
[7.1/40]

406 CHINA TABLE
c.1900
Mahogany

The serpentine top is surrounded by a low fretwork gallery set on an open lattice frieze outlined with mouldings; the straight L-section legs, pierced by long slots punctuated with gothic blocks, are headed by fretted spandrels carved with leafy scrolls and end in fronded block feet on castors. Mahogany with a veneered frieze rail.
H.74 (29); W.76 (30); D.53 (21).

406

The fresh wood, weak carving and liberal use of dark stain indicate this is not a period table; mid eighteenth century examples were normally provided with cross stretchers. Many delicate tables of 'Chinese Chippendale' character were made around 1900.

EXH: Temple Newsam, *Thomas Chippendale*, 1951 (103).

PROV: Mildenhall Manor House, Suffolk; the David Dunstan Schofield Bequest 1962. [18.28/62]

407 TEA TABLE
By Albert Horner, Leeds
*c.*1925
Mahogany; oak

The circular tip-up top with an applied 'pie-crust' edge, is raised on a short baluster shaft set on tripod legs ending in pad feet. The modern top and one of the legs are executed in mahogany, the cut-down column and other legs being of oak liberally coated in mahogany stain.
H.52 (20½); Diam.69 (27).

Albert Horner owned a cabinet maker's and house furnishing business at 19, Kendal Road, Leeds during the inter-war years. This table is a typical example of cheap reproduction style furniture incorporating old components.

PROV: Bequeathed by Mrs L. I. Wright 1965. [14.2/65]

408 COFFEE TABLE
By Design Workshops (Shelley) Ltd, Huddersfield, Yorkshire
1964
Rosewood and glass

Of oblong rectangular plan; the four square uprights support a framework of rails with terminal extensions united to the posts by open self-locking cruciform joints. The 15 mm plate glass top rests on rubber plugs.
H.39 (15½); W.101(40); D.76 (30).

This table, produced in 1964 to the design of John Hardy, was the prototype of twenty models sold over six months to Heal & Son Ltd., and private buyers. All were made of Brazilian rosewood supplied by Times Veneer Co, Edmonton, London and the glass came from James Clark & Eaton.

In 1975 a range of modern furnishings and fittings for the new Oriental Gallery and Shop at Lotherton Hall were commissioned from Design Workshops. The items – all built of solid pitch pine, bleached and sealed – comprised: a glass topped display table; three broad bench seats; two narrow wall benches; two sales display units; a slide display box and a shop counter. A third display unit and an L-shaped counter were commissioned in 1976. Copies of the original designs for these pieces are preserved in the museum files.

PROV: Bought from the Lotherton Endowment Fund 1975. [28/75]

409 COFFEE TABLE
By John Makepeace (Farnborough Barn, Ltd) Banbury
1964–5
Sycamore and glass

Rectangular in design; composed of four square uprights united by four rails overlapped at the corners and secured by screws with satin-chrome covers; the posts capped with rubber friction pads, support a plate glass top. Knock-down construction, finished in white wax.
H.32 (12½); W.68 (26¾); D.68 (26¾).

The table was designed by John Makepeace and made in his workshop at Farnborough Barn. This model was produced in batches of about fifty, either in beech, teak or sycamore and was sometimes dyed scarlet, green, yellow, magenta, turquoise, cobalt blue and charcoal. Heals of London, Dunn's of Bromley and many other high grade retailers marketed the table. The glass was supplied by Glass (Coventry) Ltd. The table was regularly shown at the Design Centre and featured in periodicals such as *Good Housekeeping*, 1968. The author has remarked 'It was designed for production in a craft workshop in order to make use of our machine facilities with minimum of handwork, in order to leave the hand cabinet makers free to concentrate on making individual pieces'. In 1976 an expensive centre display case was commissioned from John Makepeace for Lotherton Hall.

PROV: Bought from the Lotherton Endowment Fund 1976. [40/76]

408

409

TABLES, DINING

410 DINING TABLE
Mid 17th century
Oak

The plank top rests freely on six plain turned supports with simple ring collars and blocked ends united by rails, stretchers and a medial brace.
H.84 (33); L.254 (100); W.81 (32).

The top, of thick rough-hewn timber with plugged knot holes, is not original and the frame has been rebuilt. Chiselled joint numerals show that the six supports, two long stretchers and two side rails although repaired, are original; the other members are all later restorations using old wood.

PROV: Bought by Colonel F. R. T. Gascoigne for Lotherton Hall about 1910 from Mrs Langdale (Antiques), Market Weighton, Yorkshire; the Gascoigne gift 1968. [7.141/68]

411 DINING TABLE
c.1800
Mahogany; pine

Constructed in three sections united by stirrup-clips, consisting of a centre with rectangular hinged flaps supported on single gates and two semi-circular ends with veneered rails bordered by an ebony string; raised on square tapered legs on swivel castors; laminated pine frieze and rails. The ends, when detached could serve as pier tables.
H.72 (28½); L.295 (116); W.125 (49).

EXH: Leeds Art Gallery, *English Furniture*, 1930 (107).

PROV: Unknown.   [1929/F.1]

'IMPERIAL' DINING-TABLE, mahogany
By Gillows, Lancaster, 1810
Under Cat. No.496 (illustrated)

412 DINING-TABLE
c.1845
Mahogany; beech

Only the two rectangular end sections with rounded corners remain; each has a concertina-type extending underframe with wooden knuckle hinges supported on six slightly shaped turned legs ending in brass socket castors stamped 'LOACH & CLARKE'S PATENT'; when folded away the rails are locked in position by pairs of brass bolts; the missing leaves were united by stirrup-clips. Mahogany; with a veneered frieze and beech underframe.
H.72 (28½); W.152 (60).

This method of enlarging dining tables was devised by Richard Brown, who in 1805 patented a design in which 'the two ends of the table frame are connected by pieces of wood, so joined together as to form what are commonly called lazy tongs'.

Loach and Clarke, brassfounders, occupied premises in Little Charles Street, Birmingham. John Loach took out a

413

patent for castors in 1812 and another when in partnership with Clarke in 1841 (No.8788). The castors on this table were manufactured to the latter specification.

PROV: Probably from Parlington Hall; the Gascoigne gift 1968.   [7.217/68]

413 EXPANDING DINING TABLE
*c.*1870
Mahogany

The broad circular top rests on a heavy bulbous support ornamented with a turned base pendant and a gadrooned moulding; the pedestal is raised on four large spreading legs styled with scroll borders and terminating in massive eagle talon and ball feet concealing castors. The circumference can be enlarged by fitting six additional segments in a ring around the perimeter, the sections being supported on twelve lopers concealed in the frieze and secured from below by thumb screws; the table top is set on a wide cross board and reinforced underneath with radial bearers. Designed to seat either eight or twelve persons.
H.72 (28½); Diam.155 (61) extended 191 (75½).

PROV: Edmund Leatham, Wentbridge House, Yorkshire; inherited by Lady Gascoigne; the Gascoigne gift 1971.
                                                    [23.11/71]

TABLES, DRESSING

414 DRESSING TABLE
*c.*1710
Oak; elm

The rectangular top with a moulded edge and a long drawer below, is raised on turned double-baluster and knop-pattern legs united by flat cross stretchers centering on a finial, stump feet. The drawer front, outlined by a twin fillet bead, was originally fitted with two circular pulls later replaced by a brass loop handle, elm drawer linings; the finial is not original.
H.74 (29); W.87 (34½); D.57 (22¼).

PROV: Bought about 1920 by Edmund Leatham of Went- bridge House, from a dealer in York; inherited by Lady Gascoigne; the Gascoigne gift 1970.   [41/70]

415 DRESSING TABLE
18th century, second quarter
Oak

Rectangular with a moulded top and shaped front apron fitted with one long and two narrow cockbeaded drawers; the square 'country cabriole' legs end in undercut block feet.

414

The handles are not original.
H.69 (27); W.72 (28½); D.44 (17½).

PROV: Bequeathed by Sir George Martin 1976.   [51.29/76]

416 LADY'S DRESSING TABLE
*c.*1770
Mahogany; oak

The rectangular dressing chest is raised on straight chamfered legs with a recessed shelf below enclosed on three sides by lattice screens in the Chinese taste; the hinged top opens to reveal a shallow tray and the lid incorporates a swing glass; the front and back are faced with dummy drawers and there is one true and one false through drawer on each side. Brass buckle handles and locks, the original stay braces, to support the top when open, replaced by a wooden arm, castors removed. The tray almost certainly once contained a central folding glass surrounded by partitions, lidded compartments, etc. Partitioned mahogany drawer linings, the false drawer fronts veneered on to oak.
H.77 (30½); W.62 (24½); D.46 (18½).

PROV: Christie's, 7 Dec. 1922, lot 27; M. Harris & Sons; Sir George Duncombe, Wood Hall, Herts; bequeathed to Lord Deramore, Heslington Manor, York; bought from his widow (Lady Martin Bequest Fund) 1967.   [19.2/67]

417 DRESSING TABLE
*c.*1805
Mahogany; oak, pine

Compass front with reeded edge and gallery behind, con- taining a shallow drawer above the kneehole flanked by deep

416

417

Rectangular top with rounded corners, bordered on three sides by a gallery (missing); two frieze drawers with mahogany linings, quarter-beading and wooden knobs; raised on four turned legs with peg feet. Veneered pine and oak rails, medial brace birch.
H.71 (28); W.122 (48); D.61 (24).

Printed paper label on underside of drawer 'J. KENDELL & CO'. inscribed 'No.89837' and 'Workman's Name. J. Wood, Jr'. (Several other labelled pieces bearing the same name are known.)

The firm of Kendell is recorded in Leeds Trade Directories from 1790 onwards; they worked at Harewood House during the 1820s and, by the mid-century, became one of the largest upholsterers and cabinet makers in Leeds. The business was taken over by Marsh & Jones in 1863. Kendell & Co probably started to label their furniture in the late 1840s and a systematic study of the serial numbers suggests this table dates from 1859–60 although it does not differ greatly from bedroom tables made by Constantine & Co of Leeds for Broughton Hall, Yorkshire in the 1840s.

PROV: Bought from J. B. Hamilton 1922.   [1922/F53]

drawers; turned tapering legs on stump feet, the ringed shafts rise to reeded tower corners at the front. Oak drawer linings with quarter-beads. Stamped brass handles not original; evidence of towel-rail fixture on end panels. Printed paper label on back inscr. 'C 14291'.
H.82 (32¼); W.118 (46½); D.56 (22).

A typical example of medium quality bedroom furniture inspired by Sheraton's designs.

PROV: Agnes and Norman Lupton Bequest 1953.
                                        [13.380/53]

DRESSING TABLE, mahogany
By Gillows, Lancaster, 1811
Under Cat. No.500 (illustrated)

DRESSING TABLE, papier-mâché
Birmingham, c.1851
Under Cat. No.516 (illustrated)

418 DRESSING TABLE
By John Kendell & Co, Leeds
c.1860
Mahogany; pine, birch, oak

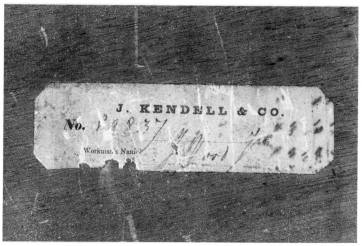

418

419 BUREAU DRESSING TABLE

*c.*1760 and *c.*1866
Mahogany; satinwood, pine, oak, ebony

The serpentine-front is fitted with nine drawers surrounding an arched knee-hole with a cupboard in the recess; the top is gadrooned and inset with a satinwood border between ebony strings; the canted corners are mounted with richly carved and pierced swags of floral foliage, drapes and oak sprigs headed by the Crewe crest 'out of a ducal coronet or, a lion's jamb erect arg'; the recess is flanked by pilasters and the spandrels ornamented with scrolled foliage incorporating masks applied onto a satinwood ground; the elaborately carved escutcheons are fitted with bronze loop handles of rococo design; corbelled base on bracket feet. Pine carcase veneered with mahogany; oak drawer linings; the mahogany carvings backed by satinwood.
H.85 (33½); W.129 (51); D.67 (26½).

Although the table is a standard design type it shows every appearance of having been embellished during the Victorian period. The use of satinwood for banding the top and as a ground veneer behind the applied carvings is inconsistent with mid Georgian cabinetwork. Plugged holes indicate the escutcheons and handles are not original and since the Crewes were not elevated to the peerage until 1806 the heraldic swags must be later additions. Following a serious fire in 1866 Crewe Hall was rebuilt, the interior being elaborately styled with armorials; the table which reflects Victorian concepts of elegance, could well have been embellished at this time. The secondary woods, traditional construction and features such as round-topped drawer linings show that the carcase itself is genuinely old.

There was a strikingly similar example at Eaton Hall (Dukes of Westminster) while another closely related dressing table was sold by Christie's, 15 July 1976, lot 86.

419

LIT: F. Moss, *Pilgrimages to Old Homes*, V, 1910, p.355 (repr. *in situ* at Crewe Hall); *L.A.C.*, No.21 (1953),p p.6–7, repr.; *Antique Collector*, Aug. 1953, p.138, repr.; *Apollo*, Aug. 1956, p.52, repr.; F. Davies, *A Picture History of Furniture*, 1958, pl.241; A. Coleridge, *Chippendale Furniture*, 1968, pl.230.

EXH: London, Royal Academy, *English Taste in the 18th Century*, Winter 1955/56 (176).

PROV: By descent to the Marquess of Crewe, Crewe Hall and Madeley Manor, Staffs; sold by his executors to W. Waddingham (Antiques); bought 1953.   [8/53]

420 DRESSING TABLE
*c.*1884
Walnut; kingwood, oak, birch, various coloured woods

The rectangular top with ovolo ends is fronted by a long drawer lined with kingwood; the hinged top opens on a retaining bar to reveal an oval mirror set into the underside with a shelf and sliding tray for toilet requisites below, flanked by half-round lidded wells on either side. The top, veneered in walnut with a trellis design, centres on a musical trophy combining a harp, mandolin, flute and scroll with crossed palm and olive sprays executed in marquetry on an ebonized ground; the frieze is decorated all round with a *trompe l'oeil* zig-zag and angular fret pattern in various stained and coloured woods; fluted tapering legs on turned

420

feet united by shaped X-stretchers centering on an oval tablet inset with diaperwork. The top, lower edge, legs and mirror are ringed by enriched gilt metal beads; engraved lock. Walnut with inner structures of oak and birch.
H.69 (27); W.71 (28); D.43 (17).

The mirror plate is backed by a copy of *The Standard*, London, 15 October 1884. The table is typical of much medium quality reproduction Louis XVI style furniture produced by firms such as Edwards & Roberts during the late Victorian period. An identical table was auctioned by Henry Spencer & Sons, Retford, 3–4 May 1962, lot 242, repr.

EXH: Temple Newsam, *L.A.C.F. Members Exhibition*, 1952 (202).

PROV: Given by Miss M. E. Jackson 1952.   [24.2/52]

421 DRESSING TABLE
By Marsh, Jones and Cribb, Leeds
*c.*1908
Walnut; rosewood, cedar

The rectangular swing mirror with an arched top and shaped shoulders is suspended between square-capped pillars above a low shelf with projecting wings at each side incorporating small drawers; beneath the table top is an arrangement of two long drawers flanked by cupboards and the structure is raised on turned legs ornamented with mushroom columns, rings and ball feet concealing castors. The solid drawer and cupboard fronts are crossbanded in rosewood and fitted with pear-shaped pulls with quatrefoil back-plates executed in bronze; the façade is outlined with plain half-round mouldings and the standards simply styled with channelling; cedar drawers. The doors, which open on pin-hinges, have ball catches impressed 'WALTERS / PATENT / IMP'D / BALES'; the mirror suspension fitment is stamped 'CROFT & ASSINDERS PATENT' and the locks are marked 'J. BRAMAH / 100 NEW BOND STREET / M 1 & 2 D9' and 'J. T. NEEDS / 100 NEW BOND STREET / M 1 & 2 D9 / Late J. BRAMAH / 142 PICCADILLY'. The back bears a brass tablet inscribed 'ESTABLISHED 1760 / MARSH JONES & CRIBB Ltd / FURNISHERS AND DECOR-ATORS / LEEDS'.
H.152 (60); W.114 (45); D.61 (24).

According to an article in *Country Life*, 9 July 1910, p.62 the original furnishings of Heathcote were designed by the architect Edwin Lutyens who completed the house in 1908. The author asserts 'it is rarely the case as at Heathcote that the architect has the opportunity of designing every piece of furniture for the house and choosing every hanging and carpet'. The illustrious design of this dressing table, when compared with the routine high-class furniture of Marsh, Jones & Cribb, tend to confirm Lutyen's hand although no manuscript designs have been traced. A trade catalogue issued by M, J & C in 1911 reveals that some of their later furniture betrays the influence of their Heathcote commission

421

(esp. a dressing table p.13). The donor owns other items from this suite.

PROV: J. T. Hemingway, Heathcote, Ilkley; Stanley Waddi-love who purchased Heathcote in 1937; sold (Dacre, Son & Hartley, Ilkley, uncatalogued sale) in 1964; Rev. John Beardsmore, Burley-in-Wharfedale who gave it to Leeds 1969.   [2/69]

422 DRESSING TABLE
By Christopher Pratt & Sons, Bradford
*c.*1910
Walnut; pine, oak, plywood

In the form of a William and Mary style bureau-dressing table surmounted by a tall framed mirror with an arched top and shaped shoulders suspended between tapering standards

with acorn finials. The flap, faced with a lobed panel out-lined by boxwood stringing, opens on self-advancing lopers to reveal two white plastic bottle-slabs and a mirror-backed recess, there are two long drawers below with turned oak knobs; the base, designed with arcaded aprons, is raised on short turned legs ending in turnip feet. The locks are stamped 'CHANCE SON & CO. BIRM'M.' Solid walnut with a veneered pine stand; plywood back, dust boards and drawer bottoms; machine cut mouldings.
H.168 (66); W.59 (23); D.39 (15½).

This dressing table is from a suite which also included a wardrobe, chest of drawers and bed – the whole group was exhibited at Bradford in 1969 (q.v.). The original manuscript design (11 × 15 in.) executed in pencil by Christopher Pratt II, a grandson of the founder of the firm, survives together with a contemporary photograph of the cabinet pieces. The companion items now furnish a manse in Shipley, Yorkshire.

EXH: Bradford Art Gallery, *Victorian and Edwardian Furniture by Pratts of Bradford*, 1969/70 (32 & 41).

PROV: Made for stock about 1910 and in 1918 annexed by the designer Christopher Pratt for his own home; given by his widow Mary in memory of her husband 1969.   [1/69]

423 DRESSING TABLE
By Gordon Russell Workshops, Broadway
1928
Oak; pine, plywood

423

Built in three main sections; the low stand with a central kneehole is raised on six chamfered legs connected by deep rails with spandrel profiles and a simple top moulding; the base supports a block of two drawers at each end with a tall narrow mirror suspended between faceted standards within the central recess. The two boxes containing drawers are constructed with revealed dovetail and pegged joints. Pine back and drawer linings, ebonized oak finger grip handles; the bevelled mirror backed by plywood originally had a moulded frame.
H.127 (50); W.140 (55); D.51 (20).

The underside of one drawer bears the following partly printed, part hand-written label 'THIS PIECE OF / FURNITURE / design No. *621* / was made throughout in / The Russell Workshops / Broadway, Worcestershire / Designer: Gordon Russell; Foreman: Edgar Turner / Cabinet Maker: *A. Harrison* / Metalworker: (blank) / Timber used: *English Brown Oak* / Date: 30/7/28'.

Gordon Russell Ltd retain the original workshop drawing (dated 30 June 1927) for this piece which was made for stock and featured in one of the firm's illustrated catalogues, p.15 (No.621). It was available in walnut, oak or brown oak, the latter version costing £27.

PROV: Purchased directly from the Russell workshops in 1928 by Dr. I. Henry, Branfield House, Branfield, nr. Birmingham; by descent to his daughter Ruth Bentall; bought 1974. [8/74]

TABLES, GATE-LEG

424 GATE-LEG TABLE
*c.*1680
Oak

The oval moulded top with a narrow centre section and deep, rule-jointed flaps, is supported on square fluted pillars with blocked tops and bases connected by rails and corner moulded stretchers; the arcaded underframe originally contained a small drawer at each end but only the fronts, now converted into fixed panels, remain; knurled feet; iron butterfly hinges, pegged construction, two joints incised 'X'.
H.64 (25); W.86 (34); D.77 (30½).

LIT: *Collectors Guide*, March 1970, p.90, repr.; G. Wills, *English Furniture 1550–1760*, 1971, p.93, pl.75.

PROV: Maxwell Joseph; Christie's, 19 Dec. 1969, lot 137; bought from the Oxley Bequest Fund 1969. [28/69]

425 GATE-LEG TABLE
Early 18th century
Walnut; elm

The plain oval top with rule-jointed flaps, is set on eight turned legs profiled as slender columns with vase-shaped bases, and shaft rings; the blocked tops and knurled feet support a system of rails and stretchers; the underframe is of elm with arcaded end panels (one replaced in mahogany); pegged construction, iron hinges.
H.72 (28½); W.117 (46); D.104 (41).

PROV: Agnes and Norman Lupton Bequest 1953. [13.387/53]

424

425

TABLES, LIBRARY AND WRITING

426 LIBRARY WRITING TABLE
c.1758
Mahogany; pine

Of rectangular design with massive corner pedestals forming through kneeholes on all four sides; the longer sides are fitted with three shallow frieze drawers and each pedestal contains three graduated drawers enclosed by a cupboard door; the corners are ornamented with engaged three-quarter clustered columns in the gothic taste having shaft rings and foliate capitals; the frieze is carved with interlaced quatrefoils enclosing florets and the pedestals filigreed with gothic tracery medallions centering on a foliate rosette encircled by frond bosses; slightly recessed kneeholes bridged by spandrels; the solid plinth and crossbanded top, lined with green morocco leather, have lobed corners; brass locks, pin-hinges and loop handles on the inner drawers; the frieze drawers are grooved for partitions and set with turned pulls; each pedestal conceals a large brass castor fitted with friction-rollers and a leather wheel. Solid mahogany doors with applied carving, the pedestals and plinth veneered on to a pine foundation; drawers mahogany throughout with corner beads; the top is constructed of mahogany panels set in a pine framework. Two spandrels, various sections of tracery, foliate carving and areas of veneer renewed.

H.82 (32½); W.203 (80); D.173 (68).

The top bears an old engraved brass tablet 'WILLIAM: GERARD: HAMILTON / KNOWN: AS / SINGLE-SPEECH: HAMILTON / M.P. FOR: 42 YEARS / BORN: JAN'Y: 29. 1729 / DIED: JULY: 16. 1796'; the inscription is coloured in red and black. The underside of one pedestal retains a damaged label, written on the back of a Victorian London Dairy Company's trade-card: 'The D[ean of] Sa[lisbu]ry.'

The table can be dated to *c*.1758 when the Countess of Pomfret's Gothic Revival London house, Pomfret Castle, in Arlington Street was completed. Her architect was Sanderson Miller, but Michael McCarthy has pointed out that the interiors (*Country Life Annual*, 1970, pp.138–9, figs.2–6) were almost certainly conceived by Henry Keene or Sir Roger Newdigate (members of the same circle) both of whom sometimes designed furniture, although, apart from stylistic analogies with the decor, evidence that either was responsible for the table is lacking. The Ashmolean, Oxford, owns a large double-portrait of the Earl and Countess of Pomfret in a spectacular Gothic Revival frame and a painted gothic cupboard, also from Pomfret Castle, survives at Easton Neston.

426

LIT (only the more important references are cited):
E. E. Watson, *Life of Bishop Wordsworth*, 1915, p.179; *Apollo* Nov. 1950, p.159, repr.; *L.A.C.*, No.17 (1952) p.4 repr.; Nos.46–7 (1961), p.19, fig.3; A. Coleridge, *Chippendale Furniture*, 1968, pl.245; *Antiques*, May 1969, p.682, repr.

EXH: Temple Newsam, *Thomas Chippendale*, 1951 (114).

PROV: Made for the Countess of Pomfret's house (Pomfret Castle) in Arlington Street, London; following her death in 1761 the Castle was occupied by Lady Sophia Carteret (1762–4) and Horace Walpole refers in 1779 to W. G. 'Single-Speech' Hamilton residing there; he gave the table to his nephew Walter Kerr Hamilton, Bishop of Salisbury in about 1860. E. E. Watson's *Life of Bishop Wordsworth* refers, on p.177 to 'The large central writing-table, an heirloom from Bishop Hamilton's days, having been a present to him from his uncle "Single-speech" Hamilton'. The table passed into the ownership of the Ecclesiastical Commissioners on 1 April 1946 under an Order in Council, and when The Palace, Salisbury, ceased to be the official residence of the Bishop and became the Cathedral School it remained there until sent to Christie's for sale, 5 Oct. 1950, lot 129; W. Waddingham (Antiques); bought with the aid of a government grant and a contribution from the vendor 1951. [24/51]

427 LIBRARY WRITING TABLE
By Thomas Chippendale, London
*c.*1771
Rosewood; oak, pine, mahogany, beech, tulipwood, satinwood, sycamore, holly and various woods

Of rectangular, slightly break-sided design, the red morocco leather top with tooled and gilt borders; fitted on one side with three frieze drawers and, in each pedestal, three graduated drawers enclosed by doors; the opposite side contains a central dummy flanked by true drawers in the frieze with partitioned cupboards below forming letter-holes and vertical folio divisions. The exterior is enriched with banding and engraved marquetry designs in the neo-classical taste on a faded rosewood ground; the frieze is ornamented with linked rosette medallions and the four cupboard doors are decorated with festooned vases surmounted by anthemion motifs among interlacing husk festoons and formal acanthus scrolls; the end panels are inset with large rosette medallions bordered by husk wreaths and foliate sprays with tulipwood and satinwood bands between green-stained strings; the inside cupboard doors and drawer fronts are veneered with rosewood. The cabinetwork is lavishly mounted with festooned ram's-mask pilasters with anthemion pendants and volute capitals headed by blocks, enriched ormolu mouldings, bands paterae and rings; the frieze drawers have laurel wreath pulls

427

and the internal drawers standard loop-handles. Original pin-hinges, locks and four massive brass castors with friction rollers screwed to beech sleepers. The framed sides of each pedestal, the internal rails, drawer linings and document partitions are oak; pine top, dust boards, base and plinth; the doors veneered on to a mahogany foundation; beech sleepers; the rosewood ground, banded with tulip and satinwood, is inset with various stained, shaded and natural woods. H.84 (33); L.207 (81½); W.120 (47½).

The dark chocolate-coloured rosewood on the inside door and drawer surfaces indicates how far the external countenance has bleached during two centuries exposure to light; it clearly once provided a much stronger contrast to the inlay and mounts. Many of the mounts bear positional numbers repeated on the carcase; the tops of the pedestals are incised 'F' over the front containing drawers and before assembly the inner face of both end panels was inscribed in white chalk 'Out Side'; an old paper label tacked underneath one pedestal is inscribed 'SCREWED / From / BOTTOM of CASE'.

Although Thomas Chippendale's existing account for furnishing Harewood House does not refer to this table there is evidence that it was entered in an earlier bill amounting to £3,024.19.3 which has not survived. The Steward's *Day Work Book* 1760–74 (Leeds Archives Department, Harewood papers, M.S. No.492) contains a section headed 'Mr Thos Chippendale & Co' recording various jobs done at the house by the firm's representatives. It shows that between 18–25 April 1772 Chippendale's foreman-in-charge William Reid

was partly occupied 'makeing covers for the Library Table & Stool', the latter item can be identified as the matching library steps still at the house which fold away into a stool. Cabinet makers normally supplied dust covers for costly furniture and it is inconceivable that Chippendale would provide such equipment for a piece made by a rival firm.

This library writing table was universally regarded by the post-war generation of furniture historians as the finest example of marquetry furniture in the neo-classical taste in existence. It must, however, be stressed that the magnificent inlaid furniture which Chippendale supplied for the principal reception rooms at Harewood is definitely superior in both the technical finish of the cabinetwork and quality of the ormolu mounts. In the eighteenth century library furniture was generally less sumptuous than pieces commissioned for state apartments and the irregular execution of the frieze rosettes provides one indication that this table is not of the highest possible standard; the companion library stool (incorporating steps) which served a more obviously prosaic function is relatively meanly embellished. Two superb reproductions of the library table dating from *c.*1910 are known.

LIT (only the most important references are cited):
P. Macquoid, *Age of Satinwood*, 1908, pls.46–8; M. Jourdain, *English Decoration and Furniture of the Later 18th Century*, 1922, pls.302, 316; *D.E.F.*, III, p.252, pl.25; R. S. Rowe, 'The Library Writing Table from Harewood House', *Burlington*, June 1966, pp.294–8; *L.A.C.*, No.58 (1966), pp.6–12; C. G. Gilbert, 'Chippendale's Harewood Commission', *Furniture History*, IX (1973), pp.1–32.

EXH: Temple Newsam, *Thomas Chippendale and his Patrons in the North*, 1968 (43).

PROV: By descent from Edwin Lascelles of Harewood House to the 7th Earl of Harewood; Christie's, 1 July 1965, lot 57, pl.34 and colour frontispiece; bought with the aid of four local benefactors, H. Blairman & Sons and grants from the government and the N.A.C.F. (voted from the Eugene Cremetti Fund) 1965.   [21/65]

428 LADY'S WRITING TABLE
*c.*1770–5
Harewood; rosewood, kingwood, holly, pine, oak

Shaped rectangular top with a baize-covered writing-slide below and a drawer at the right-hand side, supported on keeled cabriole legs joined by a shelf surrounded on three sides by a pierced brass gallery; the top, frieze and shelf veneered with panels of harewood crossbanded with kingwood, veneered rosewood back and legs; the main surfaces decorated with marquetry designs in transitional rococo – neo-classical taste, the shelf ornamented with informally grouped flowers. The top and shelf edged with a brass band, mortice lock embedded in drawer front. Pine carcase, oak drawer lined with red paper, formerly divided; the shelf is set on peg brackets.
H.71 (28); W.62 (24½); D.40 (15½).

427

428

EXH: Leeds Art Gallery, *English Furniture*, 1930 (132).

PROV: Bequeathed by Mrs Frank Gott, Weetwood Garth, Leeds 1941.   [7.20/41]

429 HARLEQUIN WRITING AND DRESSING TABLE
c.1790
Mahogany; harewood, tulipwood, box, oak

Of rectangular design, the divided folding top opens on to lopers revealing a leather-lined writing flap backed by a horse with lidded document compartments at each side and a till fitted with letter-holes and small drawers at the rear; the harlequin, operated by two coiled springs, can be raised or lowered and secured in either position by a catch; the front contains a dummy drawer, a partitioned dressing drawer with a folding glass and a pair of concave tambour cupboard doors below, the spines alternating in mahogany and harewood; this decorative treatment is continued as a veneer around the sides; raised on square tapered legs with corner strings ending in brass socket castors; the surfaces are veneered in harewood with tulipwood crossbanding, plain and chequered strings; mahogany carcase, brass hinges, locks and catches, handles replaced, original leather tag-pulls.
H.85 (33½); raised 101 (40); W.64 (25) open 127 (50); D.53 (21).

This piece is based on two slightly variant designs in *The Cabinet-Makers' London Book of Prices*, a practical trade manual

429

issued by the London Society of Cabinet-Makers in 1788. It contained detailed price schedules to help masters and journeymen estimate the cost of labour involved in making various standard articles. It included twenty plates of which seventeen are signed by Thomas Shearer and three are anonymous, the harlequin table reproduced on pl.19 is by Shearer and a slightly cheaper version on pl.10 is unsigned. The present example is a close copy of the latter design, although Shearer's was consulted for certain minor features,

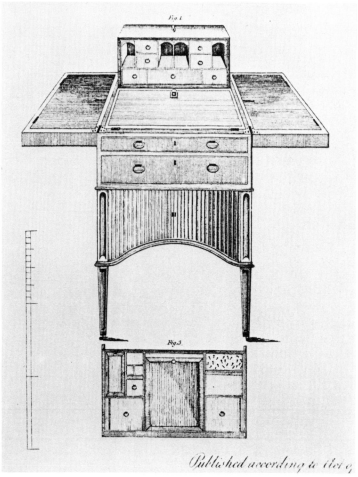

Published according to Act &c.

429

the boldest departure being the narrow reeds used to decorate the upper legs and sides. The specification is as follows:

'A HARLEQUIN TABLE
as in Plate 10, Fig.1,

Two feet two inches long, one foot nine inches from back to front, three feet high, folding tops and taper'd legs, a writing flap in the top, square clamp'd, with a horse under ditto, the harlequin to rise and fall with springs, seven drawers and four letter holes inside, one drawer and one sham ditto in front, cock beaded, a cupboard below with hollow tambour to run right and left, and an astragal on the edge of the bottom. . . .£3.6s.0d'.

This terse description of the basic model is followed by a table of prices for optional extras, but none of the more expensive refinements were introduced by the maker.

An undated drawing of a harlequin table by the London cabinet maker George Speer may be the original design for the unsigned engraving in the *London Book of Prices* (A. Coleridge, 'George Speer', *Apollo*, Oct. 1970, pp.274–83, fig. 16). Another closely similar model was published in Thomas Malton's *Compleat Treatise on Perspective* (2nd ed.) 1779, pl. xxxiv. Many examples corresponding closely to the present one are recorded e.g. Sotheby's, 20 Oct. 1972, lot 105, repr.; *Apollo*, May 1949, p. xxiii, repr.; there is another at Althorp and a fifth in the Ashmolean, Oxford.

LIT: *L.A.C.*, No.19 (1952), p.14, repr.; C. G. Gilbert, 'A Shearer Harlequin Table and its Design', *Furniture History*, II (1966), pp.40–47, figs. xx & xxi; G. Wills, *English Furniture 1760–1900*, 1971, p.131, pl.102.

EXH: Temple Newsam, *L.A.C.F. Members Exhibition*, 1952 (225).

PROV: David Dunstan Schofield Bequest 1962.   [18.21/62]

430 TAMBOUR WRITING TABLE

c.1785–90
Rosewood; tulipwood, satinwood, mahogany, sycamore, pine oak, beech

Rectangular, with frieze drawer, the leather-covered desk top, backed by small drawers and letter-holes, is enclosed by a tambour shutter; raised on four square tapered legs terminating in block feet with socket castors; veneered with rosewood and crossbanded in tulipwood with engraved marquetry designs in satinwood and sycamore; the D-shaped ends are inset with swags of drapery and the frieze ornamented with roundels; the drawer front is inlaid with an arcaded frond-pattern, while the legs, headed by fluted corner blocks, have outlined panels, shuttle-shaped medallions and diminishing husk pendants on all four sides; brass handles, locks and castors with leather rollers. Veneered on to a mahogany foundation, inner structures pine, oak drawer linings, the lower front rail beech; mahogany desk fitments; the tambour is faced with alternating strips of rose and satinwood.

430

Much engraved pen-work on the upper stage has been skinned.
H.92 (36½); W.77 (30½); D.65 (25½).

The brand-mark 'W v L' in a cartouche occurs under the lower front rail.

This type of tambour writing table was made in large numbers; one of standard form designed by Thomas Shearer was illustrated in the widely consulted *Cabinet-Makers' London Book of Prices*, 1788, pl.13, fig.2.

LIT: *Apollo*, June 1938, p. v, repr. (advert. of M. Harris & Sons).

PROV: M. Harris & Sons; given by Frank H. Fulford 1939.
[9.45/39]

431

431 CHAMBER WRITING TABLE
*c.*1805
Mahogany; satinwood, rosewood, pine, oak, box

The mahogany top crossbanded and edged with satinwood
has a well at the back, covered by a hinged flap, containing
a tip-up pen tray and bottle divisions; the frieze, fronted by a
drawer, is inset with simple outlined panels while the band
of chequered herringbone on the lower front edge is continued
as a lozenge-pattern on the other three sides; the legs are
inlaid with strings rising to a point headed by Prince of Wales
plumes with rosewood insets on the corner panels above,
corresponding to the decorative design on the frieze. Original
lock, stamped brass knobs and square socket castors. Solid
mahogany top and legs; the internal rails, well bottom,
drawer sides and glue-blocks are of oak; pine frieze, drawer
front and bottom (with old blue lining paper).
H.71 (28); W.63 (24¾); D.44 (17½).

An interesting example of medium quality provincial
furniture probably made in the Leeds district. The craftsman
has clearly attempted to give the piece a fashionable countenance by introducing Prince of Wales feathers, inset rosewood
panels, simple string outlines and decorative bands.

PROV: The spinning-wheel (Cat. No.349) and a pair of chairs
(Cat. No.90) in the same bequest are known to have come
from Armley House, Leeds; a common provenance can be
claimed for this table which is of comparable date and

431

quality and also passed by descent to Mrs Frank Gott of
Weetwood Garth, who bequeathed it to Leeds in 1941.
[7.11/41]

THREE CHAMBER WRITING TABLES, mahogany
By Gillows, Lancaster, 1811
Under Cat. Nos.502, 503, 504 (illustrated)

432 WRITING TABLE
Attributed to Holland & Sons, London
*c.*1855
Burr maple; mahogany, beech, ivory, ebony, etc.

The rectangular top, with a gilt moulding below the bevelled
edge, is inset with a maroon bordered panel of green leather
and fitted with two frieze drawers of unequal width faced to
match the opposite frieze which centres on a tablet. The end
pillars are tied by a turned and faceted stretcher ornamented
with gilt collars and a central laurel knop; the splay legs,
bordered by parcel-gilt mouldings, are decorated with carved
fronds, laurel bands, rosette bosses and cartouche-shaped
clasps, in gilt mahogany. The top is outlined with ebony and
box strings merging at each end with an elaborate linear
composition of scrolled foliage incorporating flowers, fruit,
rings and hounds' heads in engraved ivory; the side margins

centre on lesser foliate designs. The pedestals and legs are embellished on both faces with strapwork systems including floral pendants, classical wreaths and foliage; the scroll feet conceal castors. Veneered mahogany carcase, stretcher, drawer linings and applied carvings, beech base rail; new mahogany tie brace inserted beneath the top; the pedestals are incised 'I' and 'II' underneath.
H.74 (29); W.122 (48); D.66 (26).

The marquetry designs incorporating hounds' heads and classical elements amid scrolling foliage are reminiscent of Pergolesi's engravings.

A companion table was acquired by the V. & A. (W.31–1969); it has a fully veneered top with variant marquetry enrichment, but is otherwise identical. Both can be ascribed to Holland & Sons on the evidence of quality and stylistic analogy with documented work at Osborne House, the reputed source of this pair. (See E. T. Joy, 'Holland & Sons and the Furniture of Osborne House', *Antiques*, April 1971, pp. 580–5, esp. fig.5).

432

LIT: G. Wills, *English Furniture 1760–1900*, 1971, p.251, pl.201.

PROV: Reputed to have been commissioned by Queen Victoria for Osborne House or possibly Windsor Castle and purchased privately from the royal collection; John Parker (Antiques), London; bought 1969.   [16/69]

432

433 LIBRARY WRITING TABLE
Late 19th century
Mahogany; oak, pine

Built of three separable units – the top and two pedestals; each side is fitted with one long and two short frieze drawers, the pedestals contain three graduated drawers on one front and cupboards with upright folio partitions on the other, enclosed by indented panel doors on the reverse side; square feet with shaped brackets; the top covered with tooled and gilt buff morocco leather; brass drawer and lifting handles. Solid mahogany top, sides drawer fronts, doors and base, the drawer linings and inner structures oak with mahogany facings, stained pine folio partitions. The locks stamped 'JDB & Co LD / LONDON / IMPROVED / 4 / LEVER'. H.81 (32); W.155 (61); D.104 (41).

This library table is conceived in Chippendale's 'Director' manner, but certain features indicate that it was produced by one of the firms making Chippendale-style furniture during the late nineteenth century. The absence of flat drawer runners, presence of machine-made screws and modern locks, the French polished surfaces, evidence of shoddy internal workmanship and design details such as the open plinth are inconsistent with an eighteenth century date.

PROV: Bought by Sir Gervase Beckett of Kirkdale Manor who bequeathed it to his son-in-law Vice Admiral H. J. Egerton; bought at the Sheriff Hutton Park sale (Henry Spencer, Retford) 28 July 1950, lot 24. [25.1/50]

434 WRITING TABLE
Late 19th century
Zebrawood and walnut; mahogany, oak, pine, cedar

The rectangular top is lined with green leather framed by a burr walnut border crossbanded in tulipwood and a brass edge moulding with shell-pattern corner clasps. The serpentine frieze containing a pair of narrow drawers is faced with three shaped panels of floral marquetry crossbanded in tulipwood and set into a zebrawood ground; the ends and back are styled with marquetry panels similar to those on the front. The keeled cabriole legs veneered in zebrawood are embellished with foliated rococo knee mounts and *sabots*. The mahogany carcase with pine and oak tie bars is veneered in zebrawood, burr walnut, tulipwood, satinwood and various green-stained and shaded woods; the cedar drawer linings have quarter-beads; brass locks.
H.76 (30); W.101 (40); D.56 (22).

This table is a typical example of high quality reproduction Louis XV style furniture dating from the turn of the century. Numerous allied models are illustrated in contemporary furniture trade catalogues.

PROV: Agnes and Norman Lupton Bequest 1953.
[13.383/53]

434

435 WRITING TABLE
By Gillow & Co, Lancaster
1907
Walnut and purplewood; mahogany, box, oak

The kidney-shaped top, edged by a matted brass rim, is fitted with a recessed central drawer flanked by narrow deeper drawers; the top, drawer fronts and full frieze are surfaced with walnut parquetry panels set in a trellis pattern of boxwood strings within crossbanded borders; the keeled cabriole legs are veneered with purplewood and ornamented with classical knee mounts and fronded lion's-paw toes; cast-brass ring handles, the central drawer set with a cartouche and laurel spray escutcheon. Veneered onto an oak foundation.
H.76 (30); W.115 (45½); D.64 (25).

435

PROV: Bought by Sam Wilson in 1907 from Gillow & Co for the drawing room at Rutland Lodge, Leeds and recorded in his notebook as '1 Kidney Shaped Table with fine Marqueterie top & sides. Trellis design with fine ormolu mounts £76'; the Sam Wilson Bequest 1925.   [S.W.223]

436 WRITING TABLE
*c.*1920
Mahogany; oak

The lower stage is in the form of a rectangular table fitted with a fall front which pulls out on divided front legs to reveal a baize-covered writing slide with six compartments (two containing drawers) below; the straight chamfered legs and front are embellished with blind frets in the Chinese taste; the superstructure of six drawers flanking a central niche is backed by an open lattice-work screen of pagoda design with mushroom corner finials supporting three galleried shelves; ormolu drawer pulls. Mahogany throughout apart from oak baseboards in the desk drawer and rear stage. H.165 (65); W.114 (45); D.66 (26).

The design is based on a writing table in the 'Chinese Chippendale' style at Nostell Priory, Yorkshire; repr. A. Coleridge, *Chippendale Furniture*, 1968, pl.262.

This table was purchased about 1920 from Solomon Myers Harris who owned a shop on Montpellier Parade, Harrogate between 1901 and 1925. He is listed in contemporary Trade Directories as a 'Fine art, antique furniture and curio dealer' but much of his stock consisted of reproduction furniture made by a relative, H. Harris of Regent Street, Cheltenham.

LIT: *Connoisseur*, June 1956, p.10; A. Coleridge, *Chippendale Furniture*, 1968, pl.263.

PROV: S. M. Harris (Antiques) Harrogate; Mrs A. Walsh from whom it was acquired by the L.A.C.F. 1955.
[L.A.C.F./F.11]

TABLES, PEMBROKE AND SOFA

437 PEMBROKE TABLE
*c.*1780
Mahogany; harewood, oak, pine, ash

The top is of serpentine design outlined by a corner moulding with fall-flaps supported on hinged ash brackets. The frieze contains a through drawer on one side and a dummy drawer on the other, both fronts being veneered, bordered by obliquely chequered strings and fitted with later ebonized knob handles. The straight, tapering legs of square section are headed by inlaid fan paterae and end in blocked feet mounted with socket castors. Oak and pine carcase.
H.72 (28½); W.52 (20½) closed, 91(36) open; D.77 (30½).

PROV: Probably from Parlington Hall; the Gascoigne gift 1968.   [7.147/68]

436

437

438 HARLEQUIN PEMBROKE TABLE
Late 18th century
Mahogany; satinwood, rosewood

The rectangular top with side flaps supported on hinged brackets, is fitted with an oval till, containing a nest of four true and eight dummy drawers (two of the false fronts opening as cupboards) which can be raised or lowered into the specially deep underframe and secured in either position to serve as a work table or form a level top; the inner spring apparatus consists of two steel arms which, when depressed, advance sliding battens into slots in the side rails, the release mechanism is operated by a third hinged strut; the superstructure is raised on square tapering legs with socket castors. The table top and till are veneered in mahogany with satinwood borders crossbanded in rosewood and the panelled surfaces have been embellished at a much later date with painted decoration in the manner of Pergolesi; the oval top is enhanced with a pastoral scene, the small drawers with drapery swags, the flaps portray classical compositions and the legs are ornamented with berried festoons; the baseboard is pierced for hand grips; brass locks and door bolts. Mahogany carcase braced with modern beech rails.
H.74 (29) raised 89 (35); W.106 (42) extended; D.71 (28).

The use of mahogany throughout, even for the hinged brackets, and absence of traditional secondary woods is unexpected, but a strong timber was obviously essential because

438

of the stresses imposed during use. The suspiciously fresh painted details are consistent with the taste for beautified satinwood furniture fashionable in Edwardian days and most of the enrichments apparently date from that time. An antique harlequin pembroke table of identical design and styling, but without painted decoration is illustrated in *Connoisseur*, Feb. 1958, p. xxxviii.

LIT: C. G. Gilbert, *L.G. & R.F.*, 1972, p.7, repr.

EXH: Temple Newsam, *Pictures and Furniture*, 1938 (45).

PROV: From the Hon. Mrs Clive Behrens, Swinton Grange, Malton, Yorkshire.

438

439

439 PEMBROKE TABLE
*c.*1790
Mahogany; tulipwood, satinwood, oak, pine, beech

The oval top, crossbanded in tulipwood and centering on a large shaded shell medallion, has two hinged flaps supported when raised, on beech brackets. The frieze contains one through drawer opposed by a dummy drawer front, both crossbanded and inset with ivory key escutcheons; the square tapered legs are outlined with corner strings and headed by oval rosette paterae; brass socket castors; handles missing.
H.71 (28); W.100 (39½) extended; D.84 (33).

PROV: Bought in Moscow in 1929; bequeathed by Sir George Martin 1976. [51.27/76]

440 PEMBROKE TABLE
By J. Edmonds, London
*c.*1795
Mahogany; satinwood, rosewood, oak, pine, beech

The oval top has D-shaped drop-leaves supported on hinged wooden brackets and centres on an oval shell in shaded satinwood; the veneered mahogany top and rounded drawer fronts are crossbanded with rosewood; moulded and tapered legs headed by wrythen paterae in ovals; square socket castors, handles replaced, the single true drawer fitted with a thread escutcheon and brass lock. The fixed top is veneered on to a pine foundation with mahogany facing bars along the rule joints and moulded edge; mahogany flaps, drawer front and legs; pine underframe, oak drawer linings, one pair of brackets beech, the other mahogany.
H.70 (27½); W.48 (19) closed, 95 (37½) extended; D.75 (29½).

440

The drawer underside is inscribed 'J. Edmonds' (an ink-run along a crevice superficially distorts the initial into an 'F'). The firm of 'J Edmonds, cabinet maker, 6, Old Compton Street, Soho' is recorded in the list of Master Cabinet-Makers printed in Thomas Sheraton's *Cabinet Dictionary*, 1803.

PROV: Given by Sir William Burrell, Hutton Castle, Berwickshire 1944. [22.1/44]

441 PEMBROKE TABLE
*c.*1795
Satinwood; mahogany, oak, pine

Oval top with D-shaped drop-leaves supported on pairs of hinged ash brackets, crossbanded with mahogany between strings, the edge moulding and rule joints painted black; one true and one dummy drawer with crossbanded fronts, veneered tapering legs with corner strings headed by an astragal which continues below the drawers. Brass handles replace the original turned wooden knobs. Oak carcase except for the drawer fronts which are veneered on to pine; oak drawer, the bottom lined with blue paper.
H.71 (28); W.52 (20½) closed, 100(39½) extended; D.76 (30).

PROV: Agnes and Norman Lupton Bequest 1953. [13.374/53]

442 SOFA TABLE
By J. & A. Semple, London
1809
Kingwood and rosewood; mahogany, tulipwood, pine, beech, oak

The oblong top with rounded end-flaps supported on beech brackets is veneered with kingwood surrounded by a wide band of oyster-figure mahogany bordered by stringing lines and tulipwood crossbanding; the frieze, edged with a brass moulding, contains two true opposed by a pair of dummy drawers outlined with pearl beading; the bed is raised on twin reel-turned end standards connected by two matching rosewood stretchers; the squared base rails, styled with beaded corners and ring-turned discs corresponding to the drawer

440

fronts and pulls, are mounted with scrolled bracket lion's-paw feet in ormolu concealing castors. Mahogany drawer linings and top braced by oak struts, inner structures pine and beech.

H.70 (27½); W.89 (35), 148 (58½) extended; D.71 (28).

This sofa table is exceptionally well documented for the original bill on tradesman's card, cheque paying it and receipt all survive. The trade card, designed by Thomas Sheraton, portrays a fashionable dining room and is inscribed 'SEMPLE'S / Upholstery Warehouse, No 2 Berner's Street / From No. 78, Margaret Street. / T. Sheraton delin. – Barlow sculp.' The bill made out on the back reads 'London / Mr Wm Shadbolt To J & A Semple / 1809 March 12 To a fine Kingwood / Sophatable with orangewood / border 2 Drawers on solid turned / standards & Rich Brass Lions paws / & scroll castors the whole superbly / ornamented with ormolu mouldings / complete £22.0.0.' The cheque on Messrs Rogers, Olding & Rogers dated 16 March 1809 is signed 'Wm & C Shadbolt' while the receipt is signed on behalf of the partnership by 'H. Metcalf'.

The reference to 'orangewood borders' has aroused keen interest; this is a pale timber and might have been used for the light border strings but is more likely to be a capricious trade term for the vivid tulipwood crossbanding.

442

LIT: *Country Life*. 14 June 1962, p.1420, fig.1; *Connoisseur*, June 1963, p.71 repr.; *Collectors Guide*, June 1963, p.57, repr.; *L.A.C.*, No.52 (1963), p.5, fig.1; *Furniture History*, I (1965), pp.59–60, pl. x; M. Jourdain, *Regency Furniture* (rev.ed. 1965), pls.135–6; *Antiques*, April 1971, p.576, repr.; C. G. Gilbert, *L.G. & R.F.*, 1972, p.34, repr.

PROV: Bought directly from the makers by two brothers William and Charles Shadbolt of Bankside; by descent through the former's son William (d.1876) and his daughter Maria (d.1913) to Alice Lloynd (d.1961) who bequeathed it to Miss Ruth Shadbolt (great, great grand-daughter of Charles the original co-owner); Claremont Auction Rooms (Arthur F. Dunk), Hastings, 29 March 1962, lot 253; G. E. Field (Antiques) Sevenoaks; R. L. Harrington, Ltd; Stanley J. Pratt, Ltd; Hotspur, Ltd; H. Blairman & Sons; bought 1962.   [25/62]

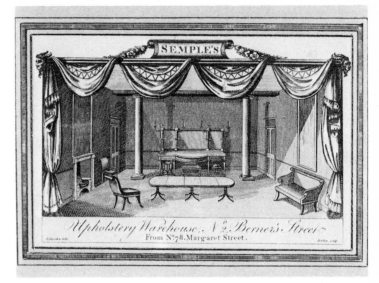

442

TABLES, SIDE
Console, Pier

443

443 SIDE TABLE
*c.*1705
Gilt pine

Rectangular top enriched with a central medallion amid a formal system of interlaced strapwork with acanthus foliage, husks and *lambrequin* motifs against a cross-hatched ground bordered by a gadrooned edge; the frieze with a central pendant, trellised ground, leafy and beaded mouldings is raised on four tapering vase-shaped legs headed by Ionic capitals, the panelled sides enriched with husk drops; the gadrooned feet are joined by pierced cross-stretchers of reversed scroll design, the members carved with acanthus and centred by a circular dished platform.
H.84 (33); W.127 (50); D.59 (23).

A side table of virtually identical design is illustrated in *Connoisseur*, Dec. 1928, p.228.

EXH: Leeds Art Gallery, *Works of Art Presented by the L.A.C.F.*, 1924 (51); Leeds Art Gallery, *English Furniture*, 1930 (43).

PROV: Bought from T. W. Richards (Antiques) Leeds, by the L.A.C.F. 1914.   [L.A.C.F./F2]

444 PAIR OF SIDE TABLES
*c.*1730
Pine and beech

Shaped, rounded aprons centering on female masks with plumed head-dresses, ear-rings and pearl necklets, flanked by formal designs of elaborately scrolling foliage, strapwork and palmettes; the side aprons centre on scallop shells; the angular cabriole legs on knurl feet are richly carved with acanthus fronds and pendants within strapwork borders; the gesso-gilt surfaces are decorated with stamped enrichment; Portovenere marble tops (one damaged). Pine frame with beech legs, the corner posts and rails impressed with joint numbers.
H.79 (31); W.90 (35½); W.59 (23).

The tables were probably ordered following the remodelling of Boynton Hall, Yorkshire *c.*1730.

LIT: *L.A.C.*, No.14 (1950–1), p.13, repr.

PROV: By descent from Sir William Strickland, 4th Baronet of Boynton to the Rev. J. E. Strickland; purchased at the Boynton Hall sale (Henry Spencer, Retford) 21–23 Nov. 1950, lot 318.   [42.4/50]

444

445 SIDE TABLE
c.1735
Pine

The vigorously carved and gilt frame with canted corners, is supported on scroll supports headed by shells, pierced aprons; the legs are decorated with scales, stylized foliage, husks and horizontal channelling within raised borders; below the frieze floral swags and acanthus fronds centre on a shell cartouche the garlands trailing across the front legs to link with interlaced side aprons; the frieze, ornamented with scrolled foliage and low-relief husk patterns, is surmounted by a ribbon and rosette moulding and acanthus cornice; the gesso surface is enriched with circular stamps and cross-hatching. Mottled yellow Siena marble top bedded on a black marble slab. H.87 (34½); W.137 (54); D.69 (27).

The marble top is not original and plugged screw sockets on the inner rails show the table at one time had a wooden top. A Victorian coating of wainscot brown paint which had preserved much of the original gilding was removed in 1949.

The frame displays remarkable refinement of detail, but at present no firm attribution can be made.

LIT: *L.A.C.*, No.12 (1950), p.4, repr.; *D.E.F.*, III, p.287, fig. 40; *Antique Collector*, April 1964, pp.57–8, figs.1 & 2; F. Davis, *A Picture History of English Furniture*, 1958, pl.190.

EXH: Royal Academy, London, *English Taste in the 18th Century*, Winter 1955/6 (12).

PROV: Ronald A. Lee (Antiques); Hotspur, Ltd; bought 1950. [13/50]

446 PAIR OF SIDE TABLES
Attributed to Matthias Lock, London
c.1740
Pine, painted white with gilt details

The rectangular tops of yellow Siena marble are supported at the front on coupled consoles headed by corner blocks, the

445

446

446

446

panelled sides being carved with husk pendants, suspended from shells; the foot scrolls are united to the single rear consoles by solid base runners; the architectural frieze is ornamented with a fronded Vitruvian scroll pattern between enriched mouldings and the pierced front apron is carved in high relief with a mask of Hercules draped with the skin of the Nemean lion hung through carved rings; the end elevations are of arched design with side scrolls and acanthus sprays centering on a large concave fronded shell. The main joints are marked with cuts, crosses and simple geometric devices; the back of one shell is roughly incised with trial cuts. H.86 (34); W.173 (68); D.89 (35).

The design corresponds very closely to a drawing by Matthias Lock in the V. & A. (2848.98), suggesting he made these tables. It may, however, be significant that a schedule among the Ditchley papers (Oxford Record Office: DIL. 1/p/3a) records that the architect Henry Flitcroft supplied five designs for table frames in 1740–1.

Several virtually identical tables and many variants of this design type exist, only examples offering a near exact analogy are cited: a pair at Wentworth Woodhouse, Yorkshire (where Flitcroft also worked); a pair at Shugborough Hall, Staffs (Earl of Lichfield); one in the Metropolitan Museum of Art (ex. Hamilton Palace); and another is illustrated by H. Cescinsky, *English Furniture*, 1929, p.259.

LIT (only the more important references are cited): *Country Life*, 20 May 1933, p.515; *Country Life*, 14 Aug. 1942, p.318, fig.2; Edwards and Jourdain, *Georgian Cabinet-Makers*, 1956, pl.82; *D.E.F.*, III, p.124, fig.3; *L.A.C.*, No.26 (1954), pp.4–5, repr.

EXH: London, Royal Academy, *English Taste in the 18th Century*, Winter 1955/6 (43).

PROV: By descent from the Earls of Lichfield, Ditchley House, Oxfordshire to the Viscounts Dillon; Sotheby's, 26 May 1933, lot 139, repr.; Ronald Tree; the Earl of Wilton; bought from Mallett & Son 1954.   [9/54]

447 PAIR OF CONSOLE TABLES
c.1740
Pine

The veneered *verde antico* marble slabs, with decorative brass beading, rest on richly carved and gilt frames with winged eagle-head supports of double-scroll design; the frieze is ornamented with a fluted band between twisted ribbon and egg and dart mouldings and the front apron centres on a female mask backed by fringed drapes linked to the supports by swags of fruit and flowers, half the design being repeated on each side; the frame is raised on a surbase painted to simulate the marble top, with gilt acanthus mouldings and a fronded shell set between the feet. The inner surfaces are painted black; one rail bears a metal tag stamped '2463'. H.90 (35½); W.138 (54½); D.79 (31).

There is an unconfirmed tradition that the tables were made to a design by the architect Henry Flitcroft for Wentworth Woodhouse, Yorkshire, which he greatly enlarged for the Marquess of Rockingham between *c*.1734–50. Flitcroft certainly designed tables and mirrors for interiors at Ditchley (Earl of Lichfield) in 1740–1 and his name has always been associated with a pair of tables from Wentworth Woodhouse sold at Christie's, 15 July 1948 (*D.E.F.*, III, p.286, figs.37 & 39); they also relate to a pair formerly at Alnwick illustrated by R. W. Symonds, *Furniture Making in 17th and 18th Century England*, figs.213–4, and another at Lamport Hall, Northants, but Flitcroft's authorship is far from proven.

LIT: *L.A.C.*, No.38 (1957), p.30, repr.; H. Hayward (ed.), *World Furniture*, p.129, fig.469.

PROV: Said to come from Wentworth Woodhouse, Yorkshire (Earl Fitzwilliam); Major Fermor Hesketh; Frank Partridge & Sons; the Earl of Wilton; Mallett & Son; bought 1958.   [7/58]

448 PAIR OF SIDE TABLES
c.1745
Gilt pine

Each supports a rectangular slab of Marmo Fior marble raised on four scrolled cabriole legs richly carved with gadrooned borders, husk chains, palm fronds and acanthus foliage; the front apron, styled with flamework, acanthus loops and paired shells, centres on a contorted rococo formation with fleshy wings clasped by a shell and acanthus spray; the side aprons display similar fleshy frills and shells; the frieze is bordered by an acanthus moulding. Pine throughout with riven corner blocks, two cross rails and pegged joints. H.87 (34½); W.183 (72); D.140 (55).

The auricular central feature, perhaps based on an engraved source, the vigorous mannerist carving and slightly unorthodox design may indicate a provincial origin.

LIT: *Apollo*, June 1937, p.371, repr.

PROV: Spero Antiques; Edwards & Sons; sold by auction (Arber, Rutter, Waghorn & Brown) 8–9 June, 1937; A. Cook (Antiques); given by Lady Martin 1944.   [20/44]

449 SIDE TABLE (Irish)
c.1740–50
Mahogany; pine

The Breccia Violetto marble top is supported on cabriole legs vigorously carved with floral foliage and shells, terminating in hocked and knuckled lion's-paw feet; the front apron formed of paired laurel swags, centres on a medallion featuring an antique head in profile suspended from tied ribbons; the swags bearing shells are repeated on the side aprons; the

447

448

449

rounded frieze is enriched with diaper patterns. Pine rails faced and veneered with mahogany; the blank studs below the shells once anchored decorative elements.
H.85 (33½); W.165 (65); D.74 (29).

The lavish carving of the legs, the deep, vigorously styled apron centering on a mask, diapered frieze and traces of a black finish, simulating bog oak, indicate an Irish origin. A very similar Irish side table with wooden top and central profile medallion between swags was sold at Christie's, 27 Nov. 1975, lot 109, repr.

PROV: Purchased about 1924 by Sir Henry Sutcliffe Smith for Ingerthorpe Grange, Markington, Yorkshire; bought from his widow 1945.   [20.1/45]

450 PAIR OF CONSOLE TABLES
By James Pascall, London
1746
Gilt mahogany and pine

The shaped top board is surfaced with a thick layer of gesso embellished in low relief with a central flame cartouche surrounded by a finely balanced system of leafy rococo scrolls, palm fronds, floral sprays, husks, flamework and trellised panels against a punched and stippled ground; sanded frieze with enriched mouldings and pierced aprons

below composed of leafy fruit and floral garlands centering at the front on a cherub mask backed by a sunburst; the console supports, carved with beaded acanthus and ferns, rest on shell toes; the shaped surbase, stained black with a trellised ground and gilt corner moulding, is bridged by a rococo wave. Mahogany top, pine frame.
H.90 (35½); W.122 (48); D.64 (25).

For evidence of authorship see Cat. No.45.

LIT: F. Moss, *Pilgrimages to Old Homes*, V, 1910, p.321, repr.; F. Lenygon, *Furniture in England 1660–1760*, 1914, pl.210; *L.A.C.*, No.3 (1947), p.2, repr.; *D.E.F.*, III, p.292, fig.53; *Burlington*, Dec. 1955, p.380, fig.20; C. G. Gilbert, 'The Temple Newsam Suite of early-Georgian Gilt Furniture,' *Connoisseur*, Feb. 1968, pp.84–88, fig.7.

EXH: London, Royal Academy, *English Taste in the 18th Century*, Winter 1955–6 (130).

PROV: Recorded in an inventory of Temple Newsam made in 1808 '10th Room Picture Gallery First Floor – 2 smaller tables carved and finished in burnished gold and carved and gilt tops and serge covers to ditto lined'; removed to Hickleton Hall, Yorkshire in 1922 and sold by Lord Halifax at the Hickleton Hall sale (Hollis & Webb, Leeds) 18–22 March 1947, lots 278 & 279, repr.; Charles Thornton (Antiques); W. Waddingham (Antiques); given by Councillor F. E. Tetley 1947.   [30.1/47]

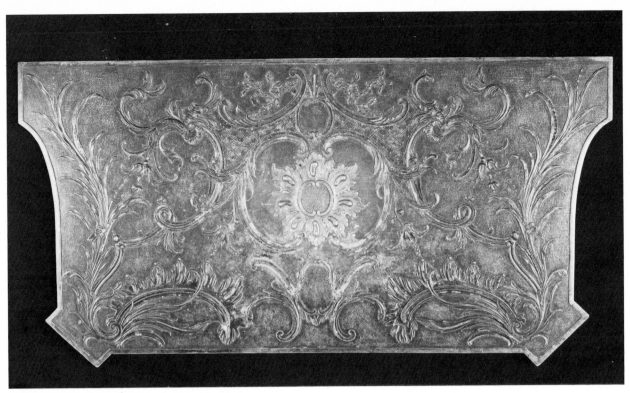

450

450

451 SIDE TABLE
*c.*1755
Gilt pine

The Florentine marble slab is supported on cabriole legs lavishly carved in the rococo taste with fronded scrolls, palm branches, ribband ornament and bold satyr-masks, ending in spurred volute feet; the frieze is styled with a vigorous flame border and the front centres on a pierced apron featuring a basket of grapes surrounded by leafy C-scrolls and spiky foliage; the gilt surface is richly tooled, burnished and textured.
H.99 (39); W.170 (67); D.84 (33).

Inside rear rail lightly incised 'W'. The Bacchic masks and grapes suggest this table was intended for a dining room.

LIT: A Tipping, *English Homes* (Period III), 1927, fig.383; *Country Life*, 17 Aug. 1935, p.171, repr.; *Apollo*, Dec. 1941, p.138, repr.; *D.E.F.*, III, p.290, fig.47; *Burlington*, Dec. 1955, p.383, pl.24; *Antiques*, Sept. 1968, p.360, repr.

EXH: London, Royal Academy, *English Taste in the 18th Century*, Winter 1955/6, (133); Munich, *The Age of Rococo*, 1958 (869).

PROV: By descent from Sir John Mordant Cope of Bramshill, Hants, to Sir Denzil Cope; Bramshill sale (Knight Frank & Rutley) 1938; A. Cook (Antiques); given by Lady Martin 1940.   [16/40]

451

451

452 PAIR OF CONSOLE TABLES AND PIER GLASSES
(See colour frontispiece and illustrations Vol.1, pp.218–19)
By William Vile and John Cobb, London
1761
Pine, painted white and gilt

The mirror plates are set in oval frames enriched with a band of guilloche enclosing florets running between an inner bead of twisted-ribbon design and an outer rope moulding with a border of cusped demi-rosettes and rococo wave motifs; the elaborately pierced forward-tilting crest is formed of a large crimped shell backed by a fronded cartouche supporting a smaller shell; scrolling acanthus branches, which spring from the central leaf clasp with fronds appearing to wind under the frame, terminate in long tapering grape swags falling clear of the shoulders; the base is richly styled with a similar shell and system of scrolling rococo fronds with pendant grape bunches; original glass plates.
H.244 (96); W.137 (54).

The Breccia Corallina marble table tops rest on console frames; the frieze rails, bordered with enriched mouldings corresponding to the mirror surrounds, centre on a rococo shell amid scrolling acanthus plumes which give the illusion of curling under and through the frieze; the cabriole supports, carved at the knees with husk drops and richly styled with frond work, terminate in volute feet set on blocks; the corners are festooned with swags of grapes which fall in 'icicle' clusters behind the legs; the side aprons exactly repeat half of the front design; medial braces renewed in oak.
H.89 (35); W.152 (60); D.79 (31).

The Royal cabinet-makers William Vile and John Cobb, the corner of Long Acre, London, invoiced this pair of console tables and pier glasses to the Earl of Coventry on 6 Dec. 1761:

'For 2 Large Oval Glasses, in Handsome Carv'd and part painted, and part Gilt in Burnish'd Gold frames . . . £173
For 2 Handsome Carv'd Table frames, to Stand under the Oval Glasses, part painted, and Gilt in Burnish'd Gold
£33.12.0'

The tables and glasses were commissioned for the piers of the saloon at Croome Court together with three window cornices *en suite*, although faint pencilled inscriptions on the table frames 'Right Hand / Yellow Room' and 'Left Hand Door / Tapestry' indicate they occupied a different position at some time. The marble slabs are not recorded in Vile and Cobb's accounts, they must have been provided separately, perhaps by John Wildsmith who supplied marble for another table top in the house. A set of window cornices *en suite* are now displayed at 7, Charlotte Square, Edinburgh. The mirrors relate interestingly to the left-hand design for 'Glass Frames' (dated 1760) in the 3rd edition of Chippendale's *Director*, pl. clxxii (repr. p.219). It is possible Chippendale

452

was specially commissioned to supply the design since he worked at Croome Court and supplied a plate of looking-glass for a frame designed by Adam for the Earl of Coventry's London house. A pair of large oval carved and gilt pier mirrors from the Earl of Mansfield's collection, Kenwood sale (C. B. King, Ltd) 6–9 Nov. 1922, lots 1040–1, repr., provide a striking analogy to the Croome Court pair; Chippendale was also involved in the furnishing of Kenwood.

LIT: H. Hayward, 'Splendour at Croome Court: New Light on Vile and Cobb', *Apollo*, May 1974, pp.350–52 (illustrated *in situ* at Croome, fig.1); *L.A.C.*, No.75 (1974), p.3.

EXH: London, Partridge (Fine Arts, Ltd) Summer Exhibition, 4–28 June 1974 (25).

PROV: By descent from the 6th Earl of Coventry to the Trustees of the Croome Court Estate; Frank Partridge & Sons; bought with the aid of a government grant, contributions from the N.A.C.F., the Pilgrim Trust, the L.A.C.F., Sir George Martin, an anonymous benefactor and assistance from the vendor 1974.   [13/74]

453 SIDE TABLE

*c.*1770
Mahogany and calamander; pine, satinwood, box, etc.

Serpentine front and sides with angular cabriole legs; the top and frieze crossbanded in calamander, bordering shaped mahogany panels; the top is decorated with a marquetry design of musical trophies (a lyre, horn, recorder, sheet music and a mask) suspended amid floral festoons from tied ribbons and encircled by a leafy rococo cartouche with floral sprays at either side; the inset frieze panels are plain apart from a central husk pendant; the legs are faced with calamander in front and mahogany behind, the keeled leading edge and moulded top being bound with brass strips; ornamental brass knee and toe mounts. Pine carcase, the top of twin framed-panel construction, laminated front rail, the underside coated with dark stain; the marquetry is executed in various green-stained, shaded and engraved woods; the brass mounts not original.
H.85 (33½); W.158 (62½); D.62 (24½).

The design and decoration of this table reflect the idiom

453

453

of the immigrant French ébéniste Pierre Langlois, although the affinities with his proven work do not justify an attribution. The top of a commode at Aske Hall confidently ascribed to his hand (*Apollo*, Sept. 1967, p.224, fig.15) offers perhaps the closest analogy.

PROV: Bought from Dowling & Bray (Antiques), Looe, Cornwall 1944.   [24/44]

454 PAIR OF PIER TABLES

c.1785
Satinwood; rosewood, sycamore, maple, pine, beech

Semi-elliptical tops veneered with satinwood, crossbanded in rosewood and decorated with engraved marquetry designs in shaded and green-stained sycamore, maple and box; the central ovals portray a standing female in classical robes with upraised pointing finger (similar to figures in the published designs of Pergolesi); the medallions are suspended by riband ties and flanked by husk-chains, scrolling arabesques and olive sprays within a border of cross-hatched lunettes; the friezes are carved with a band of scrolled flowering stems centering on paterae between an upper acanthus and lower beaded moulding; tapering turned legs enriched with stiff leaves. The veneered tops, sleepers and laminated rails are in pine; carved and gilt beech legs, gilt frieze ornament on a re-painted pale green ground.
H.87 (34½); W.148 (58½); D.52 (20½).

The decoration of the tops is strikingly similar to an unpublished marquetry piano case inscribed on the name board 'Robertus Stodart, London, fecit 1784'.

PROV: Sold at Christie's, 18 May 1961, lot 36, repr.; Ronald A. Lee (Antiques); Biggs of Maidenhead; F. E. Rhodes of

Thorpe Underwood Hall, Yorkshire who gave the tables in memory of his wife 1966.   [5/66]

455 HANGING CONSOLE TABLE

c.1790
Satinwood; tulipwood, pine

The semi-circular top and frieze are veneered in figured satinwood crossbanded in tulipwood with border strings; the frieze, outlined with string panels, centres on an inward curving console support headed by a tablet, the tail-end being secured to the wall in the manner of a bracket. The top, console and laminated frieze are of pine; a narrow strip has been added to the back.
H.53 (21); W.75 (29½); D.29 (11¼).

PROV: Agnes and Norman Lupton Bequest 1953.
[13.370/53]

456 PIER TABLE

c.1790
Mahogany; satinwood, rosewood, oak, pine

Elliptical front and rounded ends; the mahogany top has a satinwood border and various crossbandings between string inlays veneered on to an oak foundation; the frieze is ornamented with a central tablet, outlined panels and bands, raised on square tapered legs with applied harewood collars and inlaid lozenge design, the upper part of the legs stand proud of the frieze. Pine underframe and corner blocks, the curved frieze rail built up from laminated strips.
H.84 (33); W.145 (57); D.39 (15½).

PROV: Bought by Sam Wilson from the London Curio Club, Ltd. in 1913 for Rutland Lodge, Leeds; the Sam Wilson Bequest 1925.   [SW/227]

454

454

457 SIDE TABLE
Various dates
Mahogany; pine

The shaped frieze centres on an elaborately fronded cartouche formed of paired C-scrolls with leafy flower-filled cornucopia at either side; the end rails are profiled as twin pendants and the cabriole legs, ornamented at the front with acanthus carving, end in claw and ball feet; the pink and white mottled marble slab rests on a rosette-pattern moulding. Stained pine back rail and cross braces.
H.81 (32); W.143 (56½); D.66 (26).

This table originally supported a wooden top, the frieze has been faced with 'Chippendale-style' carving, the side rails profiled, the legs embellished and the top moulding added. It may be entirely Victorian, but the framework appears to date from the Georgian period. The table is typical of much heavily improved or reproduction furniture stocked by dealers in the early years of this century.

PROV: Bought by Sam Wilson in 1907 from Thomas Sutton of Eastbourne and entered in his notebook as 'Fine Old side table £45'; the Sam Wilson Bequest 1925.   [S.W.217]

TABLES, VARIOUS
Night, Work, Wine

458 NIGHT TABLE
c.1775
Mahogany; oak, pine, beech

Shaped tray-top with pierced lifting handles, the serpentine-front contains a cupboard enclosed by a tambour shutter with two drawers under and simply styled aprons; the lower part originally contained a close-stool with sham drawer fronts which pulled forward on divided legs to form a seat with pan below, this section has been rebuilt as two drawers.
H.75 (29½); W.59 (23); D.51 (20).

PROV: By descent to Mrs Frank Gott of Weetwood Garth who bequeathed it to Leeds 1941.   [7.16/41]

NIGHT OR 'DECEPTION' TABLE
By Gillows, Lancaster, 1810
Under Cat. No.498 (illustrated)

NIGHT TABLE OR POT CUPBOARD, mahogany
By Gillows, Lancaster, 1810–11
Under Cat. No.499 (illustrated)

459 WORK TABLE
c.1765–1770
Mahogany

The hexagonal top veneered with six radial segments of richly figured mahogany and a crossbanded border is supported on a tripod stand. The tapering fluted column has a gadrooned knop at the base while the moulded legs, ending in volute toes, are carved with sunk gothic panels and slight fronds. The top has an undercut lip moulding.
H.72 (28½); Diam.64 (25¼).

In 1765 Chippendale invoiced a table of similar design to Sir Lawrence Dundas, as a 'work table'.

PROV: Bequeathed by Frank Savery 1966.   [1.15/66]

459

460

460 WORK TABLE
Late 18th century
Mahogany

Plain rectangular top with astragal moulding, raised on extremely slender turned legs braced by stretchers of H-form; the top secured by glue blocks.
H.69 (27); W.70 (27½); D.44 (17½).

Tables of this design probably relate to the 'spider' tables recorded in late eighteenth century furniture bills. As a type it displays affinities with the light quartetto tables illustrated in Sheraton's *Cabinet Dictionary* (1803) and described by him as 'a kind of small work table . . .'. Harold Tweed of Bradford owns an almost identical table inscribed under the top 'A Yeoman's Table given her by Mr Watson in 1783'.

PROV: Given by Sir William Burrell, Hutton Castle, Berwickshire 1944.   [22.2/44]

WINE OR SOCIAL TABLE, mahogany
By Gillows, Lancaster, 1810
Under Cat. No.494 (illustrated)

461 VITRINE
c.1900
Kingwood; beech

In the form of a small table with slender, keeled cabriole legs supporting a shallow display case, the serpentine front, sides and hinged sloping lid panelled with curved glass; the case is

461

outlined with ormolu borders and the legs set with fronded rococo-pattern knee and toe mounts, ormolu key handle. Beech carcase veneered in kingwood.
H.85 (33½); W.57 (22½); D.39 (15½).

PROV: Recorded in the 1930s Lotherton inventory; the Gascoigne gift 1968.   [7.151/68]

TEA CADDIES

462 TEA CADDY AND EQUIPAGE
c.1735
Mahogany and silver

The rectangular casket has chamfered corners and a coved shoulder moulding while the top and sides are faced with crossbanded mahogany panels outlined by strings; the interior, lined with red plush is partitioned to receive three silver boxes, a cream jug, set of twelve tea-spoons, a mote-spoon, sugar nippers and a pair of pistol-handled knives with detachable steel blades. The case is mounted with a

462

463

silver scroll-handle backed by an elaborately profiled engraved plate centering on an oval heraldic cartouche displaying 'Or, on a fess azure between three acorns slipped argent as many bezants or' (Boissier) impaling 'argent a moor's head sable, between three mullets pierced gules (Berchere); the shaped lock plate and cast corner feet are chased with fronded rococo scrolls and shells. The rocaille tea equipage by Paul de Lamerie bears London hallmarks for 1735–6, the mounts are unmarked apart from a control stamp 'A'. The two caddies (engraved 'G' and 'B' for green/black tea); the sugar box (marked 'S'); the cream-jug and each tea-spoon are embellished with the same armorials as the handle escutcheon.
H.16·5 (6½); W.29·5 (11½); D.16·5 (6½).

This equipage is believed to be the only complete set of its kind in existence.

LIT: M. Clayton, *The Collector's Dictionary of Silver and Gold*, 1971, p.298, fig.618; A. Wells-Cole, 'Two Rococo Masterpieces', *L.A.C.*, No.79 (1976), pp.13–24, figs.1–4.

PROV: The armorials are for Jean Daniel Boissier, son of Guillaume (a Burgess of Geneva who settled in England) and Suzanne Judith, third daughter of Jaques Louis Berchere, merchant jeweller and banker, sometime of Paris and of Broad Street, London. The couple were married in April 1735 at St Peter Le Bow, London and thus the equipage was presumably a wedding present. It is quite possible that Paul de Lamerie knew the bride and bridegroom's families. By descent to P. E. Boissier; Sotheby's, 8 April 1954, lot 51; Christie's, 21 June 1967, lot 88; Frank Partridge & Sons; Palladio Stiftung; Christie's, 26 June 1974, lot 111; S. J. Shrubsole, Ltd; bought with the aid of a government grant 1975.   [15/75]

463 TEA CADDY
*c.*1765
Mahogany; ebony

Rectangular, veneered in figured mahogany with ebony corner strings, facings and base band, the coved lid mounted with a scrolled brass loop handle; the interior is fitted with a slip lining divided to receive two caddies, the lid and underside covered in green baize; mahogany carcase, silvered lock.
H.13·8 (5½); W.15 (6); D.12 (4¾).

PROV: Given by Charles Roberts, Farfield Hall, Yorkshire 1941.   [11.3/41]

464 TEA CADDY
1768–9
Mahogany and silver; pine

Oblong, veneered in figured mahogany and outlined with ebonized corner strings; the coved top is set with a scrolled silver handle and pierced escutcheon incorporating an oval tablet engraved with the arms of Mills quartering Pitfield; the box is fronted by an elaborately pierced key-plate of foliate rococo design, backed by acanthus-pattern hinges and raised on claw and ball feet with fretted corner mounts, all in silver. The interior, lined with red plush and silver gimp, is divided into three shaped wells containing silver caddies of serpentine design ornamented with husks, beading and fruit

464

finials; the engraved armorials are repeated within garlanded rococo cartouches and each lid bears a lion-rampant – the crest of Mills.
H.20·3 (8); W.29·5 (11½); D.14·7 (5¾).

The caddies bear the mark of John Langford and John Sebille with the London date letter for 1768–9. A caddy box with identical bracket feet stamped 'IW' (1765) is illustrated in *D.E.F.*, III, p.340, fig.4.

PROV: The Mills family of Gloucestershire, Middlesex and Surrey; R. F. Tetley, Beechfield, Boston Spa, Yorkshire; bought from his executors 1969.   [19/69]

465 TEA CADDY
*c.*1785
Sycamore; tulipwood, satinwood, mahogany, oak

Oblong, panelled in harewood with tulipwood crossbanding and chequered strings; the top, front, back and inside lid are

465

decorated with oval shell medallions executed in shaded satinwood on a green-stained ground, the ends are inset with ovals enclosing butterflies; the interior contains three foil-lined compartments with veneered lids and ivory knobs, mahogany carcase, oak base, lock renewed.
H.12·5 (5); W.22·2 (8¾); D.13·3 (5¼).

EXH: Temple Newsam, *Pictures and Furniture*, 1938 (21).

PROV: Given by Mrs Clive Behrens, Swinton Grange, Yorkshire 1940.   [18.9/40]

466

466 TEA CADDY
*c.*1790
Sycamore; satinwood, pine, etc.

Of oval design with a pine carcase and hinged lid veneered in harewood; the top bears an oval satinwood panel engraved with sprigs of wild rose and bramble outlined by corner strings and a feather band; the front is decorated in various stained and shaded woods with two white birds perched on the branches of an orchard tree; chequered base band, oval ivory escutcheon, lock missing, the interior lined with foil.
H.12 (4¾); W.18·4 (7¼); D.10·8 (4¾).

A caddy decorated with an almost identical but reversed design was sold at Sotheby's, 29 July 1977, lot 85, repr.

PROV: Given by Charles Roberts, Farfield Hall, Yorkshire 1941.   [11.4/41]

467 TEA CADDY
*c.*1790
Satinwood; pine, rosewood, box, etc.

In the form of a rectangular oblong box, bordered with ornamental strings and green-stained bands inset with

467

alternating motifs; the sides and top are transfer-printed with pairs of stipple-engraved medallions depicting classical scenes of putti and animals, the backgrounds over-painted in maroon; the interior is fitted with two hinge-lidded slip canisters lined with foil and a central well containing a circular cut-glass bowl; relined with pink paper, silver ring handle, new lock. Veneered on to a pine foundation. The green stain is unusually vivid.
H.15 (6); W.30·5 (12); D.15 (6).

The rear medallions are taken from a print entitled 'The Nuptials of Cupid and Psyche' drawn by G. B. Cipriani and engraved by F. Bartolozzi, but the immediate source can be traced to a plate in Michelangelo Pergolesi's *Designs for Various Ornaments etc.*, pl.101; the other subjects are presumably based on illustrations in similar works.

PROV: Given by Miss K. E. M. Cooper-Abbs, Mount Grace Priory, Yorkshire 1968.   [29/68]

468 TEA CADDY
*c.*1795
Mahogany; satinwood, harewood, pine

Of oblong, slightly tapered design with a bevelled lid; veneered in figured mahogany outlined with satinwood corner strings and a base band; the top is inset with a single and the front a pair of oval green-stained medallions representing the Prince of Wales feathers; partitioned foil-lined interior, pine carcase. The brass key plate, basket-pattern handle mounts and shell feet are later additions.
H.14·5 (5¾); W.30 (11¾); D.13·8 (5½).

PROV: Given by Mrs Clive Behrens, Swinton Grange, Yorkshire 1940.   [18.5/40]

469 TEA CADDY
*c.*1795
Satinwood; sycamore, pearl shell, rolled paperwork

Of pointed shuttle design; the lid and sides are outlined by raised satinwood borders inset with chequered strings forming sunk panels surfaced with powdered pearl shell; the front centres on a coloured stipple engraving of a kneeling female holding two torches bordered by gilt rolled paper and flanked by bouquets in the same media; the back is similarly decorated with an urn amid coloured sprays and the top bears floral motifs; the divided, foil-lined interior is closed by a hinged satinwood lid, sycamore carcase, silvered lock and buckle-pattern handle.
H.12·5 (5); W.19·5 (7¾); D.8·8 (3½).

PROV: Bought from P. H. Gillingham at the Antique Dealers' Fair, 1936 (label inside lid); given by Mrs Clive Behrens, Swinton Grange, Yorkshire 1940.   [18.1/40]

470 TEA CADDY
*c.*1800
Sycamore; pine

Of oblong octagonal design, the pine carcase veneered in harewood outlined by box corner strings; the hinged lid is engraved with a green-stained and shaded basket of garden flowers while the front is similarly styled with a basket of roses, pinks and ferns between two vases of flowers on the side panels. The tinted designs have been engraved on the veneer and enhanced with penwork details. The interior is lined with foil, partition missing.
H.12·5 (5); W.18·3 (7¼); D.10 (4).

PROV: Given by Frank H. Fulford 1939.   [9.50/39]

468

470

471 TEA CADDY

*c.*1800

Mahogany; satinwood, pine

Of hexagonal design; the top and sides are veneered with panels of figured mahogany bordered by satinwood bands patterned with ebony dice. The front panels are inset with masonic emblems including the motto 'IN HOC SIGNO VINSIS' and a star inscribed 'G'. The interior is partitioned as two foil-lined compartments with lids bearing brass knobs; pine carcase, brass hinges and lock.
H.12·5 (5); W.26·7 (10½); D.11·5 (4½).

The emblems and symbols on the tea caddy are those commonly associated with Freemasonry and certain of its additional degrees and orders; the Latin motto occurs in the Masonic Order of Knights Templar. There is a virtually identical caddy in the Freemasons' Hall Museum, London. Many domestic objects bearing masonic emblems were produced for Masons to own, few were intended exclusively for lodge use.

PROV: A private collection in Cumbria; bought from Milton Holgate (Antiques), Knaresborough 1975. [14/75]

471

472 TEA CADDY

*c.*1800

Mahogany; satinwood, pine

Of oblong octagonal design; the top and sides are veneered with panels of figured mahogany crossbanded in satinwood with border strings; the interior is partitioned as two foil-lined compartments enclosed by lids inset with rosettes; pine carcase, brass lock.
H.12·5 (5); W.22·2 (8¾); D.14·5 (5¾).

PROV: Given by Mrs Clive Behrens, Swinton Grange, Yorkshire 1940. [18.13/40]

473 TEA CADDY

*c.*1800

Satinwood; tulipwood, mahogany

Of oblong rectangular design veneered in satinwood with narrow crossbanded tulipwood borders and box corner strings; the interior is lined with red plush and contains a central well for a glass bowl flanked by slip box caddies with oval necks closed by hinged lids; the top has a bright-cut silver ring handle and the front is set with a round key plate; mahogany carcase.
H.16 (6½); W.30·5 (12); D.15·5 (6¼).

PROV: Given by Mrs Clive Behrens, Swinton Grange, Yorkshire 1940. [18.14/40]

474 TEA CADDY

*c.*1800

Mahogany; satinwood, rosewood, tulipwood, box

Oblong, veneered in mahogany, the corners and oval panels on the top, front and back are outlined with multiple strings and the ends enriched with circles; the interior is lined with foil and divided into three lidded compartments capped by finger-grips; the circular central grip features a fan-patera with raised oval blocks at either side, the pattern being reflected by satinwood insets inside the lid; mahogany carcase, brass lock.
H.13·8 (5½); W.28·5 (11¼); D.13·8 (5½).

PROV: Given by Mrs Clive Behrens, Swinton Grange, Yorkshire 1940. [18.10/40]

475 TEA CADDY

*c.*1803

Burr yew; mahogany, sycamore, pine, rosewood

Rectangular, the sides and top decorated with oval panels outlined by chequered strings and bordered with herringbone crossbanding between strings in various light, dark and green-stained woods; the interior enriched with similar patterns and divided by sycamore partitions into three wells

475

477

containing a pair of cut-glass tea canisters and a circular sugar bowl; the compartments are lined with red plush bordered by silver tape; the Waterford glass containers are ornamented with faceted diamonds, swags, fluting and stars. Silver ring handles by William Pitts, London, 1802–3; base lined with leather, original lock. Veneered in burr yew on a mahogany foundation, sycamore lining, internal blocks pine.
H.17·6 (7); W.36 (14¼); D.17·6 (7).

EXH: Temple Newsam, *L.A.C.F. Members Exhibition*, 1952 (227).

PROV: David Dunstan Schofield Bequest 1962.   [18.20/62]

476 TEA CADDY
*c.*1810
Rosewood; box, pine

Of slightly tapered oblong design with a pitched, diagonally panelled lid; veneered in rosewood with box corner strings and an ivory keyhole lozenge. The brass rosette-pattern ring-handles and turned bun feet are not original, fitted with new internal partitions and walnut lids, the central well contains a blue glass bowl.
H.14 (5½); W.30·5 (12); D.15·8 (6¼).

PROV: Given by Mrs Clive Behrens, Swinton Grange, Yorkshire 1940.   [8.6/40]

477 TEA CADDY
Probably by Humphrey Burrows, Tunbridge Wells
*c.*1840
Sycamore and rosewood; walnut, tulipwood, pine

Of rectangular casket design, the chamfered base and lid are veneered in rosewood and the sides decorated with a broad

'Van Dyke' band in sycamore and walnut; the top, patterned with perspective cubes in sycamore, rose and tulipwood, is enriched inside with a star motif; the divided interior is fitted with two lids having turned ivory knobs; pine carcase, silvered lock and hinges.
H.13·2 (5¼); W.20·3 (8); D.12·5 (5).

PROV: Given by Mrs Clive Behrens, Swinton Grange, Yorkshire 1940.   [18.2/40]

478 TEA CADDY
*c.*1840
Birch; pine, box

In the form of a rectangular, slightly tapering casket with hinged bevelled lid; the pine carcase is veneered in birch scorched to simulate natural tortoiseshell with box corner strings; the interior is divided into two lidded compartments; side handles missing, the brass escutcheon added.
H.12 (4¾); W.19·5 (7¾); D.11·4 (4½).

PROV: Given by Mrs Clive Behrens, Swinton Grange, Yorkshire 1940.   [18.3/40]

479 TEA POY
Mid 19th century
Walnut; pine oak,

In the form of a shallow oval box raised on a pillar and claw; the hinged top, veneered in figured walnut, opens to reveal two oval caddies and a pair of circular cut-glass bowls fitted into wells lined with purple plush; the gadrooned base is set on a fluted shaft with an egg and dart collar and the tripod stand, enriched with stamps rests on scroll toes terminating in

TRAYS

479

481 TEA TRAY
*c.*1790
Mahogany; sycamore

The oval base is veneered with figured mahogany quarters centering on an oval shell medallion in shaded and green-stained sycamore; wave-cut gallery of three-ply construction faced with mahogany; brass handle grips; the underside formerly ringed with green baize.
W.72 (28½); D.52 (20½).

PROV: Agnes and Norman Lupton Bequest 1953.
[13.373/53]

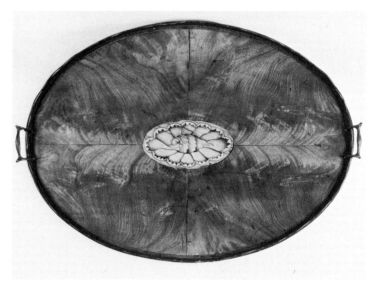

481

swivel castors impressed 'COPE PATENT'; circular lock plate, pine carcase, the caddies have oak bottoms.
H.74 (29); W.51 (20); D.39 (15½).

EXH: Temple Newsam, *L.A.C.F. Members Exhibition*, 1952 (203).

PROV: Given by Miss M. E. Jackson 1952.   [24/52]

480 TEA CADDY
Attributed to Edmund Nye and Thomas Barton, Tunbridge Wells
*c.*1860
Rosewood; pine, various coloured woods

The small rectangular box veneered in rosewood opens to reveal two foil-lined compartments, one lidded the other framed to receive a circular jar; the hinged top is decorated with two mosaic panels and lined with green silk paper; secured by a lock.
H.9·5 (3¾); W.11·4 (4½); D.6·4 (2½).

The attribution is based on labelled items in the museum at Tunbridge Wells.

PROV: Given by Mrs Clive Behrens, Swinton Grange, Yorkshire 1940.   [18.8/40]

482

482 TRAY
c.1910
Mahogany; satinwood, green-stained and shaded harewood

Kidney-shaped mahogany base inlaid with a floral spray surrounded by scrolled foliage and bordered by a gallery of three-ply construction faced with alternating strips of mahogany and satinwood; brass handle grips.
W.57 (22½); D.39 (15½).

John Finch & Co, wholesale cabinet makers, 58–64 Leonard Street, London were advertising a closely similar range of mahogany inlaid trays about 1910 (Pratt Collection of Trade Catalogues) at 19/– each.

PROV: Bequeathed by Mrs Frank Gott, Weetwood Garth, Leeds 1941. [7.14/41]

UPHOLSTERY FABRICS

A small collection of upholstery materials has accumulated over the years. It consists largely of fragments retrieved for record purposes during renovation, but includes a few more luxurious furnishing textiles, acquired more or less by chance, which deserve special mention.

483 A YELLOW SILK DAMASK, removed from the walls of the Boudoir at Temple Newsam, carries a design of a basket of flowers suspended in a lozenge-shaped cartouche of fringed ribbons. A damask of identical pattern covers a sofa at Stoneleigh Abbey (Connoisseur Period Guide, *Early Victorian*, 1958, pl.25) it is said to have been woven by Baily and Jackson of Spitalfields, *c*.1844. A similar damask lines the walls of the Drawing Room at Charlecote.
Pattern repeat 53 (21).

484 Several pieces of **DARK GREEN PLUSH** stamped with a broad formalized leaf pattern survive from the panels which G. F. Bodley installed when the Georgian library at Temple Newsam was converted into a chapel in 1877. It may well have been supplied to Bodley's design by Messrs. Watts & Co of Baker Street. The panels are illustrated *in situ* by C. G. Gilbert, 'The Victorian Chapel at Temple Newsam', *L.A.C.*, No.62 (1968) p.6. A piece was reused to cover a stool, Cat. No.376. Goats hair, 208 × 61 (82 × 24); patt. rep. 61 (24).

485–6 Two lengths of late nineteenth century **ITALIAN SILK VELVET** with conventional floral designs in cut and uncut pile are indigenous to Temple Newsam House. One is woven in deep gold, yellow, pink and white on a cream ground, the other in red pile on an oyster satin ground, each bears a label inscribed 'Testolini Freres / Venise' and recording the name of the design 'Giardinetto' and 'floroni rossi' respectively.
Size: 116 × 59 (45¾ × 23) – not a full pattern repeat; 115 × 61 (45 × 24); patt. rep. 65 (25¾).

487 A piece of light reddish brown panne **COTTON VELVET** stamped with a floral pattern, the background filled with combing and geometric shapes, was given by Lady Gascoigne in 1973. It bears the Patent Office registration mark for Feb. 1879 and the initials 'J.M.S. & Co.' An attached printed label states 'From Cowtan & Sons, (Successors to Duppa & Co) Ltd, 309 Oxford Street London / Stock Pattern 1419c. 10/9d per yd.'
Size: 130 × 61 (51½ × 24¼); patt. rep. 54 (21½).

488 A French chair covering of **VELOURS GAUFFRE** (back, seat and four strips) dating from *c*.1770 was given anonymously in 1973. The material was originally turquoise blue, now faded to a greyish green and retains the associated gimp. This woollen velvet, chiefly of goats hair, was a popular substitute in France for silk velvet. The pattern was stamped on with heated engraved copper plates. There are two chair covers from the same set at the V. & A. Exhibited at Temple Newsam, *English Furniture Upholstery*, 1973 (46).
Size of seat panel 53 × 44 (21 × 17½).

489 A Pair of **WINDOW CURTAINS** designed by William Morris and block printed by hand at the Merton Abbey works, was purchased in 1976. The *Daffodil* pattern, introduced about 1891 (*Art Journal*, 1891, p.109), was Morris's last chintz design and the only one employing chemical rather than his usual vegetable dyes. Printed in yellow, green and red on a white ground with 'MORRIS & COMPANY' on the selvage. Morris's watercolour cartoon for the design is at the William Morris Art Gallery (A.37). The curtains formerly belonged to the Carter-Wood family, The Oaks, Dalston, Cumbria.
Size: 244 × 91 (96 × 36)

488

WASHING STANDS

490 BASIN STAND
*c.*1760
Mahogany; oak

In the form of a tripod stand on plain cabriole legs; the base, which is dished for an ewer, supports three slender columns of scrolled design terminating in a moulded basin ring; a triangular shelf fitted with two small drawers for toilet requisites accommodates a globular cup and cover for a soap ball. Mahogany with oak drawer linings and later brass pulls, the soap cup is probably a replacement.
H.79 (31); Diam. 28 (11).

Alexander Peter of Edinburgh supplied twelve basin stands of similar design to the Earl of Dumfries in 1759 (*Burlington*, Nov. 1969, fig.22).

EXH: Temple Newsam, *L.A.C.F. Members Exhibition*, 1952 (222).

PROV: David Dunstan Schofield Bequest 1962.   [18.25/62]

WASH STAND, papier-mâché
Birmingham, *c.*1851
Under Cat. No.520 (illustrated)

491 BASIN STAND
*c.*1900
Mahogany; pine

Of standard mid eighteenth century form with a plain tripod base providing a circular dished well; the three uprights of scroll and column design support a triangular box shelf fitted with two drawers and are headed by a moulded bowl ring, hooped with iron. Mahogany with pine drawers.
H.81 (32); Diam. 29 (11½).

Basin stands of this traditional pattern were reproduced in large numbers around the turn of the last century.

PROV: Given by Charles Roberts, Farfield Hall, Addingham, Yorkshire 1941.   [11.5/41]

WOOL WINDER

490

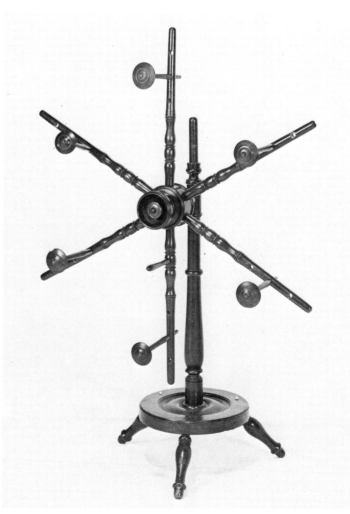

492

492 WOOL WINDER
Early 19th century
Beech, stained to resemble mahogany

Of turned construction, the central pole socketed into a circular base raised on three splayed legs; the revolving arms are bored and fitted with adjustable pegs over which the skeins were looped and the hub is surmounted by a bowl to hold balls of wool; the spokes can also be rotated on a vertical axis (as illustrated), being held in position by a terminal screw. Ornamented with white glass studs. One peg renewed.
H.84 (33).

PROV: Bought from G. L. Bulmer (Antiques) Leeds 1948.
[5.1/48]

ZOGRASCOPE

493

493 ZOGRASCOPE
1821
Mahogany

The circular dished base has a moulded rim inset with chequered strings and centres on a star design; the turned and wrythen column, headed by an enriched block set with a wooden thumb screw, is fitted with a telescopic stem supporting a baluster-turned crossbar and standards suspending a rectangular framed mirror inlaid with strings; a lead ring embedded in the baize-lined base is lightly scratched '1821'.
H.79 (31) rising to 94 (37).

The instrument was formerly equipped with an adjustable magnifying lense angled in front of the mirror; the brass pivot fitments not original. Zograscopes were intended for examining prints. When stood on a table, with the mirror correctly adjusted, a magnified reflection of an engraving placed on the table could be viewed through the lense. These optical devices are discussed by E. H. Pinto, *Treen*, 1969, p.284, pl.296; an intact model of closely similar design was sold at Sotheby's, 15 Feb. 1968, lot.139.

EXH: Temple Newsam, *L.A.C.F. Members Exhibition*, 1952 (226).

PROV: Lord Moynihan, Carr Manor, Leeds; Carr Manor sale (Hollis & Webb, Leeds) 30 Nov–3 Dec. 1937, lot 739; bequeathed by David Dunstan Schofield 1962. [18.22/62]

SUB-GROUPS

GILLOW FURNITURE FROM PARLINGTON HALL

Parlington Hall, Aberford, the ancestral home of the Gascoigne family, passed in 1810 to Richard Oliver Gascoigne who commissioned Gillows of Lancaster to refurnish the principal rooms. Colonel F. R. T. Gascoigne, who inherited the property in 1905 immediately moved to nearby Lotherton Hall taking some of the furniture with him; the remainder being dispersed at the Parlington Hall sale (Hollis & Webb, Leeds) 24–29 July 1905; however, the agent's marked catalogue records that a good proportion of the Gillow lots were bought-in. In 1937 the estate passed to his son Sir Alvary who sold more furnishings at the Lotherton Hall sale[1] (Hollis & Webb) 1–2 Oct. 1956; accordingly, only a residue of the items supplied by Gillows was included in the Gascoigne gift and of these several duplicate pieces were returned and auctioned by J. W. Watson & Son on 22 March 1972 (lots 474, 481, 483, 485).

Two pieces (both dressing tables) in the collection bear the stamp 'GILLOWS·LANCASTER' and three are signed by the craftsman responsible for making them. However, the majority are unambiguously documented in the Gillow archives at Westminster City Library, the relevant entries being in the firm's Estimate Book 1803–15 (344/199); Account Book 1811–12 (344/156), pp.53–64 and Packing Book 1809–1914 (344/186). Furthermore, two Summary Account Books (334/56 & 344/57) and a Journal (344/26) show that R. O. Gascoigne continued to patronize the firm until his death in 1834. Between October 1810 and December 1813 furnishings to the value of £2,931.16.11 were supplied and over the next twenty years work totalling £420.18.9 was received.[2]

The original order was intended to equip five bed and dressing rooms, the dining room, library and a study. The repertoire for each bedroom was almost exactly the same, but unfortunately certain items – beds, bed-steps, wash-stands, linen airers, chairs and dressing stools are not represented in the collection. A specimen schedule for furnishing one bedroom was reprinted by Susan Bourne as an appendix to 'Gillows at Parlington', L.A.C., No.72 (1973) pp.14–20. The surviving dining room furniture includes an Imperial table, port table and one chair, but not the massive sideboards, dumb waiters and supporting cast. Two of the large library bookcases (No.539) were installed in the Aberford Almshouses when Parlington was vacated in 1905 while another, which served as a gun cupboard, was taken to Lotherton.

The furniture all conforms to Gillows' conventional 'house-style' of the period, virtually identical design types being supplied from stock to Broughton Hall,[3] Tatton Park[4] and Harewood House around the same time. Complete dining and bedroom suites at Broughton give a useful idea of the corresponding items sold from Parlington, although it is clear that R. O. Gascoigne ordered 'standard' rather than the slightly more elaborate models provided for the best bedrooms at Tatton and Broughton.

[1]The auctioneer's file copy of the catalogue shows that once again several of the pieces supplied by Gillow were bought in, e.g. lot 104.
[2]An inventory of Parlington taken in 1843 (Leeds Archives Dept GC / F4/5) records the location of many items.
[3]Furniture From Broughton Hall Made by Provincial Firms 1788–1909, Temple Newsam exh. cat. 1971.
[4]N. Goodison and J. Hardy, 'Gillows at Tatton', Furniture History, VI (1970), pp.1–39.

494 WINE OR SOCIAL TABLE
By Gillows, Lancaster
1810
Mahogany

Of horseshoe design with four turned and reeded tapering legs which screw into the frieze rail; the reeded table top has a guard rim and hinged end flaps supported on lopers; a baize curtain, suspended from a hollow brass rod fixed between columns, extends across the back while a trolley, provided with decanter wells and a curved heat-shield, is attached by means of brass pivot arms to a cross rail, the apparatus being designed to coast on brass rollers in an arc around the leather-surfaced inner-lip of the table. The circular cut-glass decanters decorated with radial fluting, gadroons, facets and rings (corresponding to turning on the legs) are original. Mahogany, with a veneered frieze rail, brass socket castors, ferrules, screw fitments and a brass rib on the shield.
H.113 (44½) to table top 72 (28½); W.171 (67½); D.112 (44).

Wine or social tables were intended for after dinner drinking in front of a fire; the party, seated in a semi-circle around the table, were screened from undue heat by the curtain, while the shield on the decanter trolley protected the port as it coasted round the table.

Gillows' Packing Book, p.162 records that Case 7 despatched on 17 Oct. 1810 contained 'A mahogany social table with mahogany bottle screen'.

LIT: L.A.C., No.72 (1973) p.18, fig.7.

PROV: R. O. Gascoigne; recorded in the Parlington inventory 1843 '1 Mahogany horseshoe table and curtain'; Lotherton Hall; the Gascoigne gift 1970.   [37/70]

494

495 DINING CHAIR
By Gillows, Lancaster
1810
Mahogany; elm, oak

Of yoke-back design with a carved medial bar centering on a rosette medallion, sabre front legs; the uprights, yoke and seat rails are styled with incised reeding; the original red morocco cover, fastened by brass beading, remains beneath the later upholstery. Mahogany, with elm rails and oak corner struts. The underframe is inscribed in ink 'J. Woodhouse 1810' and on a small paper slip 'J. Savage' (both accredited Gillow employees).
H.85 (33½); W.48 (19); D.44 (17½).

Gillows' Packing Book discloses that between 2 Oct 1810 and 2 Jan. 1811 the firm despatched to 'R. O. Gascoigne, Esq, Parlington' 16 'mahogany chairs, Bute's Pattern, french stuft and covered in red-leather, brass beads bottom of rail' together with 4 matching armchairs, 4 'chairback screens covered in crimson Tammy' and a set of red cloth covers.

Nine single and four armchairs were dispersed at the Parlington sale in 1905; another was sold by Lady Gascoigne in 1972 leaving one only in the collection. In 1960 Derek Linstrum bought a pair of chairs *en suite* locally, signed by the same two workmen; they presumably once belonged to the set. A manuscript design (ink and brown wash) for a chair with an identical back occurs in the Cabinet Makers General Sketch Book (1810), Westminster City Library, Gillow archive, 344/144, p.60.

PROV: R. O. Gascoigne; recorded in the Parlington inventory, 1843 '2 armd Mahogany chairs, 16 Mahogany chairs'; Lotherton Hall; the Gascoigne gift 1968.

[7.216/68]

496 DINING TABLE
By Gillows, Lancaster
1810
Mahogany; oak

Composed of two D-shaped end sections with frieze rails, bridged by a telescopic underframe raised on ten turned and reeded tapering legs; when fully extended the top supports eight leaves, varying in width between 15 and 18 in, tied by brass stirrup clips fixed beneath the reeded edge; socket castors. Mahogany, with a veneered frieze, the underframe is constructed mainly of oak.
H.72 (28½); W.157 (62); L.488 (192).

Recorded only in Gillows' Packing Book, 2 Oct. 1810 'Two cases containing A sett of mahogany Imperial dining tables consisting of 10 boards, two of which are new ones on turn'd reeded legs'. There is a marginal plan of the top giving the size of each leaf and marking the new boards. The same schedule lists two 'Green cloths for Dining Table'.

LIT: *L.A.C.*, No.72 (1973) p.19, fig.9.

PROV: R. O. Gascoigne; recorded in the Parlington inventory 1843 'Mahogany dining table, 9 leaves & case'; Parlington Hall sale, 1905, lot 704 (bought in); Lotherton Hall; the Gascoigne gift 1968.   [7.164/68]

497 TABLE-LEAF CASE
By Gillows, Lancaster
1810
Mahogany; pine, oak

The tall narrow cupboard with a moulded cornice and plain plinth base is enclosed by a panelled door; the interior contains a rack composed of baize-covered prong divisions

496

497

and a grooved floor forming slots to accommodate eight table leaves standing upright; stamped brass turnbuckle knob. Mahogany with a panelled pine back and bottom board, the prongs tenoned into an oak medial rail. The back is inscribed with the workman's name 'Barrow' and 'O. Gasc'. H.168 (66); W.51 (20); D.51 (20).

Recorded in Gillows' Packing Book, p.161 2 Oct. 1810 Case 3 'A Mahogany rack for leaves P.E.S. 1878'. Gillows' Estimate Book, 1803–15, p.1878 contains a sketch of the case headed 'Gascoigne Esq' with the following cost analysis.

28 Sept. 1810			
A Mahogany Rack on Pedestal for Dining Tables leaves 3¾ inch Mahogany framing @ 2/4d	0.	8.	9
6 ft. ½ in Do panels 1/6d – 9/–			
1¾ ft in Do plinth & Moldgs 1/6d – 2/7½d	0.	11.	7½
23 feet inch Bay wood ends and top @ 2/–	2.	6.	0
11 ft. inch Deal 5½d – 5/6½d. 3 feet inch oak 1/3d – 3/9d	0.	8.	9½
12 feet Green Baize @ 2½d	0.	2.	6
1½ pair 2½ in Hinges 18d – 2/3d 1 Turn buckle 8d	0.	2.	11
Glue, Screws etc	0.	2.	0
Making by Mr Barrow	1.	7.	0
	£5.	9.	7

LIT: *L.A.C.*, No.72 (1973), p.19, fig.8.

PROV: R. O. Gascoigne; Parlington Hall sale 1905, lot 704 (bought in); Lotherton Hall; the Gascoigne gift 1968.
[7.178/68]

498 DECEPTION TABLE
By Gillows, Lancaster
1810
Mahogany; oak

The rectangular top, with end flaps supported on hinged wooden brackets, has a reeded edge and a fall-front pot cupboard below, the front and back panels faced as dummy drawers; raised on four ring turned and reeded legs, splayed at the base; original stamped brass knob and quadrant stay. Mahogany with an oak base, sides and brackets.
H.72 (28½); W.37 (14½) closed, 72 (28½) extended; D.40 (16).

Mentioned in Gillows' Packing Book, p.161, 2 Oct. 1810, Case 6 '2 mahogany deception tables turn'd legs turned out toes P.E.S. 1118'.

LIT: *L.A.C.*, No.72 (1973) p.16, fig.3.

PROV: R. O. Gascoigne; Parlington Hall sale 1905, lot 1154 (bought in); Lotherton Hall; the Gascoigne gift 1971.
[23.14/71]

498

499 POT CUPBOARD
By Gillows, Lancaster
1810–11
Mahogany

499

Of bow-fronted design with a low gallery around three sides of the top and simply reeded edge mouldings; the veneered door, flanked by panelled stiles, opens to reveal a cupboard with ventilation holes drilled in the base; raised on straight turned and reeded legs, stamped brass turnbuckle knob.
H.80 (31½); W.39 (15½); D.36 (14¼).

Gillows supplied ten 'round front pot cupboards' to R. O. Gascoigne, each bedroom they furnished at Parlington being provided with '2 Mahogany round front Pot Cupboards with rims and reeded legs, 3 gns. – £6.6.0.' They were identical except for minor variations in the turned feet. One pair is entered in the firm's Packing Book, p.161 on 2 Oct. 1810, the others are recorded in the Account Book under Aug. 1811. The earliest sketch of this model is dated 1806 in Gillows' Estimate Book, p.1782.

LIT: *L.A.C.*, No.72 (1973), p.15, fig.1.

PROV: R. O. Gascoigne; Parlington Hall sale, 1905 (one of four bought in); Lotherton Hall; the Gascoigne gift 1968.
[7.192/68]

500 DRESSING TABLE
By Gillows, Lancaster
1811
Mahogany; pine, oak

Of rectangular design, fronted by a concave recess; the top has a reeded edge and a low gallery around three sides with a long centre drawer flanked by pairs of narrow drawers; the corners are faced with sunk panels and the kneehole spandrels outlined with beading; raised on turned and reeded legs ending in brass socket castors; star and rosette pattern stamped brass knobs. Mahogany, with mahogany drawer linings, an oak front rail and pine inner structures. The fore-edge of the central drawer is stamped 'GILLOWS · LANCASTER'; the top right-hand drawer is signed in pencil with the workman's name 'Jon Lawson' and the front rail inscribed in blue crayon with the lot no. '490'.
H.84 (33); W.112 (44); D.59 (23).

GILLOWS·LANCASTER

Four identical dressing tables are recorded in Gillows' Account Book under 11 August 1811, a typical entry being 'To a Handsome Mahogany five drawer Dressing Table with rim and on turned reeded legs £6.16.6.' All were bought in at the Parlington sale. One other example featured the Gillows stamp and two, sold in 1972, were signed 'Thos Myers' and 'J. Dixon'. The earliest sketch of this particular model occurs in the firm's Estimate Book 1803–15 dated 12 March 1806 (for General Jones).

LIT: *Burlington*, June, 1970, p.397, fig.71; *Connoisseur*, August 1970, pp.241–49, fig.9; *L.A.C.*, No.72 (1973), p.17, fig.5.

500

PROV: R. O. Gascoigne; Parlington Hall sale, 1905, lot 490 (bought in); Lotherton Hall; the Gascoigne gift 1971.
[23.17/71]

501 DRESSING TABLE GLASS
By Gillows, Lancaster
1811
Mahogany; cedar, ivory

The rectangular 'landscape' mirror plate set in a crossbanded frame, is suspended between elaborately turned and reeded standards with ball feet and ornamental ivory finials, braced behind by two curved stays forming a trestle; the supports are united by turned crossbars. Stamped brass screw knobs, cedar back panel, one rear stay renewed, the original member is of three ply section.
H.61 (24); W.62 (24½); D.33 (13).

501

Five dressing glasses, identical in design and price are listed in Gillows' Account Book under 11 August 1811, a typical entry being 'To a Handsome Landscape Dressing Glass to place on Do with reeded stiles, plate $19 \times 15\frac{1}{2}$ in. £3.3.0.' The earliest sketch of this design occurs in the firm's Estimate Book 1803–15, p.1818 dated 1807; the ivory finials cost 3/3d each. Identical models were supplied to Broughton Hall and Tatton Park.

LIT: See Cat. No.500.

PROV: R. O. Gascoigne, Parlington Hall; removed to Lotherton Hall in 1905; the Gascoigne gift 1968.

[7.203/68]

502 CHAMBER WRITING TABLE

By Gillows, Lancaster
1811
Mahogany; oak, beech

Of rectangular design with reeded mouldings, fitted with two frieze drawers and a lidded well containing a pen-tray and bottle divisions, etc.; the rounded corners, ends and back are faced with beaded panels, the rear being styled as a dummy drawer with stamped brass pulls; the turned and reeded legs end in socket castors. Mahogany, with mahogany drawers and inner structures of oak and beech. The under-frame bears a lot ticket No.'1141'.
H.73 ($28\frac{3}{4}$); W.91 (36); D.51 (20).

According to Gillows' Account Book four chamber writing tables with reeded legs were supplied for the bed-rooms at Parlington. This example was one of a pair in-voiced on 11 August 1811 as 'To 2 Mahogany Chamber Writing Tables reeded legs and rails beaded as common £4.6.0–£8.12.0'. The companion was sold at the Lotherton

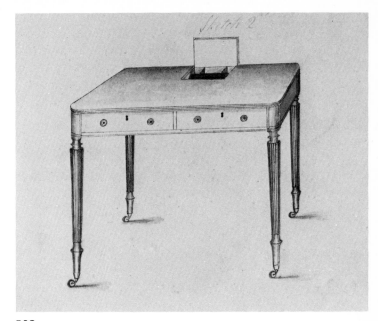

502

Hall sale, 1956, lot 206. Entered in Gillows' Packing Book 2 July 1811, case 68. There is an identical (stamped) table at Broughton Hall, Yorkshire. Based on a manuscript design (ink and grey wash) in the Cabinet Makers General Sketch Book (1810) at Westminster City Library, Gillow archive 344/144, p.11.

LIT: *L.A.C.*, No.72 (1973), p.17, fig.6.

PROV: R. O. Gascoigne; Parlington Hall sale, 1905, lot 1141 (bought in); Lotherton Hall; the Gascoigne gift 1968.

[7.209/68]

503 CHAMBER WRITING TABLE

By Gillows, Lancaster
1811
Mahogany; oak, pine

Of rectangular design, fronted by a dummy frieze drawer with true drawers in each end, the back and rounded corners faced with bead panels; the top contains a lidded well enclosing a pen-tray, bottle divisions, etc.; turned reeded legs ending in socket castors, stamped brass drawer pulls, locks. Mahogany, with oak and pine tie rails.
H.79 (31); W.86 (34); D.49 ($19\frac{1}{2}$).

Recorded in Gillows' Packing Book 24 July 1811, Case 69 'A Mahogany chamber writing table 2 ft 10 by 1 ft $7\frac{1}{2}$ a drawer at each end. Reeded edge turn'd reeded legs and castors' also in Gillows' Account Book, Aug 1811 'To 1 larger Do with a drawer at each end, say 2 ft 10 long and $2\frac{1}{2}$ in. higher than common £5.7.0'.

PROV: R. O. Gascoigne; Parlington Hall sale, 1905, lot 1550 (bought in); Lotherton Hall; the Gascoigne gift 1971.

[23.19/71]

502

504 CHAMBER WRITING TABLE

By Gillows, Lancaster
1811
Mahogany; oak, beech

The rectangular top, with rounded corners and a reeded edge, is fronted by a single long drawer; a well at the back covered by a hinged lid, contains a pen-tray, bottle divisions, etc; the sides and rear frieze are outlined with beaded panels; supported on turned and reeded legs ending in socket castors; stamped brass drawer-pulls, thread escutcheon. Mahogany, with oak drawer linings and beech cross rails; the underframe bears a lot ticket No.1172.
H.73 (28¾); W.61 (24); D.40 (16).

Recorded in Gillows' Account Book, Aug. 1811 'To a single Mahogany Chamber Writing Table on Reeded legs & a flap with ink stand under £4.6.0.'

LIT: *L.A.C.*, No.72 (1973) p.17, fig.6.

PROV: R. O. Gascoigne; Parlington Hall sale, 1905, lot 1172 (bought in); Lotherton Hall; the Gascoigne gift 1971.
[23.13/71]

505 CHEST OF DRAWERS

By Gillows, Lancaster
1811
Mahogany; pine, oak, cedar

Of rectangular design with two narrow and three graduated long drawers; the crossbanded top is outlined with black strings and an ebonized moulding under the lip; splayed bracket feet united by serpentine front and side aprons; the drawers, cockbeaded in ebony, are mounted with stamped brass lion's-mask ring handles and thread escutcheons. Pine

carcase, the top and sides veneered in mahogany, cedar drawers with mahogany sides and quarter-beading, the dust boards faced with oak rails, one bearing a printed ticket 'Lot 1376'. The lion's-mask handles carry impressed numbers.
H.112 (44); W.113 (44½); D.59 (23).

Gillows' Packing Book, 21 May 1811 Case 37 'A mahogany chest of Drawers 3 ft 6 long by 2 ft 10 ends, 3 ft 10 four heights and five drawers brass locks and nobs as common'. The stated measurements correspond to the length of a drawer, the combined height of the drawer fronts and the overall height of the structure. The firm's Account Book records under Aug 1811 '3 good Handsome Mahogany Chests of Drawers . . . four heights and five drawers, good brass Locks and Furniture, 8 gns . . . £25.4.0.' The Estimate Book, p.1833 reveals that '2 lion's face ring handles (on a pot cupboard) cost 2/10d.

PROV: R. O. Gascoigne; Parlington Hall sale, 1905, lot 1376 (bought in); Lotherton Hall; the Gascoigne gift 1971.
[23.1/71]

505

506

506 WARDROBE (CLOTHES PRESS)

By Gillows, Lancaster
1811
Mahogany; pine, ash, cedar

Of rectangular design; the upper stage, fitted with five sliding trays, is enclosed by double flush-panelled doors outlined with reeded and crossbanded borders, the moulded cornice is enriched with ebonized fillets. The lower stage, raised on square bracket feet, contains two short above two long drawers finished with ebony cockbeading and set with stamped brass lion's-mask ring handles, thread escutcheons and steel locks; the door, edged with a brass strip, is fitted with flush bolts and a new lock. Mahogany, with a pine carcase and ash rails, the drawers and trays have cedar bottom boards and quarter-beaded mahogany sides.
H.221 (87); W.132 (52); D.59 (23).

Gillows' Account Book records under 11 Aug 1811 'To 2 good Mahogany Wardrobes 4 ft long doors 3 ft 5 high solid panels lin'd fronts, good brass Locks and Furniture as Common, for N1 and N4 at 15 gns . . . £31.10.0.' They were ordered for the north wing bedrooms numbers 1 and 4. The firm's Packing Book shows that Crates 40–43, despatched on 21 May 1811 carried 'Four matted parcels containing 2 Mahogany wardrobes 4 ft, 2 long solid doors 3 ft 5, bottom ends 2 ft. Three heights four drawers brass locks and nobs as common'. The companion wardrobe was sold by Lady Gascoigne in March 1972.

PROV: R. O. Gascoigne; Parlington Hall; Lotherton Hall; the Gascoigne gift 1971.   [23.18/71]

507 GUN CUPBOARD

By Gillows, Lancaster
1811
Mahogany; pine, oak

Of upright rectangular design; the upper stage, headed by a moulded cornice, is enclosed by double doors filled with a glazed lattice composed of brass strips bearing rosettes at the intersections; the lower part contains three pairs of graduated drawers above a long one faced as two narrow drawers; the end corners are edged with reeding and the stage division masked by a simple band, plain plinth, brass drawer knobs, flush bolts and locks. Interior stained red. Oak drawers with veneered fronts and pine bottoms; panelled pine back, base and inner structures; the right end is mahogany, the left (which abutted a wall) being in deal with a mahogany stile; modern shelves.
H.229 (90); W.140 (55); D.43 (17).

Part of a range of bookcases supplied for the Study at a cost of £145. Recorded in Gillows' Account Book 11 Aug 1811 'To a large Bookcase for Angle of Room one side with folding doors in top part, trellage pannels and scarlet silk Curtains and a fast shelf inside with holes for Guns . . .

507

drawers below'. An identical bookcase, but with pigeon-holes in the upper part is sketched and costed in Gillows' Estimate Book, p.1890.

LIT: *L.A.C.*, No.72 (1973), p.15, fig.2.

PROV: R. O. Gascoigne; Parlington Hall sale 1905, lot 381 (bought in); Lotherton Hall; the Gascoigne gift 1968.
                    [7.218/68]

508 PAIR OF CURRICLE CHAIRS

By Gillows, Lancaster
c.1811
Rosewood; beech

The rounded back and arms form a continuous bow styled with incised lines ending in spirals, and the cresting is enriched with an oval panel of scrolling arabesques executed in brass inlay; the sabre forelegs are headed by carved foliate rosettes and uprights capped by ball finials; the splay rear

508

509

legs continue up to support the back frame which is channelled with a deep finger grip; the back, sides and seat, fronted by a moulded rail are caned; square socket castors. The veneered beech seat rails are lightly incised 'W'.
H.87 (34½); W.54 (21¼); D.53 (21).

Not mentioned in the Estimate, Account or Packing Books, but virtually identical to a pair of mahogany 'curricle' chairs supplied by Gillow to T. W. Egerton of Tatton Park, Cheshire in 1811 at £5 each. Originally fitted with a squab and intended for a bed or dressing room. See *Furniture History*, VI (1967), p.32 & fig.16.

LIT: *L.A.C.*, No.72 (1973), p.16, fig.4.

PROV: R. O. Gascoigne; Parlington inventory 1843 'Large Drawing Room 2 Rosewood chairs inlaid with cushions'; Parlington Hall sale, 1905, lot 286 (bought in); Lotherton Hall; the Gascoigne gift 1968.   [7.157/68]

509 SET OF ONE ARM AND FOUR SINGLE CHAIRS
Probably by Gillows, Lancaster
*c.*1825
Mahogany; beech

The curved yoke-backs with gadrooned shoulders each centre on shaped panels of figured veneer; the incised uprights terminating in volutes are connected by a pierced cross bar formed of paired lotus scrolls supporting a tablet carved with a foliate rosette; moulded seat rails, turned, reeded legs, modern upholstery. The armchair is of identical design but with high scroll-under arms ending in volutes. Mahogany, with beech seat rails.
H.84 (33); W.48 (19); D.43 (17); armchair W.56 (22).

PROV: R. O. Gascoigne; probably entered in the Parlington inventory of 1843 as 'Ladies Dining Room: 4 Mahogany chairs covered in red Leather, 1 Easy chair & Cover'; Lotherton Hall; the Gascoigne gift 1968.   [7.165/68]

ORMOLU

510 PERFUME-BURNER
By Matthew Boulton, Birmingham
*c.*1772
Ormolu

The vase, banded with lotus, Vitruvian scroll and guilloche ornament, has a perforated cover surmounted by a leafy dome; the interior contains a spring-loaded glass vessel set in a brass cylinder and there is a circular aperture in the bottom. The body is supported on three winged female terms; the

510

suspending swags of drapery. The marble vases mounted in leaf cups are raised on enriched ormolu feet and decorated with garlands, while the open scrolled foliate friezes feature rams' heads which support fronded branches ending in drip-pans and fluted candleholders, the fruit-finials reverse to form a fourth candle socket; the vases are lined with gilt-copper.
H.39 (15½).

Boulton's vases were sometimes named after the patron who had first commissioned them, this model was almost certainly known at the time as 'Burgoyne's'. Two almost identical versions, but with blue john bodies, are illustrated by Goodison, pls, 104–6. The candle branches are similar to a drawing in Boulton and Fothergill's Pattern Book I, p.13 and relate interestingly to the arms of a pair of candelabra designed by J. C. Delafosse at the Detroit Institute of Art.

LIT: N. P. Goodison, *Ormolu: the Work of Matthew Boulton*, 1974, pp.146, 150 and pl.105.

EXH: London, V. & A., *B.A.D.A. Golden Jubilee*, May 1968 (169); London, *Hotspur Ltd. Golden Jubilee*, 1974, pl.10.

PROV: Comte Stroganoff de St Petersbourg, Berlin; Ricardo and Armando Chane; Christie's, 19 March 1964, lot 85; John Aspinall; Hotspur, Ltd; bought with the aid of a government grant 1975.   [16/75]

fluted and fronded shafts, ending in paw feet, rest on a concave triangular plinth which centres on a foliate boss.
H.23 (9).

Two identical models are known, one from the A.C.J. Wall loan at Birmingham Museum and Art Gallery; the other, owned by the Earl of Jersey, is illustrated in *D.E.F.*, III, p.16, fig.2. Both have a circular lamp suspended below the vase by chains attached to the chests of the winged figures. This element, now missing from the Temple Newsam example, is illustrated in Boulton and Fothergill's Pattern Book I, p.74, with a flame issuing from the nozzle. The burner was designed to heat pastilles in the glass vessel, scented vapours escaping through the perforated cover.

PROV: By descent to Captain V. M. Wombwell of Newburgh Priory, Yorkshire; given by Charles Lumb & Sons, Harrogate, in memory of Reginald Lumb 1976.   [15/76]

511 PAIR OF CANDLE-VASES
By Matthew Boulton, Birmingham
*c.*1772
White marble and ormolu

The circular stepped marble bases, ringed with gilt-copper guilloche-pattern bands, support cylindrical pedestals ornamented with rosette paterae between four female terms

512 CASSOLET
By Matthew Boulton, Birmingham
*c.*1775
White marble and ormolu

In the form of a covered marble vase raised on an ormolu tripod bolted to a triangular marble plinth. The vase, decorated with ormolu guilloche-pattern mounts, has a leaf-pendant and the perforated cover is surmounted by a fruit-finial. The tapering fluted legs, headed by scrolls and terminating in paw feet, support a horizontal ring with guilloche enrichment.
H.31 (12½).

The design of the tripod, rings and plinth correspond to a drawing in Boulton and Fothergill's Pattern Book I, p.171 (Goodison, pl.61b) and are repeated on a cassolet supplied to Lord Digby in 1775 (*ibid*, pl.72). However, both examples are furnished with ormolu vases and sport a spiralling snake between the legs which are encircled by upper and lower rings. The pattern derives ultimately from a plate in Stuart and Revett's *Antiquities of Athens*, p.36. Goodison suggests that this tripod was also originally ornamented with two rings and a coiling snake, but Boulton's 'meccano'-like approach to assembling components weakens his argument. For the social use of cassolets, which Boulton often referred to as essence pots, see R. S. Rowe, *Adam Silver*, 1965, p.61.

511

512

513

LIT: N. P. Goodison, *Ormolu: the Work of Matthew Boulton*, 1974, p.142, pl.71.

PROV: H. Blairman & Sons; acquired by the L.A.C.F. 1967.
[L.A.C.F./M2]

513 PAIR OF CASSOLETS
By Matthew Boulton, Birmingham
c.1778
White marble and ormolu

The marble vases are lined with gilt-copper and have perforated domed covers surmounted by pineapple finials. The friezes, enriched with floret and lotus-pattern bands, are set with three leaf-scroll bracket handles suspending festoons of roses which enclose oval classical medallions. Each vase is cradled in an ormolu leaf-cup mount raised on a circular support; the triangular open bases, each with three splayed legs sheathed in foliage and resting on paw feet, are surmounted by female busts suspending floral festoons; the concave triangular plinths have gadrooned borders and centre on a fluted domed patera.
H.38 (15).

No source has been traced for the delicate classical medallions depicting sacrifice scenes, although they are based on plates in A. F. Gori's *Museum Florentinum*, 1732. Identical plaques occur on other examples of Boulton's work; the floral swags on the vase body are also repeated in the firm's repertoire and the frieze was employed on a silver tureen produced by Boulton and Fothergill in 1773–4. Tripod legs of closely similar form are shown in a sketch for a silver jug stand in Boulton's Pattern Book I, p.83. A virtually identical pair of cassolets are illustrated by Goodison, pl.158, while the Temple Newsam collection includes a comparable silver version dated 1779.

LIT: *L.A.C.*, No.62 (1968) p.3; N.P. Goodison, *Ormolu: the work of Matthew Boulton*, 1974, p.154, pl.157.

EXH: London, *Hotspur Ltd, Golden Jubilee*, 1974, pl.32.

PROV: Christie's, 6 July 1967, lot 84; Mark Horowitz; purchased from H. Blairman & Sons with the aid of a government grant and a contribution from Mr Horowitz 1968. [10/68]

514 GLOBE INKSTAND
Ormolu
*c.*1790

The hollow spherical body is constructed in two halves, the divided upper section being formed of pivoted segments which open to reveal a circular tray with stands for a set of three blue glass ink and pounce jars, penholders and dished channels. The globe is mounted in an upright circular frame consisting of two rings supported by four curved stays ornamented with lions' masks suspending floral festoons; the outspreading scroll legs terminate in hairy claw and ball feet. At the apex is a winged Victory figure operating the pressure catch which opens the globe. The inkstand rests on a galleried plinth fronted by a shallow drawer with statuettes representing 'Africa' (2); 'Asia' and 'Europe' at each corner; the sides are faced with blue glass panels contained within laurel borders and the sycamore base is set on fronded bracket feet.
H.40 (16).

An account dated 6 July 1841 for groceries supplied to 'Donald, 26 Elder Street' was found in the lining of the small drawer.

Globe inkstands became fashionable during the last quarter of the eighteenth century, the London silversmith John Robins specialized in their manufacture. An article by G. B. Hughes in *Country Life*, 13 Nov. 1969, pp.1240–1 illustrates silver and Sheffield plate examples.

PROV: H. Blairman & Sons; given anonymously through the L.A.C.F. 1969.   [L.A.C.F./M3]

514

PAPIER-MÂCHÉ BEDROOM SUITE

The suite consists of seven pieces: a bed, a wardrobe, a dressing table and mirror, a washstand, a towel horse and a what-not. Apart from alterations to the bedhead and the removal of the splash-back from the washstand the condition is good and this must be regarded as the most impressive suite of papier-mâché bedroom furniture yet recorded. It originally included a balloon back chair illustrated by De Voe (q.v.) and the what-not may not have joined the suite until a later date, although strong stylistic links suggest it is from the same factory. There are no maker's marks, but fragments of the *Birmingham Weekly* dated between June and September 1851 discovered beneath lining paper in the dressing table drawers provide a clue to its place of origin and date. A music canterbury in the V. & A. (W.59–1931) with identical decoration is also unmarked so, although Jennens & Bettridge or McCallum & Hodson of Birmingham, both of whom enjoyed a reputation for large scale papier-mâché furniture at this time, are the most likely authors, a firm attribution is not possible.

LIT: V. Wood, *Victoriana: A Collector's Guide*, 1960, pl.13 (wardrobe); *Antique Dealer & Collectors' Guide*, Jan. 1960, p.21 (full suite); S. De Voe, *English Papier-Mâché*, 1971, p.182, fig.180 (full suite); G. Wills, *English Furniture 1760–1900*, p.226, pl.29 (dressing table and mirror in colour); *Burlington*, Dec. 1971, pp.738–41, fig.52 (dressing table and mirror).

PROV: Reputed to have been shown at the Great Exhibition, 1851; bought by Lady Parker of Waddington in the 1930s from an elderly lady living in Cornwall; sold in 1958 to Quality Wood Antiques, Ousden; Lord Walston, Newton Hall, Cambs; Newton Hall sale (Knight, Frank & Rutley) 23–24 June 1970, lots 698–703 (withdrawn); bought 1970.   [16.1–7/70]

515 BED
*c.*1851
Papier-mâché; pine

The papier-mâché footboard is fronted by a large bouquet worked in mother of pearl and coloured enamels outlined by a semi-circular moulding enriched with crushed pearl shell; the serpentine top and base mouldings are similarly treated and the shaped apron is ornamented with festoons and oval tablets; the inner face has a recessed half-round panel painted with flowers. The spirally turned corner posts, with short baluster legs on bun feet and knob finials, are of wood banded with crushed pearl shell and gilt tendrils; the lower blocked sections display papier-mâché tablets bearing floral sprays while the chamfered upper blocks have circular bosses, the outer pair masking long screws which secure the foot board.

515

The original headboard was of high arched design, the top moulding, together with a tall domed panel and a lower rectangular border, being outlined with pearl shell; these decorative features perished when Lord Walston converted the bed into a pair of divans, although the central bouquet of flowers was saved and built into the restyled plywood bed-head; a new leg section has been added to the otherwise original posts in an attempt to recreate the impression of height; the modern chassis replaces green painted iron rails.
H.140 (55); L.218 (86); W.152 (60). [16.1/70]

516 DRESSING TABLE

*c.*1851
Papier-mâché

Of bow-fronted pedestal design with a central drawer, a cupboard in the kneehole and tiers of five graduated drawers at each side; the shaped top outlined with a crushed pearl shell moulding is bordered on three sides by floral festoons, rococo scrolls and a central bouquet of flowers executed in mother of pearl, coloured enamels and gold; the drawer fronts háve proud borders enriched with crushed shell enclosing floral swags; the ends and arched door panel centre on mixed bunches of roses surrounded by garlands, sprays and clumps of trailing clematis amid gilt tendrils; the plinth is banded with green palmettes and a gilt ribbon-pattern. Constructed in four parts – top, pedestals and kneehole section – made of papier-mâché throughout, the units being held together by circular brass thumb-screw components; the timber back rail, bottom boards and turned feet are not original; pearl drawer-pulls and keyhole studs; patent locks stamped 'VR' beneath a crown.
H.81 (32); W.152 (60); D.66 (26). [16.3/70]

516, 517

518

517 DRESSING TABLE GLASS
*c.*1851
Papier-mâché; pine

The boldly shaped swing mirror is suspended between scrolling uprights supported on a serpentine-fronted box base containing three drawers; the whole is lavishly styled with crushed pearl shell borders, floral festoons and bouquets in mother of pearl, enamels and gold; the top is enriched with a border of fronded scrolls and flamework in the rococo taste while the mirror surround is painted with quatrefoils and the lower moulding bears a gilt ribbon spiral; the standards are raised on ornamental brackets composed of wavy scrolls and fleshy leaves in relief. The mirror frame and supports have a pine core faced with thick layers of papier-mâché, the rest is made entirely of papier-mâché apart from the six peg feet. The brass suspension fitments are impressed 'COPE & AUSTIN PATENT' and the posts are secured to the plateau by circular brass thumb-screws; glass renewed.
H.112 (44); W.119 (47); D.40 (16).   [16.4/70]

518 WARDROBE (CLOTHES PRESS)
*c.*1851
Papier-mâché; mahogany, pine, rosewood

518

In the form of a tall upright cupboard with a deep moulded cornice and plinth, rounded forecorners and double doors fronted by arched panels; the interior contains four sliding trays, a long and two short drawers with turned rosewood knobs and mother of pearl keyholes. The recessed door panels outlined by a crushed pearl shell moulding, are lavishly decorated with tall bunches of garden and wild flowers worked in mother of pearl, enamel colours and gold, the surrounding frames and large end panels being enriched with detached floral sprays and festoons of clematis executed in the same media. The inner surface of each door bears a sub-classical design composed of gilt arabesques, husks and anthemia with painted details, clumps of fern appear in the lower corners. The straight projecting cornice is banded with crushed pearl shell, green palmettes and twisted ribbon border, the moulded plinth is similarly enriched and styled with floral swags; ornamented bun feet. The fitted interior panelled back and boarded sides are of mahogany; the pine cornice, the plinth and ends are faced with papier-mâché and the doors are entirely made of this material. Brass door furniture and bolted plate hinges; the locks are stamped 'BARRONS PATENT' beneath a crowned 'VR'.
H.218 (86); W.157 (62); D.84 (33).   [16.2/70]

519 WHAT-NOT
*c.*1851
Papier-mâché; pine

The elaborately shaped back board supports a tier of three diminishing shelves with a serpentine drawer in the base and another below the second shelf; the lower stage is raised on baluster turned rear and scrolling forelegs and the stand is crested by a pierced cartouche framing a small mirror. The lower shelf is decorated with a garlanded moonlight scene of Kirkstall Abbey worked in mother of pearl with painted and gilt details; the upper shelves and drawer fronts bear floral sprays executed in the same media, while the moulded borders are outlined either with crushed pearl shell or a gilt ribbon-twist. The main structure is of papier-mâché with curved timber stays supporting the middle shelf, ebonized pine legs and a later plywood back to the cresting. The wooden members are secured by brass screw fitments; the castors are stamped 'COPE'S PATENT' and the drawers lined with mauve sprig-pattern paper.
H.137 (54); W.56 (22); D.40 (16).   [16.7/70]

520 WASHSTAND
*c.*1851
Papier-mâché; pine

Of double serpentine-fronted design with a white veined marble slab and a central frieze drawer; the single spiral-column end supports are mounted on flat runners connected by a base platform bearing two circular jug rings. The frieze is richly decorated with floral swags alternating with clumps of fruiting clematis executed in mother of pearl, gold and enamel colours; the platform, centering on a bouquet of flowers and the plinths are styled in the same taste, while the frieze moulding, jug rings and runners are banded with crushed mother of pearl; castors missing. The framework is of wood faced with papier-mâché, the platform is panelled with papier-mâché boards and the drawer, frieze moulding and runner caps are of the same material. The marble top is drilled for a splash back, removed when a previous owner used the washstand as a writing table.

H.74 (29); W.117 (46); D.61 (24).   [16.5/70]

521 TOWEL-HORSE
*c.*1851
Pine; papier-mâché

The ebonized frame is composed of two spiral-twist end supports each with twin scrolling upper arms connected by rib-turned cross bars; the splay bracket feet, decorated with domed papier-mâché ornaments and the arms are styled with painted and gilt acanthus foliage while the standards, which rise from papier-mâché collars, are banded with gilt vine and lily trails. The cross bars are enriched with a pattern of palmettes and classical foliage executed in blue, green and gold; plain base stretcher.

H.107 (42½); W.87 (34½); D.35 (14).   [16.6/70]

519

520

521

THE SALT FURNITURE BY MARSH AND JONES

This exceptional group of High Victorian furniture in the 'old English style' includes every item from the best bedroom at Milner Field, one of the most lavishly appointed houses built for a Yorkshire mill owner, plus the grand piano and companion duet ottoman from the drawing room and a richly carved oak rug chest. The ensemble was made by John Marsh and Edward Jones of Leeds who had purchased John Kendell's old established business in 1864 and opened a London show room in Cavendish Square. Their manuscript account for the bedroom suite has been kept by the Salt family (photocopy in V. & A. Library, 47 H 66) and the majority of pieces bear the firm's trade label inscribed with the order number and a workman's (probably the polisher's) name (Cat. No.521b).

The grand piano and duet ottoman were illustrated in *The Building News*, 1 March 1867: the descriptive text states that not only the piano case, but 'the whole of Mr Salt's furniture' was designed by 'Mr Charles Bevan, 66 Margaret Street, Cavendish Square, London.' This evidence, combined with their individual 'Medieval' character, confirms that the entire group was executed after Bevan's designs. The commentary also notes that the inlays 'are cut by Mr Vert' proving that, according to long established practice in the cabinet trade, the marquetry work was sub-contracted to a specialist. Vert, a Spaniard, is at present a shadowy figure, but he was clearly also responsible for the profuse marquetry ornament on the bedroom furniture. The rug chest (Cat. No.521p) cannot be associated with Charles Bevan but was perhaps designed by Bruce Talbert about 1872. Henry Cribb, who agreed the final settlement of Titus Salt's account (reprinted in *Furniture History*, III, pp.66–91) was taken into partnership in 1872. Milner Field was demolished in 1927.

It is obvious from Marsh and Jones's account that they offered Titus Salt, Jun., a complete house furnishing and decorating service, even invoicing the toilet wares for the washstand (Cat. No.521e), but the merino upholstery fabric may well have been woven at the Salt mills. Items from the walnut, birch and oak bedroom suites recorded in the bill have descended in the Salt family, they are fine, but less magnificent than the sycamore furniture commissioned for the best bedroom which was used by the Prince and Princess of Wales when they stayed at Milner Field in 1882. The seat furniture was specially reupholstered in the present silvery-grey brocaded fabric interwoven with gold thread for the Royal visit; the luxurious window curtains, bed furniture, seat cushions, pelmets and many other trappings were taken down and carefully stored following the royal couple's departure and survive in pristine condition (10.16/

78). I am grateful to the Misses S. M. I. and N. K. Salt for historical information about this suite.

LIT: *The Building News*, 1 March 1867, pp.158–61; *The Builder*, 15 March 1873, p.204; Edward Healey, *Picturesque Views in Yorkshire*, Bradford, 1885, No.26; L. O. J. Boynton, 'High Victorian Furniture: the Example of Marsh and Jones of Leeds', *Furniture History*, III (1967) pp.54–91; Christopher Hutchinson, 'Furniture by Marsh and Jones of Leeds 1864–1872', *L.A.C.*, No.80 (1977) pp.11–17.

PROV: Commissioned by Titus Salt, Jun., (d.1887) in readiness for setting up home on his marriage to Catherine Crossley in March 1866; installed initially at Baildon Lodge, Baildon and removed in 1872 to their new home Milner Field, Saltaire, Yorkshire. By descent to Catherine Salt who gave up Milner Field in 1902 and rented Denton Hall, Ilkley until 1911 when the furniture was taken to The Old Rectory, Thorp Arch, Yorkshire; on Catherine's death in 1930 the furniture passed to her eldest son Gordon Locksley Salt (d.1938) and so to Olive Mary Gorton, the widow of Gordon's eldest son John Salt (d.1947). The rug chest passed to the Salt Family Trust. Purchased with the aid of a government grant and a contribution from Mrs Olive Gorton in memory of her husband John Salt 1978.

521a CONCERT GRAND PIANO

Action by Erard, the case made by Marsh and Jones, Leeds, to the design of Charles Bevan
1866
Satinwood; amboyna, walnut, purplewood, alder, orangewood, harewood and other coloured woods, pine, beech, oak

The satinwood case is bordered with decorative bands and circular florets; the treble end, styled as a Romanesque arcade, frames four panels inlaid with botanical designs executed in various coloured woods on an ebony ground, while the bent-side and tail are ornamented with eight formalized marquetry panels edged by gilt chamfers. The keyboard cover is enriched with dogtooth, palmette and lunette patterns expressing the reformed gothic taste. A section of the top, faced with four rectangular panels enclosing geometrical inlays, turns back to reveal a folding adjustable music rest flanked by candleslides pierced in the gothic style. The richly figured top, supported when open on a strut, is outlined with four panels defined by bands. The veneered case rests on three sturdy coupled columns headed by carved capitals and corbels, linked at the base by a long blocked and chamfered side, and shorter front stretcher which supports the lavishly inlaid pedal box faced with brass mounts. The carcase is mainly of beech and oak bedded on a complex cradle of pine struts and bars; the inner structures include a polished pine sound board, wide metal hitch-plate and six long iron braces; elaborate gilt brass castors.
H.107 (36); L.254 (100); W.142 (56).

Erard special repetition double escapement action with under dampers and felt hammers serving eighty-five ivory and ebony keys giving a seven octave compass AAA to a''''; tri-chord except for the lowest seventeen notes which are overspun bi-chord (8) and single (9); damper and *una corda* pedals. The cover, which functions when raised as a nameboard, is inlaid in gothic script 'C. BEVAN del / PATENT ERARD LONDON'; the interior is impressed 'C. MARTIN', with the number '9276' and pencilled signature 'G. F. Collinson', while the lowest key stave is stamped 'H. G. RAPKIN'.

The piano is not entered in Marsh and Jones's surviving account of household furniture supplied to Titus Salt, Jnr. between July 1865 and August 1866, but was published as their work in *The Building News*, 1 March 1867, pp.158–161 under the heading 'Medieval Furniture / Designed by C. Bevan'. One illustration shows ornamental details, the other a general view of the instrument together with the duet ottoman (Cat. No.521b) invoiced in November 1865 and a music canterbury whatnot invoiced on 2 July 1866 which has not been traced; there was also an adjustable music stand *en suite* which has disappeared (*Furniture History*, III, pl.24).

The commentary states 'We give this week an illustration of a grand piano by Messrs. S. and P. Erard. The case was made by Marsh and Jones, Leeds, and was designed for Mr Titus Salt, Jun., of Saltaire, by Mr Charles Bevan, 66, Margaret Street, Cavendish Square, London. The ground-work is of satinwood; the inlays of amboina, purpleheart, orangewood, black and harewood, etc., are cut by Mr Vert.

The mouldings round the panels are relieved with gold. On the same sheet will be seen a canterbury and duet ottoman, designed to match. The whole of Mr Salt's furniture is designed by the same artist. We select the piano to show the successful manner in which it has been treated. On the opposite sheet will be seen some of the details, one-fourth the real size. The lower framing of the piano together with the arrangement of the pedal possesses considerable merit'. The Mr Vert alluded to was a Spaniard who established an exclusive marquetry workshop in London; his commissions included finishing a famous table at Alnwick Castle for the Duke of Northumberland in 1865 (information from Clive Wainwright).

LIT and PROV: see p.394. [10.1/78]

521b DUET OTTOMAN

By Marsh and Jones, Leeds, to the design of Charles Bevan
1865
Satinwood; mahogany, various coloured woods

The oblong seat, stuffed over a mahogany frame, is raised on X-pattern end supports united by stretchers centering on lunettes and attached to the standards by sham wedged joints. The frame members are richly styled with gilt chamfers and inlaid with florets, banding and spots. The seat, originally upholstered in brown silk with a deep gold silk fringe, was re-covered about 1902 in the present green,

521b

521a

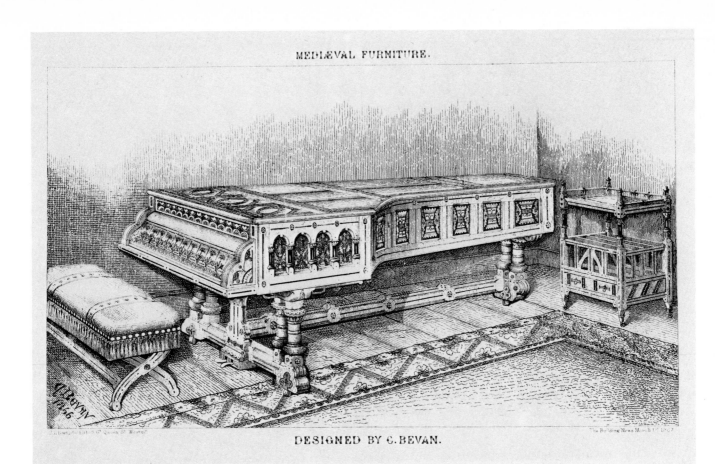

MEDIÆVAL FURNITURE.

DESIGNED BY C. BEVAN.

521a

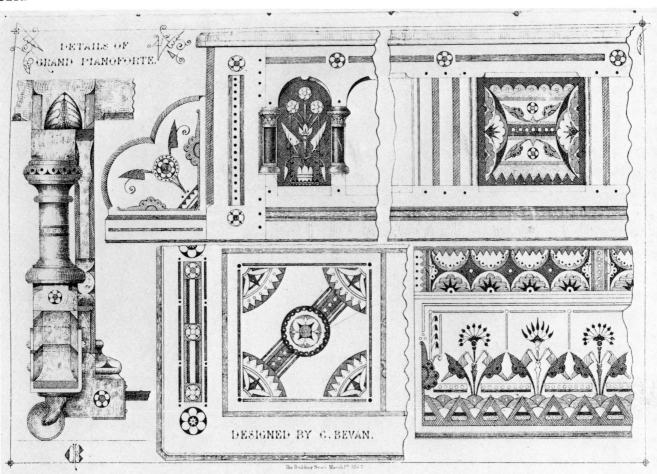

DETAILS OF GRAND PIANOFORTE.

DESIGNED BY C. BEVAN.

521a

521b

yellow and purple brocade reflecting medieval fashions. The legs are reinforced with brass plates.
H.46 (18); L.122 (48); W.43 (17).

The medial brace is impressed 'L. HANSON' and bears Marsh and Jones's printed trade label inscribed in ink '99127' and with the workman's name 'Stevenson'.

Invoiced 16 November 1865 (Drawing Room)
'A Satinwood duet Ottoman, on X standards, chamfered and inlaid with colored woods, canted stretcher, gilt chamfers, stuffed with best hair in canvas. Polished £8 10 0.'

En suite with, and illustrated alongside, the grand piano (Cat. No.521a) in *The Building News*, 1 March 1867, p.160. The brocade cover was presumably chosen to harmonize with wallpaper in the drawing room at Denton Hall (*Furniture History*, III, p.124).

LIT and PROV: see p.394.   [10.2/78]

521c HALF-TESTER BED
By Marsh and Jones, Leeds, to the design of Charles Bevan
1865
Sycamore; amboyna, alder, purplewood, ebony and various coloured woods, oak, pine

The bed consists of a sumptuous footboard connected by side rails, supporting a sprung box mattress, to plain headposts fitted with a padded and buttoned headboard backed by a draped rear structure crested by an ornamental half-tester fitted with external brass curtain rods. The foot is constructed of massive turned and faceted corner columns with inlaid and notched base blocks resting on stump feet; the squared cappings are surmounted by domed finials with carved and gilt dogtooth enrichment. The posts are united by four lavishly styled lunette pattern marquetry panels in the gothic taste with a boldly shaped bottom rail and a heavily moulded parcel-gilt top rail with eight open panels below. The framework is inlaid with alder and purpleheart banding, florets and spots. The half-tester, which is bolted to the corner posts, consists of three pierced and scalloped rails with moulded battlements and inlaid corner blocks with faceted pendants and tower finials. The side rails are mounted with brackets supporting brass curtain rods fitted with decorative terminals. The buttoned headboard has been re-covered in pink plush and the rear structure sports a silvery brocade, curtains missing, the box mattress retains its original blue check linen case.
H.261 (102); L.224 (84); W.153 (60).

521c

The tester bears Marsh and Jones's printed trade label (see Cat. No.521b) inscribed in ink '99080' and with the workman's name 'Hirst'. The footboard is inscribed 'East Room' and the pine rear structure 'Gordon Salt' in chalk, while the headboard is pencilled '79056 T. Salt Esq. Sycamore bed'.

521d

Invoiced 16 November 1865 (Best Bedroom)
'A 5 ft Sycamore Tudor Bedstead to design, handsomely inlaid with alnus and purple, paneled footboard, chamfered and moulded capping, turned and thurmed posts, moulded and battlemented cornice, supported by brackets and gilt chamfers. Polished   51 18 0
A 5 ft Spring Mattress on strong deal frame,
in linen case   5 10 0
A 5 ft Upper Mattress of Wool and Hair in
linen case   3 18 0
A Feather Bolster and 2 down pillows   3   3 0
2 Toilet Quilts   4 16 0'

Grey merino was used for the bed hangings, and the 'tufted headboard' was trimmed with 'Cerise. Grey and gold silk lace, trellis fringe and twine fringe.' The present silvery-grey brocade bed furniture dates from the visit of the Prince and Princess of Wales to Milner Field in 1882.

LIT and PROV: see p.394.   [10.3/78]

521d WARDROBE

By Marsh and Jones, Leeds, to the design of Charles Bevan
1865
Sycamore; amboyna, purplewood, alder and various coloured woods, ash, pine, oak

Constructed of two units raised on a plinth and surmounted by a moulded, notched and banded cornice with corbelled ends. The larger left-hand section is fronted by double doors enclosing two long and two narrow deep drawers with four sliding trays above; the right-hand wing, designed for hanging clothes, is lined with waxed calico and contains eight ebonized brass dress pegs below a shelf. The middle door, which frames a looking-glass, is headed by three chevron pattern marquetry panels repeated on the side doors which centre on large V-jointed panels with blocks of four framed marquetry panels at the base, creating an overall lozenge design surrounded by lobes and stylized floral motifs. The door frames are inlaid with florets and bands executed in alder and purplewood while the V-joints and chamfers are gilt. Mounted with elaborately shaped and

521d

engraved strap hinges, lock plates and drawer handles in the gothic taste. The latch-locks impressed 'COPE & COLLINSON' and the door stay 'COPES'. The interior fittings are of ash, pine back and dust boards faced with oak rails.
H.218 (86); W.203 (80); D.61 (24).

Invoiced 16 November 1865 (Best Bedroom)
'A 6 ft.6 three door Wardrobe, to design, the centre fitted with trays and drawers, enclosed by plate glass door; the wings fitted as dress closets, lined with print, enclosed by paneled doors, with inlaid panel chamfered and v jointed, moulded cornice, mounted with handsome brass strap hinges etc. Polished £75 12 0.'

LIT and PROV: see p.394.   [10.4/78]

521e WASHSTAND

By Marsh and Jones, Leeds, to the design of Charles Bevan
1865
Sycamore; alder, purplewood, pine

The blue-grey *bardiglio* marble slab streaked with dark veins is raised on four turned column supports with faceted and inlaid shaft rings. The chamfered rear stretcher is united to the bridge rails by sham wedged joints while the end friezes are fitted with towel rails. The rear structure consists of pierced triangular wings supporting a galleried shelf with a panelled marble splash-back below and tall standards suspending a brass curtain rod between bracket mounts. The frame members are chamfered, notched and enriched with inlaid spots, bands, florets and marquetry segments executed in alder and purplewood. Brown pottery castors stamped 'C & C PATENT'.
H.137 (54); W.135 (53); D.61 (24).

The pine back rail bears Marsh and Jones's printed trade label (see Cat. No.521b) inscribed in ink '99086' and with the workman's name 'Pattison'.

Invoiced 16 November 1865 (Best Bedroom)
'A 4 ft. solid Sycamore Washstand to design, inlaid with alnus, on canted and thurmed standards and cross block, back and ends with shelf supported by brackets, brass muslin rods and holders, fitted with bardilla marble slab and tiles. Polished £20 16 0.'

LIT and PROV: see p.394.   [10.5/78]

521f DRESSING TABLE

By Marsh and Jones, Leeds, to the design of Charles Bevan
1865
Sycamore; alder, purplewood, pine, ash

Of rectangular kneehole design with a swing glass. The pedestals, styled with chamfers and gilt V-jointed sides, rest on moulded plinths and have galleried tops; each contains five graduated drawers outlined with alder bands and spots. The kneehole, fronted by enriched spandrels, is backed by two framed panels with diagonal V joints. The mirror, set in a

521e

parcel gilt and inlaid chamfered frame, is suspended between splayed standards headed by notched roundels inset with purplewood and alder rosettes. Pine back, bottom and dust boards, ash drawer linings. Gilt brass ring handles, brown pottery castors impressed 'C & C PATENT', the locks stamped 'COPE & COLLINSON' and the suspension fitments 'COPE & AUSTIN PATENT'.

H.174 (68½); W.146 (57½); D.55 (21½).

Invoiced 16 November 1865 (Best Bedroom)
'A French Pedestal Toilet Table to design of solid sycamore, inlaid with alnus and purple; the ends framed flush and v-jointed, fitted with drawers, mounted with polished brass handles: Glass in canted frame supported by shaped standards. Polished £38 2 0.'

LIT and PROV: see p.394.   [10.6/78]

521f

521g DRESSING STOOL

By Marsh and Jones, Leeds, to the design of Charles Bevan
1865
Sycamore; alnus, ash

The rectangular upholstered seat stuffed over an ash frame is raised on chamfered and notched X supports inlaid with spots and united by a turned bar. The seat re-covered in a silvery brocade with pink plush facings and a decorative fringe.
H.46 (18); W.56 (22); D.46 (18).

The seat frame bears Marsh and Jones's printed trade label (see Cat. No.521b) inscribed in ink '99089' and with the workman's name 'J. Bell Senr.'

Invoiced 16 November 1865 (Best Bedroom)
'A Dressing Stool on X standards chamfered and inlaid, stuffed with best hair, covered in merino. Polished £4 15 0.'

LIT and PROV: see p.394. [10.7/78]

521g

521h

521h CENTRE TABLE
By Marsh and Jones, Leeds, to the design of Charles Bevan
1865
Sycamore; alder, purplewood, mahogany, ash

The circular moulded top with a mahogany foundation and the laminated ash frieze are veneered in sycamore inlaid with bands and clusters of spots. The cruciform underbrace is supported by four turned columns with shaft rings and alder bandings inset with purple spots, the blocked bases rest on cruciform stretchers styled with chamfers and inlays, the shaped feet conceal brass castors.
H.71 (28); Diam. 91 (36).

The underside bears Marsh and Jones's printed trade label (see Cat. No.521b) inscribed in ink '99094' and with the workman's name 'Jackson'.

Invoiced 16 November 1865 (Best Bedroom)
'A 3 ft.6 Circular Table, on four columns and cross blocks, inlaid with alnus. Polished £9 13 0.'

LIT and PROV: see p.394.   [10.8/78]

521j PEDESTAL CHAMBER CUPBOARD
By Marsh and Jones, Leeds, to the design of Charles Bevan
1865
Sycamore; alder, pine

Of pedestal design fronted by a door enclosing two shelves, the chamfered plinth and galleried top inlaid with alder bands and spots. The sides and door are constructed of solid sycamore staves united by gilt V joints, the central door panel featuring a stylized ball flower and circular rosettes on a harewood (stained sycamore) ground. Mounted with decorative gilt brass strap hinges and a ring handle in the gothic taste. Pine shelves, bottom and back.
H.84 (33); W.36 (14½); D.39 (15¼).

The back bears Marsh and Jones's printed trade label (see Cat. No.521b) inscribed in ink '99092' and with the workman's name 'Seaman'.

Invoiced 16 November 1865 (Best Bedroom)
'A Pedestal Chamber Cupboard to design of solid sycamore, inlaid with alnus, v jointed enclosed by paneled door, inlaid, mounted with brass strap hinges, polished and engraved £9 0 0.'

LIT and PROV: see p.394.   [10.9/78]

521k COMMODE STOOL
By Marsh and Jones, Leeds, to the design of Charles Bevan
1865
Sycamore; alder, mahogany, oak, pine

The stool, of circular coopered construction with gilt V joints, is raised on a veneered pine plinth headed by an alder fillet and the hollow interior is closed by a hinged padded seat. The lid, stuffed over an oak board inscribed '99093 sycamore', opens to reveal a polished mahogany seat with a white pottery pan below; pine inner structures. The main gilt brass stay-hinge is impressed 'COPE & COLLINSON' while the small inner hinge is stamped 'HORNES PATENT'. The loose seat cover is not original.
H.48 (19); Diam. 38 (15).

The underside bears Marsh and Jones's printed trade label (see Cat. No.521b) inscribed in ink '99093', with the workman's name 'Davis' and in pencil 'Sycamore'.

Invoiced 16 November 1865 (Best Bedroom)
'A sycamore Bedside Seat, inlaid with alnus, fitted with luted pan, the top stuffed with best hair covered in merino. Polished. £3 18 0.'

LIT and PROV: see p.394.   [10.10/78]

521k

521j

5211

521m

5211 EASY CHAIR
By Marsh and Jones, Leeds, to the design of Charles Bevan
1865
Sycamore; alder, beech

The X-pattern frame, united by side rails and moulded stretchers, is built of chamfered members supporting a square stuffed seat, padded armrests and a curvilinear solid upholstered back; the main joints are inlaid with alder spots simulating pegged construction. The legs terminate in lobed brass clip castors; beech seat base and armrests. Re-covered in a silvery brocade with pink plush facings and a decorative fringe.
H.91 (36); W.53 (21); D.64 (25).

The seat frame bears Marsh and Jones's printed trade label (see Cat. No.521b) inscribed in ink '99152' and with the workman's name 'Jackson'.

Invoiced 16 November 1865 (Best Bedroom)
'An Easy Chair to design of sycamore, stuffed with best hair, covered in merino, handsomely trimmed. Polished £8 10 0.'

LIT and PROV: see p.394.   [10.11/78]

521m SET OF THREE CHAIRS
By Marsh and Jones, Leeds, to the design of Charles Bevan
1865
Sycamore; alder, ebony

Of rectangular design with original caned seats; the back-posts, yoke crest rail and notched medial bar are chamfered and inlaid with alder and ebony spots. The finely turned front legs are banded with spots and end in round toes; box stretchers.
H.77 (32½); W.42 (16½); D.38 (15).

Invoiced 16 November 1865 (Best Bedroom)
'3 sycamore chamfered Chairs, inlaid, finely caned seats 38/-. Polished £5 14 0.'

Three flat seat cushions covered in silvery brocade with pink plush facings and tapes were made for the visit of the Prince and Princess of Wales in 1882. They were used on only this one occasion and survive in pristine condition.

LIT and PROV: see p.394.   [10. 12 & 16/78]

521n BOX OTTOMAN COUCH
By Marsh and Jones, Leeds
1865
Pine

Of solid fully upholstered design; the box base is rounded at the foot and has a scrolled head, while the stuffed seat, which is hinged, opens to reveal a well, lined with waxed calico. Pine carcase, the plate castors are impressed 'COPES PATENT' and the hinges 'HORNES PATENT'. Recovered in a silvery floral brocade trimmed with a decorative fringe, the plinth faced with pink plush. Chalked on the bottom '14 ft 3 y ⅞ ret' – evidently a reference to upholstery fabric.
H.71 (28); L.168 (66); W.62 (24½).

Invoiced 16 November 1865 (Own Room)
'An Ottoman Couch, with scroll head, stuffed with best hair, covered in merino, handsomely trimmed. Polished. £12 12 0.'

LIT and PROV: see p.394.   [10.13/78]

521p RUG CHEST
By Marsh and Jones, Leeds
c.1872
Oak

Designed as a cupboard in the form of a chest, the fixed moulded top framing six flush panels. The ends and double doors are each divided by moulded rails and stiles into four panels carved with roundels enclosing floral garlands. The front centres on a broad muntin finely carved with naturalistic flowers and foliage, mounted with an elaborate brass lock incorporating a bolt and hasp mechanism, while the doors are fitted with large curved hinge plates fashioned in the gothic style. The interior contains a single sliding tray and the backboard is pierced by holes.
H.71 (28); W.115 (45½); D.56 (22).

The underside bears Marsh and Jones's printed trade label (see Cat. No. 521b) inscribed in ink '35933' and with the workman's name 'Wright'.

Not recorded amongst oak furniture listed in the 1865–6

521p

account, presumably part of a later order for furnishing Milner Field, the firm continued to use their old style label for up to three years after Henry Cribb was taken into partnership in 1872. The Salt Family Trust owns a large oak centre table of similar character.

The chest displays many points of resemblance to designs published in Bruce Talbert's *Examples of Ancient and Modern Furniture*, 1876 which illustrates a sideboard designed by the author for 'Messrs Marsh Jones & Cribb' on pl.33. The possibility that this chest is also after one of Talbert's designs clearly exists.

LIT and PROV: see p.394.   [10.14/78]

FURNITURE IN THE CHAPEL AT TEMPLE NEWSAM

In 1877 Mrs E. C. Meynell Ingram commissioned the architect G. F. Bodley to convert the early Georgian library at Temple Newsam into a private chapel. Bodley's contract included the provision of furnishings, all of which were supplied by firms regularly employed for his church work. A full account of the chapel by C. G. Gilbert appeared in *L.A.C.*, No.62 (1968), pp.5–9 and No.76 (1975) pp.18–20. Bodley frequently engaged Messrs Rattee and Kett of Cambridge for ecclesiastical woodwork; prior to the destruction of their archives in 1930 a volume listing the firm's commissions was compiled, titled *Record of Jobs from 1843*, which yields the following entry on p.81:

'1877 Temple Newsame Church. G. F. Bodley, Archt Altar, Kneelers (2), Litany desk'

The altar offers no problems of identification but there are two litany desks, two pairs of kneelers and a credence table. Since the only available evidence is a rough summary of the firm's work, in which certain details were omitted, it is reasonable to assume that Rattee and Kett made the whole group. The larger desk and the slab-ended kneelers probably relate to items listed in the register. In 1876 the firm was involved in the provision of furnishings for the church which Bodley built for Mrs Meynell Ingram at Hoar Cross, Staffordshire.   [1922/F18 a–g]

522 ALTAR
By Rattee and Kett, Cambridge, 1877
Oak

Rectangular top, panelled sides bordered with applied mouldings; the front was originally panelled but is now open and hung with a fringed velvet frontal embroidered in gold thread with interlaced designs and the monogram 'I H S'.
H.96 (38); W.168 (66); D.56 (22).   [F.18a]

523 CREDENCE TABLE
Probably by Rattee and Kett, Cambridge, 1877
Walnut

The rectangular, heavily moulded slab top rests on a box-like structure formed of sunk panels set in moulded frames with ogee bottom rails; partly pegged. The open back is roughly finished indicating that this table was designed as a wall fixture.
H.79 (31); W.66 (26); D.39 (15½).   [F.18b]

524 PAIR OF KNEELERS
By Rattee and Kett, Cambridge, 1877
Walnut; oak

Each is formed of a sloped capping with moulded edges raised on solid end supports shaped and cut with ogee sections along one side; the supports are braced by a medial top rail and rest on base runners of ogee design bearing a kneeling board which has been set back on oak blocks to allow a more restful posture; pegged joints.
H.66 (26); W.168 (66).   [F.18c]

525 PAIR OF KNEELERS
Probably by Rattee and Kett, Cambridge, 1877
Walnut; oak

Each is formed of a sloped capping with shallow mouldings raised on four turned supports united by stretchers and rails, the base runners have at some time been extended with oak blocks and the kneeling boards set back a few inches allowing the body to lean forward at a more restful angle; low turned feet.
H.70 (27½); W.106 (42).   [F.18d]

525

524

526 LITANY DESK
By Rattee and Kett, Cambridge, 1877
Oak

The angled top, with a book ledge and a shelf below, is supported by solid sides set on shaped base runners and the panelled front is faced with a band of linenfold; the sides bear brass mounts for candlearms; pegged construction.
H.82 (32½); W.66 (26); D.38 (15).

EXH: *Temple Newsam Heirlooms*, 1972 (37).   [F.18e]

527 LITANY DESK
By Rattee and Kett, Cambridge, 1877
Oak

The angled top with moulded borders and two shelves below is raised on solid side supports with channelled fore-edges set on base runners; the panelled front is faced with a lower rail cut in the style of linenfold; pegged joints.
H.66 (26); W.71 (28); D.38 (15).   [F.18f]

528 PAIR OF PANELS
Pine
1877

Carved in the 'Aesthetic' taste with formal low-relief designs of roses and sunflowers in urns amid scrolling foliage and flowers; painted a dusky bluish-green with gilt details.
H.56 (22); W.92 (36).

Formerly fixed over the doors in the south alcove. A label on the back of one is inscribed 'The Honb'le Mrs Meynell Ingram / Leeds Station / Midland Rail'y / July 26th 1877 / With Care / Keep Dry / Passenger Train Immediate'.

Given together with Cat. Nos. 522–7 by the Earl of Halifax 1922.   [F.18g]

528

LIGHT FITTINGS
1877
Probably made to the design of G. F. Bodley by Messrs. Watts & Co, London (a firm established by Bodley and Garner to execute ecclesiastical metalwork). [1922/F18h–k]

529 CHANDELIER
Brass

The lightly turned stem supports fourteen elaborately scrolled and fronded candle arms arranged in two tiers of six above eight lights alternating with short scrolled members terminating in flower heads; the shaft is crested by eight floral brackets and the base features an openwork globe engraved with Byzantine designs; gothic trefoil-pattern suspension ring, plain drip-pans and holders.
H.71 (28).

The chandelier was originally hung from two wrought iron rods with a medial brass ball. [F.18h]

530 PAIR OF SCONCES
Brass

The shaped back plate centres on a convex oval panel bordered by embossed floral trails in seventeenth century Dutch taste with a phoenix at the base from which three elaborately scrolled candle arms spring.
H.39 (15½); W.26 (10¼). [F.18i]

531 PAIR OF SCONCES
Brass

Similar to the above, but with a cast cartouche-shaped plate encircled by floral trails on a stippled ground and lacking the phoenix motif.
H.43 (17); W.33 (13). [F.18j]

532 SET OF FOUR ALTAR CANDLESTICKS
Brass

The domed bases with wrythen gadrooned decoration are raised on three lions couchant; the knopped columns support large gadrooned drip-bowls centering on a candle spike.
H.33 (13).

Given together with Cat. Nos. 529–31 by the Earl of Halifax 1922. [F.18k]

533 LECTERN
Attributed to C. E. Kempe
c.1877
Cast iron and leather

533

Of folding X-design, the slender octagonal uprights have flat feet, flame finials and are united at the intersections by a cabled bar with quatrefoil terminals and at the top by narrow strips of pierced gothic tracery and rods supporting the leather book-rest laced with zig-zag thongs; the structure is painted black.
H.142 (56); W.51 (20); D.71 (28).

The lectern is identical to one which G. F. Bodley commissioned from C. E. Kempe for St Michael and All Angels, Brighton in the 1860s and there is another in the church built by Street at Upton Scudamore, Wilts. It is closely based on a medieval lectern in the Hotel de Cluny, Paris, drawn by G. E. Street for the Second Series of *Instrumenta Ecclesiastica*, published by the Ecclesiological Society, 1856, p.70, pls.29 & 30.

LIT: C. G. Gilbert, 'The Victorian Chapel at Temple Newsam', *L.A.C.*, No.62 (1968), pp.5–9, repr.; *L.A.C.*, No.76 (1975) p.19.

534

EXH: London, V.&A., *Victorian Church Art*, 1971/2 (N.9); *Temple Newsam Heirlooms*, 1972 (36).

PROV: Supplied for the private chapel which the Hon Mrs E. C. Meynell Ingram commissioned G. F. Bodley to create and furnish at Temple Newsam in 1877; given by the Earl of Halifax 1922.   [1922/F.19]

UNREGISTERED FURNITURE IN THE CHAPEL AT LOTHERTON

534 ORGAN
Built by Wordsworth and Maskell, Leeds to the design of G. F. Bodley
1877
Walnut; pine, oak, etc

The corbelled-out upper stage centering on a half-round tower is fronted by thirty-three dummy pipes of tin set in an open case with panelled sides headed by a pulvinated frieze enriched with parcel-gilt foliage; the toe boards, pipe shades and cresting are elaborately styled with carved and gilt floral foliage of scrolled openwork design; the kneehole pedestal is fitted with double panelled doors which open to reveal the keyboard and support two brass candlearms. The case is of walnut, partly veneered, with some pine and oak structures, the pierced carving is backed by blue paper bearing sketches of foliage. A tablet above the keyboard is inscribed 'WORDSWORTH & MASKELL / LEEDS'; The door lock is impressed 'CHUBB & SON / MAKERS TO HER MAJESTY / 87 ST PAULS CYD LONDON / 683637'; the catch is impressed 'HINDE'S PATENT' and the hinges are marked 'RODGERS / PATENT / LOCK-JOINT'.
H.404 (159); W.198 (78).

Single keyboard, tracker action with 56 notes giving a manual compass CC–g‴ with ten ivory draw stops and 25 pedal notes CC–C′ keyed to pipes concealed in boarded-over book cases either side; there are two combination foot levers and a swell pedal. The pipe specification is Pedal Bourdon 16′; Open Diapason 8′; Lieblich Gedact 8′; Keraulophon 8′; Principal 4′; Twelfth 2⅔′; Piccolo 2′; Hautbois 8′. The bellows were originally powered by an hydraulic engine in the basement; this mechanism was replaced in 1967 by an electric motor and during the major restoration of 1974 a modern wind chamber was installed.

The case, built by John Wood, Snr was designed by G. F. Bodley, the architect commissioned to convert the early Georgian Library at Temple Newsam into a domestic chapel in 1877. The seventeenth century Flemish style was favoured by the High Church Movement to which he and his patron Mrs E. C. Meynell Ingram belonged; Bodley's drawing perished in a fire at the organ works in 1950.

LIT: *L.A.C.*, No.62 (1968) pp.5–9, fig.1; *L.A.C.*, No.66 (1970) pp.12–14.

PROV: The Hon Mrs E. C. Meynell Ingram, Temple Newsam; given by the Earl of Halifax 1922.   [1922/F47]

535

The Norman chapel at Lotherton Hall contains an interesting group of furniture entrusted to the Aberford Parochial Church Council, but since these pieces are closely associated with the Gascoigne family and are unlikely ever to be removed, they deserve a brief mention. The chapel, which fell into disuse in 1891, was comprehensively restored between 1913 and 1916 by Colonel F. R. T. Gascoigne who introduced most of the present furnishings. An article by G. E. Kirk outlining the history of the building was published in *Thoresby Society Miscellanea*, XXXVI, pt.II (1920), pp.113–8 with photographs of the unreformed interior.

The only indigenous early woodwork is a late seventeenth century oak pulpit and the two-tier reading desk, which originally stood together in the south west corner of the nave. The pulpit (Fig.535) raised on a massive turned support, has panelled sides carved with simple lozenges reflecting local decorative traditions, a plain back-plate and an octagonal sounding board featuring a star motif.

The primitive plank pews were replaced by fifty bentwood chairs with moulded plywood seats. They are branded 'J & J KOHN WSETIN AUSTRIA 19 iii 13'; several also bear a printed paper label inscribed 'JACOB & JOSEPH KOHEN, WIEN' while many have in addition either an ivoret or a paper label indicating they were supplied by W. Richardson, Cabinet Maker, Leeds.

The communion table made way for an impressive North German oak chest (Fig.536) acquired in 1915 by Colonel Gascoigne from a Lutheran Church at Cuxhaven; it now serves as the altar. The elaborately carved front frames five panels representing biblical scenes: Adam and Eve, the sacrifice of Isaac, the Annunciation; the Nativity and the Resurrection, with a long inscription above: DAS ALTE TESTAMENT WIRT DVRCH DAS NEWE KUNT DAS NEWE HAT IM ALTEN SEINE GRUNT DAN WIE SIE IN ADAM ALLE GESUNDIGET HABEN ALLSO WERDEN SIE IN CHRISTO ALLE SALICHE WERD [EN]. The following translation is offered by Professor John Wilkie 'The Old Testament becomes known through the New, the New has its foundation in the Old; for as in Adam they have all sinned, so in Christ they will all become blessed'. The chest is six feet long with large hinges and wrought iron lifting handles. It can be assigned to about 1630 on the evidence of a closely similar example illustrated by H. Kreisel, *Die Kunst des Deutschen Möbels*, I, 1968, fig.333.

536

The chest formerly supported a tall carved, painted and gilt reredos of architectural design with three niches housing figures of St George and two martyrs, reputedly acquired in Venice. This lavish structure was presented to the Leeds Art Galleries in 1957 and is now displayed in the chapel vestibule at Temple Newsam.

Musical needs are served by an harmonium which, according to an inscription on the sound board, was restored by L. S. Burditt in October 1913. The instrument was supplied by 'Mason and Bandin / Organ Company', the interior reveals several sets of impressed and gilt serial numbers while a paper label describes the action as 'MASON & HAMLIN'S / Automatic Bellows Swell / Patented 21 Oct. 1862'.

The remaining furniture is a mixture of genuine, made-up and reproduction oak. The Italianate-style chair carved with lions rampant and grotesque masks is an Edwardian copy of a sixteenth century prototype. There is one respectable late seventeenth century West Yorkshire pattern armchair with a lozenge on the back panel and a scrolled foliate cresting, but the other two oak armchairs contain very little old work; the same is true of the organ bench and a prayer desk. However, a large and picturesque settle possesses art-historical interest as a vigorous example of nineteenth century antiquarian oak furniture. The panelled back embellished with 'Romayne' heads incorporates a tablet carved '1690 MC'; there are two drawers beneath the seat and the arms terminate in lion masks. The settle, composed entirely of old, new and re-carved members documents a fascinating aspect of Victorian taste.

UNREGISTERED FURNITURE IN THE ABERFORD ALMSHOUSES

In 1974 Leeds City Council acquired the picturesque Gothic Revival almshouses, built at Aberford by Mary and Elizabeth Gascoigne of Parlington in 1844. They are scheduled to become a conservation centre for works of art and thus form an outstation of the Leeds Art Galleries. Before the sale the Trustees disposed of many original furnishings and some verminous items were subsequently destroyed: what remains has been placed on permanent loan.

Almshouses furniture is an interesting sub-group on the fringes of the English vernacular tradition and the Aberford pieces, being documented, are of particular significance. An account book among the Gascoigne papers (GC/E2/46 & 7) deposited at Leeds Archives Department, reveals that during the six months up to 1 July 1846 Messrs Henry Atkinson and A. Barker were paid £100 'on account of their Bill as Upholsterers' and later the same year received the balance of

537

£115.3.10. in full for 'Bedsteads, Tables, Chairs &c'. Atkinson's separate account for £44.7.6. was settled at the same time. Henry Atkinson is recorded in White's *Leeds Directory*, 1853 as a cabinet maker at 119 Park Lane, but Barker has not been traced.

The furniture falls into three groups: common domestic wares from the eight dwellings; impressive pieces made for the communal refectory and the cloister passage; intrusive items imported from other local buildings.

The dwellings, which each consist of a ground floor living room and an upstairs bedroom, were uniformly furnished with painted pine sideboard dressers, writing tables, chests of drawers, dressing tables, wash stands, chamber tables, cricket tables, cupboards and elm chairs. None of the original beds remained when a census of the movables was taken in 1975. Of this repertoire only one chamber table on chamfered legs, a single writing table with profiled end supports and seven robust elm chairs (representing two different patterns) now remain. The yoke-back chairs with octagonal legs (Fig.537) possess a severe simplicity which separates them from 'cottage and farmhouse' furniture; their austerity may have been inspired by the gothic character of their setting.

538

A pair of eight-foot corridor benches (Fig.538) and two massive twelve-foot refectory tables, one designed with long drop-leaves, are more consciously Gothic Revival, even ecclesiastical, in concept; the choice of oak, revealed wedged joints and complex profiles suggest they may well have been designed by George Fowler Jones, architect of the alms-houses, who also built the nearby church of St Mary at Garforth in 1844.

When the Gascoigne family vacated Parlington Hall, Aberford in 1905 two towering library bookcases supplied by Gillows of Lancaster in 1811 were installed in the almshouses. They are of mahogany with doors in the lower stage and open shelves above. Decoration is confined to simple reeding, a crossbanded frieze set with circular paterae and outlined door panels. A drawing (Fig.539) for one of the units (8 ft 6 in. high, 6 ft wide) exists in Gillows' Estimate Sketch Books at Westminster City Libraries Archives Department (344/ 99a, p.1900). The cost analysis records that two matching units were commissioned by Richard Oliver Gascoigne in 1811 at an estimated price of £15.12.0. each.

Finally, a large oak Stolzenberg patent roll shutter filing cabinet of *c*.1910 incorporating ten tiers of sliding document trays each closed by a hanging lid, was removed from the Aberford Estate Office to the almshouses after the last war. It is a spectacular example of Edwardian office furniture.

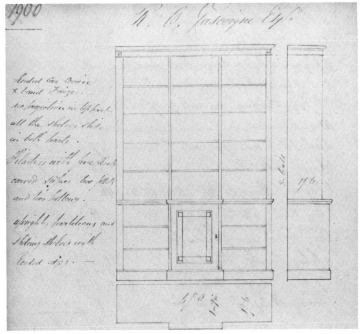

539

Part Two

CONTINENTAL FURNITURE

DUTCH AND FLEMISH

540 CUPBOARD
17th century, first half
Oak and walnut; pine

Built in two heavily moulded stages with a deep cornice and prominent blocked corners featuring free-standing columns, backed by pilasters, of Composite and Tuscan design; each section is enclosed by double doors ornamented with walnut parquetry and applied mouldings arranged in geometrical patterns; the sides are formed of elaborately moulded raised panels and the base contains two drawers; the blocked front centres on two engaged standing figures of St Mary Magdalene *pentant* holding a skull with a vessel of ointment at her feet and, above, Christ as the Good Shepherd wearing the crown of thorns and carrying a lamb on his shoulders. The doors swivel on pin-hinges and the locks, concealed in the thickness of the doors, operate rising bolts; a section of the Magdalene's drapery is fashioned as a keyhole cover. Oak carcase, the doors and side panels veneered with walnut, pine drawers sliding on side runners and united by nails.
H.221 (87); W.208 (82); D.74 (29).

Although largely intact the cupboard has been provided with a new panelled back and extensively reconditioned; the carved frieze ornament is not original and the structure was probably raised on low globular feet. The design is similar in many respects to a cabinet engraved by Paul Vredeman de Vries, *Verscheyden Schrynwerck*, 1630, pl.5.

EXH: *Temple Newsam Heirlooms*, 1972 (22).

PROV: The biblical figures suggest that this piece stood in the sacristy of a church; it was presumably acquired by the Hon. Mrs E. C. Meynell Ingram during the late Victorian era on one of her periodic visits to the Low Countries; purchased at the Temple Newsam sale (Robinson, Fisher & Harding) 26–31 July 1922, lot 430.   [1922/F25]

541 DRAW TABLE
c.1630–50
Oak

The top and leaves are of plank construction set in a mitred frame and the rails are simply styled with a corner bracket and scroll profiles centering on a pendant drop; the turned supports with large plain bulbous knops of unequal girth are connected at floor level by wide flat stretchers. Built of riven and adzed timber united by pegs with traces of red ochre.
H.79 (31); W.62 (24½); L. 137(54) closed, 249 (98) open.

One new plank and minor repairs to the top. The surface has been refinished but the frame displays convincing signs of wear; the supports may originally have been raised on block bases. The design is similar in many respects to engavings for tables by Paul Vredeman de Vries, *Verscheyden Schrynwerck*, 1630, pl.12.

PROV: The Gascoigne gift 1968.   [7.140/68]

542 TWO FRAMES
Mid 17th century
Oak

Of oval cartouche-form with flattened volute crestings and bases; one surround is embellished with fleshy leaves in the auricular style and headed by a ram's mask; the other is ornamented with cornucopia and backed by a lion *affrontée*, the head, paws and tufts of hair being shown. The frames contain lead-faced panels painted with the armorials of past owners of Temple Newsam.
H.81 (32); W.69 (27).

These surrounds may originally have served as internal window frames and are similar to examples portrayed in room interiors by the Dutch artist Pieter de Hooch and his contemporaries.

PROV: The frames were almost certainly acquired in Holland by the Hon. Mrs E. C. Meynell Ingram who decorated the Great Hall at Temple Newsam with family armorials; they were displayed during her time in the entrance porch; given by the Earl of Halifax 1922.   [1922/F29]

543 CABINET ON STAND
17th Century, third quarter
Lignum vitae; pine, oak, walnut, ivory

The large rectangular cabinet enclosed by double doors with two shallow frieze drawers above, is raised on six front and three rear wave-turned supports connected by flat veneered stretchers; the front, inner door surfaces, sides and base rail are faced with oyster parquetry patterns and ripple mouldings in lignum vitae; the interior is fitted with an elaborate façade of revealed and concealed drawers centering on an architecturally styled cupboard; each side is flanked by a spiral-turned column, having gilt-brass capital and base mounts, which pulls out to disclose a nest of drawers, the column units are inserted between head and foot blocks, also backed by document compartments; there are tiers of five large drawers outlined with ribbed mouldings either side of the central section which is designed as a portico embellished with precise architectural details; the cupboard doors, ornamented with three spiral-turned columns matching the lateral fixtures, are articulated with baroque niches, cornices, consoles and

541

542

543

similar elements; the richly moulded entablature and broken pediment front two shallow drawers and the blocked base is backed by a third; the doors open to reveal a mirror-lined recess with turned central and corner colonettes, the floor is inlaid with lobed ivory medallions; an alcove at the back contains false side panels painted with figures of Ceres and Bacchus concealing tiers of four small drawers. The main drawers are mounted with winged dragonhead pulls in brass; the hinges, door bolts and outer key escutcheon are gilt metal; steel locks. All visible surfaces are veneered in lignum vitae, pine carcase and doors, solid turned members; the drawer linings are of oak except for the very small internal drawers which are in walnut. The stand is a later replacement, the turned uprights are too numerous and slender for such a cabinet and the rail displays inferior ripple mouldings. The original was almost certainly lower with robust spirally-turned corner supports on bun feet united by a central stretcher.

H.191 (75½); W.196 (77); D.59 (23).

PROV: By descent to the Hon. Mrs I. M. H. Strickland, Howsham Hall, Yorkshire; Howsham Hall sale (Hollis & Webb, Leeds) 1 Nov. 1948, lot 262; given by Colonel Grey 1948. [28/48]

544 SIDE TABLE
*c.*1680
Walnut; pine, beech

The rectangular top with a veneered border and edge moulding rests on a panelled frieze decorated around three sides with strapwork designs enhanced by husks, flower heads and diaper patterns against a stippled ground; the front apron is lavishly carved and pierced with fronded scrolls centering on a cartouche tablet featuring a husk spray; the elaborately scrolled and moulded legs, set at a slight angle, are vigorously carved with acanthus foliage, husk chains and strapwork interlace contained within raised borders; the cross stretchers,

544

styled in the same manner, centre on an oval gadrooned platform and pendant; the rear stretchers and legs are plain behind; the toes of paired scroll formation. Walnut, with a pine backrail and medial brace, the top lies on beech sleepers.

H.86 (34); W.147 (58); W.61 (24).

It has not been easy to establish the origin of this table; it is unlikely to be French or English; some authorities feel it betrays a Germanic character, others favour a Flemish source.

PROV: Sotheby's, 25 Nov. 1960, lot 122; H. Blairman & Sons; private collection; H. Blairman & Sons; bought from the Lady Martin Bequest Fund 1966. [19/66]

545 HALL SETTEE
*c.*1690–1700
Lime; oak

Elaborately carved openwork back of scroll design richly ornamented with acanthus sprays, festoons of fruit and flowers, leaf-rosettes, wheat ears and a central garland framing a profile medallion of William and Mary in low relief; the solid end supports have sunk panels containing olive branches on both faces and the scrolled openwork arms are carved with serpents and leaf ornament; the oak seat has an acanthus moulding and dentil frieze; the back is reinforced with iron straps. It may originally have possessed an apron of carved drapery swags beneath the seat rail.

H.117 (46); W.193 (76); D.38 (15).

The profile heads do not quote precisely any recorded coin, medal or engraved source, although the features leave no doubt that the conjoint busts are intended to portray William and Mary. The closest parallel is provided by effigies on medals produced by the Dutchman Arondeaux between 1690 and 1692 (*Medallic Illustrations*, pls. lxxx 5; lxxxvii 6 and lxxxix 3). The olive branches represent political peace.

Hall seats of this type were commonly placed in the entrance halls of Dutch houses and often painted to match the wall decoration. Prior to stripping in 1939 this example was grained to simulate oak and had other layers of paint underneath.

545

A large number of similar hall settees are to be found in Britain: there is one in the V. & A. with green graining; two at Arniston, Scotland; a set of four at Dunham Massey Hall, Cheshire and another figured in the Mentmore sale (Sotheby's) 18–20 May 1977, lot 899. Some are enriched with the armorials of English families suggesting they were imported from the Netherlands with blank reserved panels.

545

LIT: *Connoisseur*, April 1941, p.117, repr.; F. Davis, *A Picture History of Furniture*, 1958, pl.88.

PROV: The Earl of Balfour, Redcliff Hall, Dunbar, Scotland; Charles Thornton (Antiques); bought from the Harding Fund 1939.   [3/39]

546 PAIR OF CHAIRS
*c.*1710
Walnut; beech

Each with a broad, elaborately carved and pierced splat representing a vase of fruit and flowers surrounded by leafy scrolls; the moulded back posts of elongated S-design are surmounted by a decorative cresting composed of a *lambrequin* motif and urn-finial supported by double scrolls; the cabriole forelegs are styled with acanthus and husk pendants, raised borders and knurl feet connected to the turned rear legs by moulded side stretchers supporting an ornamental cross rail, designed as an urn between scrolls to correspond with the cresting; the seat re-covered with leather fastened over the shaped aprons with brass nails. Walnut frames with

546

beech seat rails; the splat and stretcher joints are incised with Roman numerals 'viii & iii' and 'iiii & iv'.
H.126 (49½); W.51 (20); D.44 (17½).

These chairs, which evidently formed part of a larger set, convey a vivid impression of the style introduced by the architect-designer Daniel Marot; the seats would originally have been covered in a luxurious fabric trimmed with a deep fringe.

LIT: *Apollo*, Dec. 1941, p.140, fig. v.

PROV: Said to come from Hamilton Palace, Scotland; Alfred Jowett; Charles Lumb & Sons; bought from the Harding Fund 1939.   [10.1 & 2/39]

547 LOOKING-GLASS
Early 18th century
Stained pine

The cartouche-shaped mirror is framed by a moulded surround embellished with grotesque shoulder masks and floral festoons; the pierced cresting centres on a shell headed by a plumed fan carved with husks and acanthus foliage, the base is carved with a fronded shell between openwork C-scrolls. Pine back board.
H.89 (35); W.46 (18).

PROV: The Gascoigne gift 1968.   [7.198/68]

548 CONSOLE TABLE
*c.*1730
Painted pine

The serpentine *verde antico* marble top, with curved sides and a moulded edge, is raised on legs of S-form set back, carved at the top with winged cherub heads and terminating in

548

fronded scrolls; the legs are tied by a leafy bracket supporting a third winged cherub's head in high relief and the underframe reveals heavily carved and pierced foliage; a tasselled *lambrequin* apron, ornamented with strapwork designs in the baroque taste verging on rococo, encircles the table below a heavily moulded top rail with embellished panels at the centre and corners; painted dark brown over a white primer.
H.87 (34½); W.112 (44); D.48 (19).

This table is one of a pair, the companion being in the V. & A. (W.12–1963). They probably served as credence tables standing on either side of the altar in a Flemish church and would have been painted to match the walls. The design resembles engravings by André-Charles Boulle and Daniel Marot published in the latter's *Ornamentes*, n.d. (R.I.B.A. Press Mark EW. 72: 103, 44).

PROV: Bought from Walter H. Ferry 1963.   [13/63]

549 LONG-CASE CLOCK
By Pieter Egter, Dordrecht
*c.*1730
Mulberry; oak, pine

The arched hood with a fretted frieze and corner columns is surmounted by a high dome supporting a carved and gilt figure of Atlas standing on an orb holding up a painted celestial globe; the front corners bear companion statues in loin cloths, probably originally holding a trumpet and a sun-shaped mirror; the arched side panels are fitted with ebonized arabesque fretwork on a canvas backing. The trunk, enclosed by a tall moulded door centering on a window encircled with brass and outlined by a string panel, rests loosely on a box base with a plinth moulding and restored bun feet (masked in illustration). Oak carcase veneered in mulberry, the hood and base renovated.

The low arch contains a fully engraved and silvered starspangled lunar disc with the age shown in a circular aperture at the top. The brass dial plate, with a laurel border and matted centre, has a silvered chapter ring, cast-brass spandrels emblematic of the seasons, ringed winding holes and a square date aperture surrounded by foliate scrolls. The subsidiary dial with five-seconds numbering and the face have original pointers. The arch span is engraved 'Pieter Egter Dordregt Fecit'. Eight-day, five pillar rack-striking movement with two bells of different pitch and a pump-over change using the same pin-wheel; the hours are struck on the larger bell, the lesser registers half-hours, the preceding hour being sounded on the small bell. The weights and pendulum bob encased in brass.
H.297 (117).

E. L. Edwardes illustrates two Dutch clocks, *c.*1725, of very similar character in *The Grandfather Clock*, (rev.ed.) 1952, pls.27–34. One by Jacob Hasius features the same spandrels and dial markings, the other exhibits an identical set of cresting figures.

PROV: Harold T. Eddison (d.1940), Stairfoot House, Adel, Leeds; bequeathed by Sir George Martin 1976.

[51.33/76]

550 CORNER CABINET
*c.*1770
Mahogany; oak, pine

Bow-fronted and built in two stages; the upper part is headed by a moulded cornice of flattened arch design centering on a platform concealed by an elaborately carved cluster of fronded scrolls of asymmetric rococo form, with a floral spray in low relief on the shaped tympanum; the upper cabinet contains two shelves and a pair of drawers in the base while

549

550

the lower stage is fitted with a single shelf; square bracket feet united by a curved apron. Both parts are fronted by tambour shutters which shunt into a narrow passage between the back boards. Original pierced brass drawer escutcheons and loop handles with true and false key plates. Oak carcase with a solid mahogany front, the tambour is built up of pine ribs glued to canvas and faced with mahogany reeds; the back panels are joined to the top and bottom boards by dovetails.
H.239 (94); W.106 (42); D.64 (25).

The shaped cornice crested by vigorous rococo foliage, the central platform and corner ledges, the flattened S-scroll profile of the tympanum and English style mounts reveal this cabinet was made in the Low Countries.

EXH: Temple Newsam, *Pictures and Furniture*, 1938 (186).

PROV: Bought from Charles Thornton (Antiques) 1938.
[27/38]

551 SLEIGH
c.1760–70
Oak; pine, beech, lime

The chassis, flared at the rear and tapering towards the front, is raised on six scroll supports set on iron-clad runners which sweep upwards to converge on a bold lion's-head; the inward curving backboard has a richly carved crest rail centering on a cherub mask with a hound emerging from an elaborate rococo cartouche at the base. Each side is sub-divided by rails, embellished with strapwork, shells and fronded scrolls, into three shaped panels, the front pair being painted with floral sprays, the others and the large backboard bear wintry landscapes and figures. The carved framework is painted black with gilt details and reinforced with iron straps and braces; outriders' footboard and pedal brake. The padded box seat has a loose cushion and a fringed red plush coverlet lined with lambs wool. A red and gold leather harness hung with brass bells, pair of shafts and whip belonging to the sleigh survive.
H.96 (38); L.198 (78); W.99 (39).

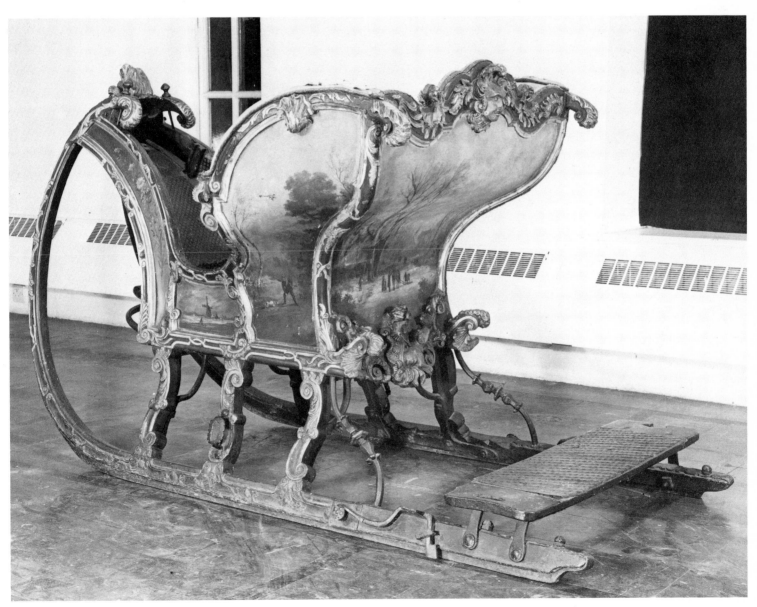

The sleigh is a fine example of the so-called *arreslede* (bellsleigh) of the Amsterdam type and was probably made in that city. The panels have been repainted during the nineteenth century; floral sprays in particular are not a traditional decorative element. A closely similar model is illustrated in the *Connoisseur*, Oct. 1929, p. lxxiv.

LIT: F. Moss, *Pilgrimages to Old Homes*, V, 1910, p.307, repr.

PROV: According to the earliest Temple Newsam guidebook (1922) this sleigh was presented by the King of Holland to the Lord Mayor of Enkhuizen, after whose death it was purchased by Joseph Morpurgo, 37, Nieuwe Hoogstraat, Amsterdam and later acquired by the Hon. Mrs E. C. Meynell Ingram of Temple Newsam. If the tradition of a Royal connection has substance the gift must date from after 1813 when the sleigh was already old and possessed antiquarian interest; given by the Earl of Halifax 1922.

[1922/F12]

552 PAIR OF CHAIRS
Late 18th century
Elm; walnut and various coloured woods

The chairs have shaped backs with rounded shoulders divided by two S-pattern splats, serpentine-fronted seats and cabriole forelegs on pad feet; the backs and shaped seat rails are veneered with marquetry compositions of scrolling seaweed, floral sprays and a pair of stylized dolphins on the cresting executed in stained and shaded woods on a walnut ground, the front legs are also inlaid with floral motifs. Elm frames united by pegs; one chair has new feet spliced on to the rear legs and blocked mortice slots beneath the back rail, one seat preserves early webbing. The crude marquetry work and inlays probably added at a later period.
H.92 (36½); W.51 (20); D.40 (16).

PROV: The Gascoigne gift 1968.   [7.152/68]

553 SECRETAIRE
Late 18th century
Olivewood; oak, pine, rosewood, satinwood

Upright and rectangular with a frieze drawer, a fall-front above cupboard doors and chamfered forecorners; veneered with quartered olivewood panels set within rosewood borders and chequered feathered strings; the drop-front and doors are inset with similar green-stained oval panels figuring fluted urns in shaded satinwood; short square tapered legs, block-banded cornice. The desk interior contains a central cupboard, four small drawers with veneered fronts and open shelves; the writing surface has a baize panel and the doors below pivot on pin-hinges, circular stamped brass escutcheons, steel locks (the top one secures both drawer and flap), brass bolts and ball feet. Veneered on to a pine foundation, the back and bottom boards, internal structures and legs are of oak, the lower doors and flap are veneered inside.
H.150 (59); W.91 (36); D.46 (18).

553

Dutch fall-front secretaires of this design are based on Louis XVI prototypes, but the simpler marquetry decoration, absence of lavish ormolu mounts and traditional features such as the block-banded cornice give them a distinctive national character. The veneer is too thin for microscopic identification.

PROV: By descent from Duke Fox to his niece Miss M. Fox Hunter who gave it to Leeds 1946.   [11.1/46]

554 COMMODE
Late 18th century
Satinwood; mahogany, rosewood, olivewood, box, oak, pine

In the form of a rectangular cabinet containing a long drawer above two cupboard doors and supported on short square tapering legs; chamfered forecorners, a veneered dentil cornice and brass spindle-gallery around three sides of the top; veneered with satinwood panels bordered by mahogany, rosewood and chequered bands; the drawer front centres on a small panel of Japanese floral lacquer and the cupboard doors are inset with pictorial medallions of lacquer, each

554

555

suspended from an engraved marquetry design of tied ribbons; the ovals portray oriental garden buildings in red and gilt on a greenish-black ground; circular cast-brass drawer handles replaced, flush bolts, pin-hinges; keyhole escutcheon and brass ball feet missing. Pine carcase with oak back, legs, rails, shelf and drawer, the doors veneered inside with olive-wood.
H.85 (33½); W.80 (31½); D.36 (14¼).

PROV: Given by Charles Roberts, Farfield Hall, Yorkshire 1941.   [11.2/41]

555 CARD TABLE
Late 18th century
Mahogany; oak, sycamore and other pale woods

Of rectangular design, raised on square fluted legs inlaid with box strings and headed by floral sprigs; the frieze drawer and ends are decorated with arabesques and sprays, the front rail centres on a small apron. The folded top opens to reveal a circular bouquet and butterfly executed in various green-stained, shaded and scorched woods with a playing card inset at each corner: ace of spades; two of hearts; three of diamonds; ace of clubs. The opened top is supported on a hinged rear leg; when closed the visible surface is ornamented with a large oval fan medallion with radial spurs and anthemion motifs at each apex surrounded by arabesques and

floral sprays inlaid into the solid mahogany board. The drawer originally had internal divisions and the knobs are replaced by modern escutcheons.
H.72 (28½); W.85 (33½); D. closed 41 (16½).

The front edge of the drawer is stamped 'EDWARDS & ROBERTS'. This fashionable Victorian furnishing firm with premises at 148–60, Wardour Street and 532, Oxford Street traded in new and antique furniture. They presumably put on the reproduction brasses and reconditioned the table, although there is no evidence of more extensive decorative improvements. See also Cat. Nos.102, 225.

PROV: Bought by Edmund Leatham, Wentbridge House, Yorkshire, about 1880; inherited by Lady Gascoigne; the Gascoigne gift 1968.   [7.153/68]

556 SIDEBOARD CABINET
*c.*1805
Mahogany; oak, pine

The top lifts to reveal an oval pewter basin fitted in a well flanked by slides; a pewter urn fixed inside the lid discharges water into the basin, the lid being held open by hinged wooden brackets which also support two pairs of folding shelves for glasses; the front contains one dummy flanked by two true drawers with a cupboard enclosed by double doors below, the adjustable shelf rests on bars fitted between notched posts; the corner colonettes are carved with tasselled drapery and have brass mummy-head and foot terminals in the Egyptian taste, short tapered legs on ball feet; the top and front surfaces are outlined with brass strings and beading. The basin and cistern stamped with Rotterdam pewter marks; modern locks, hinges and bolts. Oak carcase veneered with mahogany, front corner posts and bottom rails pine.
H.99 (39); W.120 (47½); D.59 (23).

556

Sideboards of this design type were never made in England.

LIT: *L.A.C.*, No.20 (1953), pp.9–10, repr.

PROV: Charles Roberts, Farfield Hall, Addingham, Yorkshire; Farfield sale (Hollis & Webb, Leeds) 27 May 1952,
lot 137; given by Lady Martin through the L.A.C.F. 1952.
[21/52]

556

FRENCH

557 DRESSER
*c.*1580–1600
Walnut; oak

Of architectural design, the upper part is surmounted at the
back by a crested and pedimented gallery elaborately ornamented in the renaissance style with grotesque masks,
foliage, swags and strapwork; the coved central panel is
carved in high relief with Apollo seated by a spring attended
by two female musicians in a classical landscape and there
are niches with shell-lunettes flanked by columns at either
side; beneath is a low step and shelf. The middle stage contains three shelved cupboards, the central panel features a
nymph holding a lyre set in an architectural niche; the side
doors, separated by pilasters and term figures, bear satyr
masks amid floral arabesques, below are three shallow
drawers. The lower part consists of an open platform with
two pairs of detached column supports forming an arcade,
the backboard is carved with a strapwork cartouche between
shallow niche panels; heavily moulded plinth raised on bun
feet. Wrought iron drawer pulls, two original locks, pivot
hinges on the central cupboard, the side doors move on plate
hinges embedded into the stiles. Solid walnut, apart from
renewed oak backboards, the drawers united by nailed
dovetails with rough-hewn panelled bottoms.
H.264 (104); W.150 (59); D.48 (19).

A dresser with closely similar decorative elements in the
Rijksmuseum, Amsterdam, *Catalogus Van Meubelen*, 1952,
No.433 bears the date 1591 inside, but engravings published
by S. S. Jervis, *Printed Furniture Designs Before 1650*, 1974,
show that furniture of this type was made into the 1620s.

The upper gallery is an addition presumably taken from
another dresser. The lower back and middle side panels are
of inferior quality and appear to be nineteenth century in
date.

PROV: Sir Richard Wallace, Sudbourne Hall, Suffolk; purchased with the hall by Kenneth McKenzie Clark; Joseph
Watson, 1st Baron Manton; Frances Claire, Lady Manton
who removed the dresser to Ladymead, Sussex and bequeathed it to her 4th son, the Hon. Richard Mark Watson
who gave it to Leeds in memory of his mother 1944. [5/44]

558 LOOKING-GLASS
*c.*1720
Pine

The central plate is enclosed by an inner frame of carved and
gilt bay-leaf pattern, surrounded by glass borders set within
a more elaborate outer frame. The arched top centres on a
fleshy cartouche and acanthus fan cresting backed by diaper
work and flanked by floral festoons on a sand-textured
ground. The low scrolled shoulders, decorated with acanthus

557

558

559

volutes and floral sprays, support winged dragons; the shaped bottom border is ornamented with a rococo shell and paired plumes set between C-scrolls, while the fronded corner volutes have leafy brackets. The pine backboard is inscribed in pencil 'Sold Mr Downes'.
H.180 (71); W.119 (47).

The cresting and base ornaments partly re-worked.

PROV: Bought from Mrs Emma Reid, Moor Park, Harrogate 1950. [26/50]

559 BRACKET CLOCK
By De Lorme, Paris
c.1725–30
Tortoiseshell and brass; oak

The balloon-shaped case is veneered on oak with Boulle marquetry of engraved brass and natural tortoiseshell ornamented with gilt-bronze mounts. The removable dome top has a *lambrequin* capping surmounted by a seated putto holding an hourglass and is faced on each side by an engraved female mask and fronted by a foliate panel. The arched side windows and glazed door are framed in ormolu and the case, enriched with floral trails and stylized foliate panels executed in Boulle marquetry, is set with fronded shoulder

mounts and raised on scrolling gilt-bronze feet. The door centres at the base on a pierced shell plaque above a mask of Mercury. The interior of the rear door is veneered with a floral design and the sloping floor bears a tiled perspective pattern in tortoiseshell and brass with a circular hole, presumably to bolt the clock securely to a bracket or pedestal.

The dial is of chased, matted bronze with hour numerals painted in blue on white enamel plaques and an outer minute band; original pointers. The square, spring-driven, eight-day timepiece movement has vase-shaped pillars, a crown wheel and verge escapement and a silk suspension pendulum operating via a crutch; the back plate is engraved 'De Lorme Paris'.
H.48 (19).

PROV: Given by T. Edmund Harvey 1948. [30/48]

560 SEDAN CHAIR
c.1740–5
Pine

Of rectangular design with a domed roof, outward curving back and straight sides resting on scroll feet united by shaped

rails; the corners and window surrounds are carved with gilt scrolls, flame borders and flourishes in the rococo taste and the panels are painted with *singeries* portraying monkeys masquerading as fashionable ladies: on the front – a cherry picking scene; r.h. side – a bathroom interior; back – monkey on horseback in a park with sporting trophies above; l.h. side – a dressing room scene, the pictures being set in rococo cartouches surrounded by garlands and chinoiserie decoration on a dark-green ground. The windows slide in grooved frames and may be raised or lowered by straps; the interior, containing a seat with padded armrests, is lined in red silk damask with fringed valances (curtains missing). Ornamental brass door handle impressed 'F.T', iron *fische* hinges and staple mounts to receive the lifting poles; the roof is covered in leather secured by conical headed nails.
H.168 (66); W.71 (28); D.94 (37).

LIT: *L.A.C.*, No.13 (1950), p.6, repr.　　**F.T**

PROV: Sir Jeremiah Colman; Rt. Hon. A. T. Lennox-Boyd, M.P.; Frank Partridge & Sons; given by Lady Martin 1950.　　　　　　　　　　　　　　　　[20/50]

561 WRITING TABLE
By Bernard II van Risenburgh, Paris
*c.*1745
Kingwood; rosewood, walnut, oak, pine

The rectangular top, lined with tooled red leather is rimmed by a moulded brass border set with cabochon corner clasps; the frieze contains five drawers, the long central one being slightly recessed and flanked by a narrow pair concealed behind the shaped wings of the drawer fronts at either side; the opposite frieze is faced with a blind matching arrangement. The drawer fronts are outlined with matted brass surrounds framing rich foliate bridge-handles, pulls and cartouche shell-pattern key escutcheons modelled in the rococo taste backed by shaped rosewood insets; the curved wings on the side drawers are ornamented with deep acanthus scrolls and leafy sprays; the shaped ends, similarly styled with matted ormolu surrounds, centre on *espagnolette* masks dressed with vines and scalloped head-dresses; the keeled, tapering cabriole legs bear rich knee mounts of elaborately scrolled rococo design composed of cabochons, shells, flowing water, flame borders and acanthus foliage linked by ribs to fronded

561

561

561

561

561

to design his country house at Allerton Park, Yorkshire in 1746; the table evidently formed part of the furnishings of that building or perhaps his London house. It is significant that a prominent British architect-designer, who had many opportunities for influencing the taste of his fellow countrymen, should have made a carefully scaled pictorial record of this table during the formative years of the English rococo style. The drawing reveals that it was originally surmounted by an imposing *cartonnier* with a clock, ormolu candle-branches and a sloping desk.

The earliest precisely datable *bureau-plat* by Bernard II van Risenburgh is one made for the Dauphin at Versailles in 1745. This (unstamped) example is in a considerably more fluent style than the Temple Newsam table which, in its rather severe silhouette, suggests a date round about 1740. It is difficult to reconcile the early style with the presence of van Risenburgh's stamp unless Richard Arundale deliberately ordered a slightly archaic piece. The obscure mark 'FL' may offer a clue to this puzzle. Unfortunately John Vardy's drawing is undated, but on the evidence of his designs for Allerton (1746) it can hardly be earlier than that year. Perhaps the most satisfactory provisional date for this table is *c.*1745. G. de Bellaigue, *Waddesdon Furniture Catalogue*, I, 1974, p.419 discusses the stamp 'FL' giving qualified support to Salverte's suggestion that they may be the initials of the *ébéniste* François Lebesgue (d.1765).

LIT: P. Ward-Jackson, *English Furniture Designs of the Eighteenth Century*, 1958, pp.36–7, fig.45; *Apollo*, June 1972, p.529, fig.11; *Collector's Guide*, Nov. 1972, p.102, fig.9; C. G. Gilbert, 'An Exceptional Bureau-Plat by BVRB'; *L.A.C.*, No.73 (1973), pp.15–18, figs.1–6; *Gazette des Beaux Arts*, No.1261 (Feb. 1974), p.174, fig.583.

sabots; the legs are outlined with reeding. Plank top and baseboards of pine, oak rails and legs, walnut drawer linings with dovetailed corners and rebated bottoms; veneered in kingwood with shaped inset panels of rosewood. The long rails are faintly stamped in three places 'BVRB' and impressed once 'FL'; many mounts bear file marks corresponding to cuts on the frame to ensure correct positioning. One ormolu spray has been recast from its twin component.
H.81 (32); W.211 (83); D.96 (38).

There were three Parisian *ébénistes* with the initials BVRB but only the last two employed a stamp, for Bernard I died in 1738. Bernard II, author of this table, had become a *maître-ébéniste* by 1730 and died in 1765/6. Stamping of furniture with the *ébéniste*'s name or mark was first adumbrated in some draft amendments to the statutes of the *Corporation des Menuisiers-Ébénistes* in 1743; these were given preliminary official form by letters patent in March 1744 and were ratified by the Parliament in August 1751, so there was no obligation to stamp a piece before 1751.

The Drawing Collection of the Royal Institute of British Architects contains an elegant pen and wash drawing of this table (No.K9/17) inscribed 'J. Vardy delin at Mr. Arundales'. The artist can readily be identified as John Vardy, the celebrated mid eighteenth century architect, while Mr Arundale is obviously Richard Arundale who commissioned Vardy

PROV: Richard Arundale of Allerton Park, Yorkshire; passed in 1769 to his nephew, the 2nd Viscount Galway of Serlby Hall, Nottinghamshire – the table and its companion *cartonnier* (which has since disappeared) are recorded in an inventory of Serlby dated 25 Dec. 1774 (Nottingham University Library, Galway MS. P.C. 0/3/20): 'Book Room – One writeing Table inlaid with Brass & Covered with Leather . . . A case inlaid with brass and a Clock upon it'; by descent to the Dowager Viscountess Galway; sold at Christie's, 23 March 1972, lot 97; Frank Partridge & Sons; bought with the aid of a special government grant and contributions from the N.A.C.F., the L.A.C.F., Sir George Martin and Christie's 1972.   [32/72]

BVRB

FL

562

562 WRITING TABLE

*c.*1765
Kingwood; walnut, pine, oak, maple, beech

The serpentine top, lined with a panel of gilt-tooled green leather, is crossbanded in kingwood and enclosed by a brass edge moulding. The shaped frieze contains three drawers faced with mirror veneers, the central drawer is shallower than the other two, slightly recessed and flanked by acanthus leaf mounts; the side drawers have cartouche-shaped key escutcheons, the middle is fronted by one of rococo vine-trail pattern; matching blind drawers at the back. The ends, faced with raised veneered panels are set with fronded shell-work plaques contained in a lunette. The keeled cabriole legs with matted ormolu knee mounts bordered by acanthus and headed by ram's masks are outlined with brass beading and end in foliate *sabots*. The carcase is of pine and walnut with beech legs and inner structures of maple and oak; the oak drawers are fitted with steel locks impressed 'FE'. The ormolu mounts are marked with Arabic and Roman numerals.

H.74 (29); W.115 (45¼); D.60 (23½).

PROV: By descent to Lord Swinton, Swinton Park, Yorkshire; bought at the Swinton Park sale (Hollis & Webb, Leeds), 13 May 1947, lot 110.   [18.1/47]

563 COMMODE

By Jacques Bircklé, Paris
*c.*1765–70
Kingwood; oak, pine

Of bombé design with splayed bombé sides and a serpentine pinkish-grey fossiliferous marble top; the sides and drawer fronts are veneered with shaped panels of quartered kingwood outlined by a light string and deep crossbanded borders; the forecorners, terminating in short curved legs of triangular section, are mounted at the top with pierced foliate brasses and at the feet with scrolled acanthus leaves; the three drawers are fronted with leafy rococo pattern key escutcheons and asymmetrical open-work handles with raised loops; the

563

shaped apron centres on a lavishly scrolled and pierced mount. The rough-hewn oak carcase united by pegs is fitted with dustboards and laminated drawers, the bottom panel and sides are of pine; original steel locks.
H.81 (32); W.82 (32½); D.44 (17½).

Stamped beneath the slab across each of the front corners 'J. BIRCKLE' with the monogram 'JME' (*juré des menuisiers-ébénistes*): the mark of Jacques Bircklé (1734–1803) who became *maître ébéniste* in 1764 and settled in Rue St. Nicholas.

LIT: *Connoisseur*, Aug. 1970, p.246, fig.7.

PROV: By descent from Sir Douglas Galton of Hadzor House, Worcestershire, maternal grandfather of Sir Alvary Gascoigne; recorded in the 1930s Lotherton inventory; the Gascoigne gift 1968.   [7.149/68]

J*BIRCKLE

HURDY-GURDY, maple
By T. Henry, Mirecourt, *c.*1770
Under Cat. No.290 (illustrated)

564

564

564 BELLOWS

*c.*1780
Walnut; softwood

Dual action bellows, the handles operate the main wind and a second backboard, worked with the fingers, produces a gentler gust; the front is mounted with an elaborately scrolled floral arabesque in ormolu and pierced with a vent-hole of lyre design; the concertina sides are of tooled and gilt green leather reinforced with internal wooden strips; turned pine neck fitted with a tubular brass nozzle.
L.47 (18½).

The front handle is branded: T 5613
                                 1576
                                 C.T
                                 3586 [?]

The first mark is probably a nineteenth century inventory number of the *Palais des Tuileries*; the smaller, partially effaced number appears to be the brand of Marie-Antoinette's personal *Grande Meuble*, the letters C.T standing for the *Château de Trianon*; the fourth stamp is practically obliterated. The inventories of Marie-Antoinette's personal possessions have almost all vanished. (Information from Sir Francis Watson).

The bellows were formerly mounted in an ebonized display case inscribed 'Pair of Bellows made for Marie-Antoinette. From the Grande Trianon'.

LIT: *Country Life*, 9 June 1906, p.838.

PROV: Marie-Antoinette; in 1906 the property of Alfred De Lafontaine, Athelhampton Hall, Dorset; acquired about 1920 by Mrs Cochrane; bequeathed to her niece Mrs M. Nickols of Spofforth Hall, Yorkshire who gave the bellows to Leeds 1941.   [31/41]

565 BRACKET CLOCK

By Jean-Baptiste Lepaute, Paris
*c.*1785
White marble and ormolu

The circular movement is contained in an arched marble case set on a block base, crested by a lamp and elaborately mounted with finely chased ormolu mouldings and garniture; the dial is flanked by pilasters with detached ormolu columns and engaged trusses at each side, a recessed foliate plaque below and pierced floral tablets fronting the base which is raised on six conical feet; the cresting is enriched with ormolu scrolls suspending vine swags, cable-twist bands and fruit finials.

The white enamel dial with original brass hands is inscribed 'Lepaute / H'GR DU ROI' and enclosed by a convex glass; the circular spring-driven eight-day movement with a two-train count wheel, hour and half-hour strike, pin-pallet escapement and a fine pendulum adjustment device through the dial, is enclosed by a glazed rear door.
H.53 (21).

565

An almost identical clock case, the movement by Etienne Le Noir, was sold at Sotheby's, 24 Nov. 1972, lot 11 (the catalogue cites a third example by Hoguet). Another clock case of identical design (apart from one cast ornament), the movement by A. Damson, Paris, was in the Mentmore sale, 6th Earl of Rosebery (Sotheby's) 19 May 1977, lot 487.

PROV: Pelham Galleries; bought from Hotspur, Ltd 1965.
                                              [5/65]

566 LOOKING-GLASS

*c.*1840
Pine and bone

The frame, composed of an inward-sloping bottom rail and stiles with a high shaped cresting, is completely faced with small bone plates overlaid and incised to resemble feathers; the surface is embellished with a formal array of small carved bone ornaments representing putti, emblematic shields, banners, figures in renaissance costume, eagles and, on the cresting, an heraldic display featuring the Royal Arms of France, a crown, helm, mantling, lion supporters and a ribbon inscribed 'MONTIOYE St. DENYS'; arched and bevelled mirror plate.
H.137 (54); W.89 (35).

566

567

This mirror belongs to a well-known group of bone en-crusted furniture believed to have been made in Dieppe during the mid nineteenth century. The archaic seventeenth century style repertoire of ornament, appearance of the medieval French war cry, quaint figures and heraldic motifs are an interesting expression of the romantic imagination in folk art. A pair of upholstered chairs embellished with closely similar bonework is illustrated in *Connaissance des Arts*, Mars 1967, p.48; there is a comparable set of mirrors in the dining room at Scone (the Earl of Mansfield) Scotland.

PROV: The Crozier family, Leeds; Joseph Stewart; bought from his son Dr. B. Stewart 1971.   [12/71]

567 BRACKET CLOCK
By Henry Dasson, Paris
c.1860
Bronze

Of elaborate rococo form surmounted by a cupid playing pipes; the case is flanked by heavy leafy scrolls enriched with

flowers and beneath the dial is a trophy of crossed laurel branches, a torch and quiver of arrows symbolizing love; the sides and cresting are pierced by shaped panels framing diapered grilles backed by red silk and the rear is enclosed by a solid plate door; the foot scrolls are set on a low raised platform base styled in the Louis XV taste.

The circular thirteen piece dial formed of a central enamel tablet inscribed 'HENRY DASSON A PARIS' surrounded by hour plaques, is pierced by a brocket pendulum adjust-ment device; original gilt-metal pointers of delicate scroll and shell design. Square, two-train eight-day going barrel movement with pump action hour and half-hour strike, pin-pallet escapement and half-second pendulum. The back plate is impressed with a medallion lettered 'MEDAILLE D'AR-GENT 1855 / VINCENTI & CIE' referring to an exhibition award. The movement was probably made by Vincenti et Cie and the case by Henry Dasson who was at Rue Saint-Louis-Marais in 1860.
H.59 (23).

PROV: Given by Charles Roberts, Farfield Hall, Yorkshire 1952.   [13.1/52]

568 PAIR OF VASES ON PEDESTALS
*c.*1860
Scagliola; marble, ormolu

The oval basin-shaped vases of malachite scagliola rest on Levanto Rosso marble blocks raised on black Breccia scagliola pedestals headed by Ionic scrolls and a moulded platform; the front, faced with Levanto Rosso marble tablets, and the tapered sides are panelled within raised borders; the fronts are enhanced with ormolu laurel swags, floral festoons and a foliated cartouche clasp, while the vase stems are mounted with an open system of fronded scrolls; the scagliola and marble shell encases a plaster core reinforced with iron ties; the bowl, stem and column, modified behind to stand flush against a wall, form separate sections; backpinned ormolu mounts.
H.190 (75); W.66 (26).

The florid Louis XIV styling and combination of extravagant materials indicates the Second Empire period.

PROV: Bequeathed by Mrs D. U. McGrigor Phillips 1967.
[24.42/67]

569 PAIR OF ORNAMENTAL FIRE-DOGS
19th century, third quarter
Bronze; brass

Cast in the form of recumbent whippets, their muzzles resting on outstretched paws, wearing brass collars fashioned with buckles and Greek lotus clasps. The cast sections united by bolts, hollow interior. (Illustrated in Volume 1, p.146.)
L.71 (28).

Thomas Hope's *Household Furniture*, 1807 features a couch ornamented with an identical 'greyhound after the manner of similar animals on Gothic sarcophagi.' These so-called Medici dogs were often raised on bronze plinths and are thought to be French in origin.

PROV: Bequeathed by Mrs D. U. McGrigor Phillips 1967.
[24.38/67]

570 COMMODE MEDAILLIER
Possibly by Henri Dasson, Paris
*c.*1870
Kingwood and tulipwood; oak, ebony, box

The serpentine-front and concave spreading sides are veneered with diamond trellis patterns in kingwood and tulipwood parquetry, profusely overlaid with rich ormolu mounts composed of fronded rococo borders and ribbons suspending floral festoons and clusters of antique medals with Latin inscriptions, the door and side panels centre on ormolu medallions enclosing classical figures mounted on blue composition plaques; the double doors are divided by a stile ornamented with a female mask above the shell key escutcheon; the commode is supported on four solid ormolu

570

cabriole legs headed by rams' masks on scrolled feet; each door is faced inside with quartered kingwood and encloses two drawers panelled in tulipwood with ebony bands, kingwood borders and rich ormolu handles; moulded *Rouge Griotte* marble top; pin-hinges, central steel lock. Oak drawer linings and carcase with a panelled back; some of the mounts impressed 'M'; internal side boards inscribed prior to assembly 'Droit' and 'Gauche'.
H.91 (36); W.173 (68); D.65 (25½).

The original of this commode was made as a medal cabinet for Louis XV at Versailles by Antoine Gaudreaux in 1738 after designs by one of the brothers Slodtz; in 1780 it was transferred to the Bibliothèque Nationale, Paris, and is now at Versailles. The original is illustrated and discussed by by P. Verlet, *Le Mobilier Royal Français*, Paris, 1955, pp.43–7, pl.1. Many copies of this celebrated cabinet are known: there is one in the French Embassy at Stockholm; another at Knowsley Hall, Lancashire (*Country Life*, xxxiv, p.56, repr.); Lord Hertford commissioned a copy (*Wallace Furniture Catalogue*, p.265); examples were sold by Sotheby's, 24 Jan. 1969,

lot 145 and 15 Dec. 1971, lot 173; also at Christie's, 10 Dec. 1970, lot 121 and another appeared at Hôtel Drouet, salle No.6, 28 Dec. 1943; see also *Connoisseur*, June 1976, p.164. The pencilled inscriptions show this model was made in France, possibly by Henri Dasson of Paris who specialized in high quality reproductions of Louis XV masterpieces. The following Parisian manufacturers also made high quality copies of French Royal furniture in the late nineteenth century: A. E. L. Beurdeley, François Linke, J. Allard and Jansen.

EXH: Leeds Art Gallery, *Works of Art Presented by the L.A.C.F.*, 1924 (54).

PROV: Bought from Frederick Walker, Leeds by the L.A.C.F. 1913. [L.A.C.F./F1]

GRAND PIANOFORTE
Action by Erard, the case by Jansen 1901
Under Cat. No.298 (illustrated)

GERMANIC

CHEST, carved oak, *c.*1630
From a Lutheran Church at Cuxhaven
Under Cat. No.536 (illustrated)

571 SECRETAIRE CABINET
*c.*1780 (South German)
Mahogany and birch; pine, oak, rosewood, satinwood, sycamore, tulipwood, box, holly, etc.

In two stages separated by a shelf, the upper part of break-
front design consists of three cupboards, the tall central
section flanked by lower wings, each headed by a plain frieze
and dentil cornice; the doors, decorated in marquetry with
fluted borders, corner fans and rayed medallions, are delicately painted with classical designs of paterae, husks and
anthemion motifs amid scrolled foliage and columbine trails;
the side cupboards each contain five short drawers, the
central compartment being fitted with three double-faced
long drawers and an architecturally styled, parcel-gilt niche
surrounded by letter holes above; the minutely detailed
niche, headed by a satyr mask, is flanked by Corinthian
columns supporting corner blocks set with trophies of Love
and Learning; the drawer fronts, veneered in tulipwood with
crossbanded rosewood borders, corner fans and chequered
strings are inset with green-stained panels depicting a double-
headed eagle displayed gorged with a coronet, executed in
black paint. The lower stage contains a desk drawer panelled-
out to simulate small drawers, four drawers in each pedestal
and a cupboard in the kneehole recess; the front is veneered
with birch bordered by fluting, husk strips and chequered bands
set out with small fans, medallions and lunettes, the inside
cupboard door handsomely decorated with an encircled fan

medallion; the velvet lined fall-front, supported on quad-
rants, opens to reveal a small central cupboard flanked by
pairs of serpentine drawers veneered in harewood with letter
holes above and additional compartments at each side; the
door is inset with an oval satinwood panel decorated in
penwork with a bunch of flowers in a classical vase bearing
the cipher 'J.W.' and painted cherub-head spandrels; the
pedestals are raised on fluted block feet with a plinth base in
the recess; turned laburnum and ivory pulls (replaced);
brass locks; keyhole escutcheons missing. Solid mahogany
sides, cornice, desk drawer and internal partititons, the doors
veneered on to a mahogany foundation, the central panel
quartered; the lower stage is veneered in figured birch and
the desk interior with harewood; the marquetry is executed
in satinwood, tulipwood, holly, etc. with rosewood banding;
pine carcase faced with mahogany rails; the large drawer
linings are oak, medium size mahogany with oak bottoms, the
small entirely of mahogany.
H.236 (93); W.129 (51); D.61 (24).

Geometrically rayed lunettes and circles, evidently trial
setting-out marks for marquetry designs, are lightly scored
on the pine top of the desk drawer and underneath the board
forming a shelf in the kneehole cupboard.

The proportions, marquetry decoration and selection of
timbers indicate a late eighteenth century date although the
painted door panels express rococo impulses and the enriched
niche is of distinctly archaic design. The busy, highly repetitive decorative idiom (extending even to elaborate treatment
inside the lower cupboard door) and simplified classical
vocabulary combined with stylistically retarded elements
invests this cabinet with a provincial character. The cherub-
head spandrels, multiple chequered bands (allied to straw-
work) and festive painted eagles suggest the influence of folk
traditions. Structurally the piece is consistent with English
cabinetwork, although the use of birch veneer and prominent
eagles are more in accordance with continental practice.

571

571

571

The established provenance does not rule out the possibility that the rather weird countenance of this cabinet is a product of Irish craftsmanship; however, according to family tradition it was acquired by Blayney Townley Balfour at the Prior Park sale, Bath, and had originally been made for Catherine the Great (hence the Russian eagles) but never delivered; since the Prior Park sale catalogue of 1769 does not record the cabinet this ancestry is suspect. The cipher 'J.W.' remains obscure, although it could be significant that gems and seals by James Tassie were sent to the Empress Catherine in cabinets 'executed by James Roade, one of the best cabinet-makers, after drawings by Mr James Wyatt'. The prominent double-headed eagles gorged with a coronet furnish another ambiguous clue: two English families, Loveday and Gunman, were entitled to this device but heraldically it is more likely to be continental, the Hapsburgs (Austria) and Tsars (Russia) adopting the emblem.

Both Blayney Townley Balfour (1704–88) and his grandson of the same name (1768–1805) were compulsive Grand Tourists and collectors; the elder man noted in his diary with reference to furniture purchased abroad in a single year 'To my sorrow and shame I have spent £1,000.' The available evidence favours Germany as the probable source for this cabinet. German furniture has a long tradition of repetitive intarsia-like inlay and during the late eighteenth century reflected English styles in the south. A South German chest sold at Christie's, 29 March 1973, lot 138, repr. is inset with oval pictorial panels, cherub-head spandrels and bold double-headed coroneted eagles. The use of birch veneer to simulate satinwood was also commoner in Germany than England.

LIT: *Country Life*, 30 July 1948, pp.228–31, fig.2; C. Hussey, 'Treasures of Townley Hall, Ireland', *Country Life*, 26 Nov. 1948, pp.1104–5, figs.7–12; *Connoisseur*, Dec. 1963, p.207; *Burlington*, May 1965, p.285, fig.92.

PROV: Probably purchased abroad by Blayney Townley Balfour of Townley Hall, Co. Louth, Ireland and passed by descent to Mrs Townley Balfour and thence to her nephew David Crichton; Christie's, 24 Oct. 1957, lot 127 (withdrawn); Christie's, 16 Feb. 1961, lot 102; Nyman, Bros; J. A. Lewis & Son; H. Blairman & Sons; bought with the aid of a government grant 1963. [8/63]

572 SET OF FOUR ARMCHAIRS
c.1800
Birch

The open heart-shaped backs carved with swags of fringed drapery, have central loops incorporating Prince of Wales feathers in the cresting; short bowed arms with swept supports; the rounded upholstered seats are raised on turned tapering forelegs headed by blocks and ending in lotus feet. The frames are enriched with simple overall low-relief systems of garrya chains and rosettes, circular studs, vine trails and a running leaf pattern.
H.91 (36); W.56 (22); D.46 (18).

572

The use of birch, identified as *Betula*, a species distributed predominantly in the northern hemisphere, implies the chairs are European; they were at one time thought to be of Dutch colonial origin. The timber, slender proportions and repetitive decoration suggests the set was made in Austria or Hungary. Both countries were strongly influenced by English furniture styles at this time, a German edition of Sheraton's *Drawing-Book* being published at Leipzig in 1794. See H. Szabolcsi, 'English Influence on Hungarian Furniture at the end of the 18th Century', *Furniture History*, IX (1973) pp.89–96 and *Ars Hungarica*, Budapest, 1974, pp.107–30. Lady Celia Milnes-Coates possesses two chairs of an identical design; a third owned by Edward Farmer was reproduced in *Connoisseur*, Sept. 1939, p.155.

LIT: *Country Life*, 28 May 1938, p.547, repr.; *Antique Collector*, Aug. 1940, p.32, repr.; *Apollo*, Dec. 1941, p.140, fig. vii.

EXH: Leeds Art Gallery, *English Furniture*, 1930 (129, 131); Temple Newsam, *Pictures and Furniture*, 1938 (19, 22, 41, 43).

PROV: Perhaps F. W. Greenwood & Son, York; given by Frank H. Fulford, Headingley Castle, Leeds 1939.

[9.33/39]

573

573 PAIR OF ARMCHAIRS
19th century, last quarter (probably Austrian)
Beech

The slightly shaped solid upholstered backs are framed by gilt chain-pattern surrounds with pierced crestings featuring female corner heads, fronds and central tablets portraying the head and shoulders of a male morris dancer wearing a feathered hat. The padded arms terminate in scroll elbows carved with grotesque masks; the seat rails, outlined with leafy scrolls, centre on heart-shaped cartouches ornamented at the front by a female mask. The cabriole forelegs are styled with wyverns, their forked tails coiling around the supports which end in shell and scroll pattern feet. One chair is upholstered in maroon plush, the seat, back and arm pads of the other being covered with pictorial panels of *petit-point* wool needlework edged with blue plush secured by gimp. The back is worked in muted colours with a blue cartouche, bordered by rose and carnation sprays, enclosing a shepherdess with cows and sheep, while the seat depicts a lion and mule in a landscape. The cartouches incorporate three small shields featuring a red cross, a white Maltese cross and the initial 'B'.
H.115 (45½); W.71 (28); D.61 (24).

LIT: F. Moss, *Pilgrimages to Old Homes*, V, 1910, p.314, repr.

PROV: Temple Newsam House; probably acquired by the Hon. Mrs E. C. Meynell Ingram during her frequent continental tours; given by the Earl of Halifax 1922.

[1922/F41]

574 PAIR OF ARMCHAIRS
1923
Birch; pine

The low, severely rectangular frames of uniform height are designed with open plan sides and backs simply constructed of three horizontal bars united to the corner posts which have block feet connected by plinth rails; the inner faces are lined with padded boards and the seat wells fitted with spring bases supporting flat squabs and wedge-shaped back cushions rising above the top rail.
H.64 (25); W.69 (27); D.85 (33½).

Designed by the German architect Bachen, *en suite* with a centre table. The V. & A. have a third armchair and a sofa from this suite (C. 41 & 42, 1969).

In 1972 both chairs were re-covered in a printed cotton (supplied by Liberty of London) reproducing a fabric designed in 1927–8 by Gunta Stolzl, crafts master and director of the dyeing workshops at the Bauhaus.

PROV: Commissioned for the Berlin home of L. Tell in 1923 and bought from the family by Dr. Bella Horovitz; given by the Phaidon Press 1969.

[7.2/69]

574, 575

575 CENTRE TABLE
1923
Birch; pine

The circular top built of eight wedge-shaped boards, with a pine frieze rail in six sections, is veneered with figured birch stained to resemble walnut; the top, surfaced with a pattern of sixteen radial segments, rests freely on a cruciform plank platform supported on four straight rectangular legs veneered with birch; pine carcase, pegged joints.
H.74 (29); Diam.119 (47).

Designed by the German architect Bachen, *en suite* with a pair of armchairs.

prov: Commissioned for the Berlin home of L. Tell in 1923 and bought from the family by Dr. Bella Horovitz; given by the Phaidon Press 1969. [7.1/69]

ITALIAN

576 PAIR OF ARMCHAIRS
17th century, second half (Tuscany)
Walnut

Of rectangular design, the tall backposts surmounted by carved and gilt plumes, turned and blocked front uprights, wide flat arm-rests and shaped runners with paw terminals; the backs and double-railed stuffed seats support leather

576

panels secured by rows of conical-headed brass nails; the back panels are lightly tooled and gilt with a shield-shaped cartouche depicting a plumed helm, demi-figures, lions' masks, swags and feathery fronds within ornamental surrounds. Riven seat rails united to the uprights by distinctive wedged joints; the runners and sections of turning renewed. H.138 (54½); W.61 (24); D.39 (15½).

A paper label (apparently the title to an account book) on the back of one chair is inscribed in ink 'Registro / Massa Generale di Deconto / Parle Iᵐᵃ / Entrata' with an ornamental surround featuring the arms of the house of Savoy. There is an earlier label underneath. One of the right-hand arms is lightly scratched 'Clerle / Alessandro' and 'CHAISE / Venezia'.

The chairs are very similar in design to an example from Tuscany, illustrated by A. Pedrini, *Italian Furniture*, 1949, pl.148.

LIT: *Country Life*, 8 Oct. 1904, p.425, repr.

EXH: *Temple Newsam Heirlooms*, 1972 (23).

PROV: Probably acquired by the Hon. Mrs E. C. Meynell Ingram; Temple Newsam sale (Robinson, Harding & Fisher) 26–31 July 1922, lot 646; bought by Colonel F. R. T. Gascoigne, Lotherton Hall; the Gascoigne gift 1968.
[7.142/68]

577 PRIE-DIEU
Late 17th century
Pine, ebonized fruitwood

A praying desk with a sloped front containing three drawers and a flat top for devotional books, raised on a low plinth forming a kneeling-step also fitted with a drawer; the front, top and sides are veneered in ebonized fruitwood inset with ivory strings, chequered roundels and star-patterns, the drawers have moulded surrounds and replacement cast-brass

577

loop handles; the desk is surmounted by a tall cross painted black with carved and gilt terminals, bearing a silvered figure of Christ and a scroll inscribed 'INRI' with a large gilt sunburst behind. Pine carcase with ebonized veneer and ivory parquetry.
H.239 (94); of desk 87 (34½); W.70 (27½).

578

The crucifix is a later addition.

The prie-dieu was a popular symbol of piety among High Church families during the mid Victorian period. This example, probably acquired on the continent by Mrs Meynell Ingram, was placed in one of the principal bedrooms at Temple Newsam.

LIT: F. Moss, *Pilgrimages to Old Homes*, V, 1910, p.333, repr.; *L.A.C.*, No.62 (1968), pp.5–9, repr.

PROV: Probably acquired by the Hon. Mrs E. C. Meynell Ingram, Temple Newsam; given by the Earl of Halifax 1922. [1922/F20]

578 PAIR OF SIDE TABLES
*c.*1700–10 (Rome)
Gilt pine

The rectangular slabs of Breccia Violetto marble with veneered Siena borders are let into recessed surrounds; the elaborately shaped aprons, edged with scrolls and foliage, centre on large receding cartouches; square tapered supports with leafy shoulders and panelled sides containing husk pendants, block feet united by heavy cross stretchers ornamented with acanthus and an upright shell. Traces of silver where the gilt is worn.
H.101 (40); W.165 (65); D.84 (33).

PROV: Acquired in Italy by the L.A.C.F. about 1920.
[L.A.C.F. F/15]

579 SIDE TABLE
*c.*1720–30 (North Italy)
Gilt lime

The solid Portovenere marble top is formed of two slabs braced beneath the join by a later tablet of slate; the front

579

centres on a grotesque satyr-mask with elaborately scrolled acanthus fronds issuing from the mouth and spreading to form a deep pierced apron ornamented with grapes and flower-heads, the side aprons are composed of similar acanthus sprays; the vigorously scrolled legs of open interlaced design carved with foliage terminate in chamfered blocks. The frame has been reinforced at a latter date with corner brackets and cross rails. Old photographs show the mask had a waved crest, now missing.
H.86 (34); W.211 (83); D.76 (30).

A German origin has also been suggested.

PROV: Bought by the L.A.C.F. from Gill & Reigate, Ltd 1916.   [L.A.C.F./F4]

580 CHANDELIER
c.1720–30
Rock crystal and glass

The silvered framework consists of a metal shaft with ring collars into which the square branches are screwed; the gadrooned ball and baluster stem is crested by a double tier of eighteen scrolled arms hung with crystal and cut-glass pendants; a medial set of six scrolled arms terminating in large diamond drops are linked by curved stays to the upper members of a two tier arrangement of twelve scrolled candle branches below; the top row is also mounted with hollow vase-shaped finials (*pyramides*) and the metal skeleton has been dressed at a later date with triple strings of moulded beads; the shaft terminates in a large faceted pendant.
H.152 (60).

A photograph reproduced in the 1947 sale catalogue (q.v.) shows that many of the original festoons, cut-glass floral motifs and a thick cluster of faceted drops underneath have been re-arranged or discarded; the chandelier has thus lost some of its flamboyant character. The drip pans are probably later.

LIT: *L.A.C.*, No.1 (1947), p.6, repr.

PROV: Formerly in the White Library, 14–15, Carlton House Terrace, London, home of the Earls of Lonsdale; bought at the Lowther Castle sale (Maple & Co) 15 April 1947, lot 243.   [17.1/47]

581 SIDE TABLE
*c.*1730
Pine

PROV: Purchased in Italy for the L.A.C.F. about 1925.
[L.A.C.F./F16]

The shaped and moulded Levanto Rosso marble top is supported on a heavily carved and gilt frame; the cabriole legs are bordered by leafy scrolls and richly styled with fronds headed by a ribbed shell between spirals; the cross stretchers, formed of vigorous C-scrolls tied by swirling cabochon motifs, centre on a rococo shell, the flamboyant composition being tilted forwards; the lavishly carved and pierced front apron is set with a large shell amid a balanced system of scrolls and leafy spurs, the side aprons are of cartilaginous design.
H.91 (36); W.160 (63); D.84 (33).

The harsh, rather aggressive lines, heavy elaboration and generally stiff treatment raises a possiblity that this table is a product of the German rococo revival of *c.*1830–40, although its Italian provenance and affinities with Genoese furniture in the manner of Filippo Parodi count against this idea.

582 BRACKET AND CANOPY (MENSOLE)
Early 18th century
Pine; walnut

The shaped platform base, bordered by stepped mouldings, supports an elaborately shaped cartouche-like rear structure composed of fronded scrolls, putto heads and drapery, framing a pair of vine stems; a winged putto carved in the round hovers on each shoulder and a secondary cartouche at the top is headed by a projecting canopy surmounted by an open crown of double leafy scrolls. The carved gesso surface, incised with ribbed and diapered patterns, has a gilt, silvered and brown painted finish. The modern backboard is painted blue and the base incorporates a wooden mounting block.
H.114 (45).

581

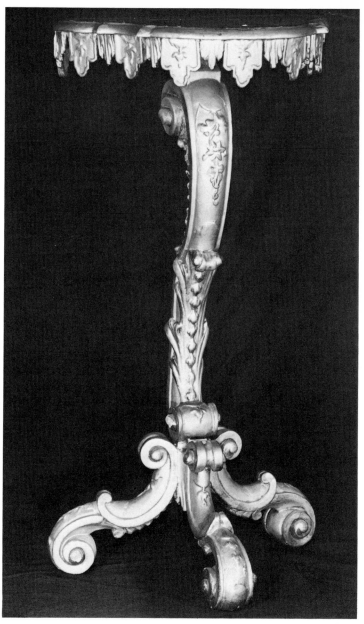

582

Mural brackets of this kind often serve in Catholic churches as monstrance stands.

EXH: Leeds Art Gallery, *Works of Art Presented by the L.A.C.F.*, 1924 (50).

PROV: Given to the L.A.C.F. by Robert Kitson, Elmete Hall, Leeds 1914.   [L.A.C.F./F3]

583

583 CONSOLE STAND (TRESPOLO)
18th century, second quarter (Venice)
Lime and pine

In the form of a small carved and gilt table; the shaped top, decorated with an apron of alternating *lambrequin* motifs and icicle clusters, is raised on a leafy console support ending in a scrolled tripod. The top, which has been painted to simulate *verde antico* marble, is of pine; the stand is executed in lime.
H.82 (32½).

EXH: Temple Newsam, *Pictures and Furniture*, 1938 (242).

PROV: Given by Charles Lumb & Sons, Harrogate 1938.
                                                    [32/38]

584 PAIR OF SOFAS
*c.*1750 (Venice)
Gilt walnut and beech

Of curvilinear rococo form with closed ends; the splayed arms and contoured back are framed by a moulded rail carved with leafy scrolls rising through a series of stippled panels to an elaborately pierced cresting centering on a flame cartouche festooned with flowers; the double-serpentine seat is bordered by shaped aprons composed of floral sprays, fronded scrolls and flame ornament, the side aprons are of simpler design; raised on five cabriole supports, the three front legs enriched with shell motifs and roses. Walnut, with beech corner braces and a medial seat stretcher; formerly upholstered in cut and figured Genoa velvet.
H.101 (40); W.145 (57); D.61 (24).

584

The frames may well originally have been painted.

PROV: Lord Swinton; Swinton Park sale (Hollis & Webb, Leeds) 13 May 1947, lots 84 & 85; given by Lady Martin 1947. [20/47]

585 SIDE TABLE
*c.*1750 (Piedmont)
Pine

The serpentine-fronted Tortosa Brocatello marble top with shaped sides and a moulded edge is supported on an elaborately carved and gilt frame. The inward curving double S-scroll legs, decorated with fleshy leaf-tongues, shell motifs suspending fruit pendants and bullrushes, are united by receding asymmetrical aprons, composed of an open system of tortuous C-scrolls centering on rococo shells. The tilted

X-shaped stretchers, formed of vigorous leafy scrolls converge on a pierced cartouche enclosing a fan palmette headed by a large frilly shell; the volute feet rest on leaf toes.
H.89 (35); W.152 (60); D.71 (28).

The design follows French precedents.

EXH: Temple Newsam, *Pictures and Furniture*, 1938 (238).

PROV: Bought in Rome for the L.A.C.F. by R. H. Kitson, *c.*1926. [L.A.C.F./F7]

585

586

586 SIDE TABLE
Late 18th century (Sicily)
Gilt pine

The top, which slides into the grooved surround, is formed of a central slab of Levanto Rosso serpentine set in immured Brescia marble borders bedded on to slate; the frieze is faced with glass panels painted behind to simulate blue-grey onyx and bordered with egg and dart, beaded and bay leaf mouldings; the front is mounted with an *espagnolette* mask flanked by cherubs blowing horns and lions' masks above the legs; the sides centre on pine-apple motifs and the square tapered legs headed by acanthus plumes are similarly panelled and ornamented with applied double-tailed *canephorae*.
H.96 (38); W.126 (49½); D.65 (25½).

The pair of cherubs blowing horns are modern restorations in gilt plaster; the casts were taken from the frieze ornament on an identical pair of tables from the collection of Lady Anne Tree, Mereworth, sold at Christie's, 4 June 1970, lot 151, repr. This table is also one of a pair, the companion being in the V. & A. (W.18–1970). It is related to a class of gilt furniture, lined with glass painted on the reverse to simulate semi-precious stones, fashionable in Sicily during the late eighteenth century. Many pieces were formerly at the Villa Palagonia and although the table does not belong to this suite it is obviously of Sicilian origin.

LIT: A. Gonzalez-Palacios, 'The Prince of Palagonia, Goethe and Glass Furniture', *Burlington*, Aug. 1971, pp.456–61.

PROV: Butler (Antiques), Market Deeping; J. R. Brudenell, Bourne; sold by auction (Lyall & Co, Stamford) 15 May 1968, lot 436; Stamford Properties, Ltd; R. L. Harrington, Ltd; Signor Ernesto di Castro, Rome; bought with the aid of a government grant 1970. [19/70]

587

587 PAIR OF LOOKING-GLASSES
19th century, second half
Pine

Elaborately carved and gilt shield-shaped frames, the enriched borders ornamented with rococo shells, foliage, flowers and *lambrequin* motifs; each is surmounted by a seated harlequin (in slightly different postures) with a valanced canopy below, and supported at each side by female terminal figures holding drapes; backboard contoured to the frame.
H.113 (44½); W.69 (27).

Many picturesque frames of this decorative pattern were made during the last century; the indifferent carving, modern glass and plain shields at the bases where candle-branches should be attached indicate a reproduction piece.

PROV: By descent from the Earls of Lindsey, Uffington House, Lincolnshire to Lady Muriel Barclay-Harvey; bought 1953. [12.1/53]

588 TWO WALL-BRACKETS
Probably 19th century (Venice)
Pine

(I) The shaped platform is designed as a canopy hung with fringed and tasselled drapes and supported by a blackamoor in festive costume; painted in various colours with silvered and gilt details.
H.40 (16).

(II) Of similar form, the shelf, enriched with a rococo edge, is supported by a gaily dressed female blackamoor backed by fringed and patterned drapes, decorated in various colours with gilt details.
H.43 (17).

LIT: *L.A.C.*, No.23 (1954), p.6.

PROV: Agnes and Norman Lupton Bequest 1953.
[13.367–8/53]

588

589

589 CENTRE TABLE
19th century, second half
Gilt pine

Rectangular top inset with a slab of grey *brocatello* marble framed by a moulded surround; each long side is carved with a pierced apron of fronded scrolls centering on a shaped cartouche crested by a coronet, simpler end aprons; supported on four square legs with broad fluted and gadrooned shoulders headed by leafy corner blocks; the panelled columns, embellished on each face with combined swag and *lambrequin* motifs, rest on base blocks connected by heavily scrolled cross stretchers carved with acanthus foliage, rising to a high moulded plinth surmounted by an octagonal urn; square bulbous feet.
H.96 (38); W.122 (48); D.65 (25½).

The coarse carving and clumsy design, particularly of the aprons betray the late date of this table.

EXH: Leeds Art Gallery, *Works of Art Presented by the L.A.C.F.*, 1924 (53).

PROV: Galerie Sangiorgi, Rome; purchased on behalf of the L.A.C.F. by R. H. Kitson 1921.   [L.A.C.F./F6]

590 PAIR OF ALTAR CANDLESTANDS
Late 19th century
Bronze; pine

The circular dished top is supported on a tall stem which rises in six diminishing stages lavishly chased with decorative mouldings, ornamental figures, masks and a varied repertoire of Italian renaissance motifs; the tripod base consists of three winged female terms on fronded feet surmounted by seated cupids with a tier of mythological figures above; the middle stage is embellished with three erect putti holding aloft flaming lamps, headed by female terminal figures of scroll design; the top section is elaborately chased with foliated masks, wreaths and engaged terms; the stand is mounted on a solid painted pine plinth. Each stand is cast in six main sections, threaded on a central iron rod, the lateral figures being screwed into position; each set of components is numbered to ensure correct assembly.
H. without plinth 125 (49).

The design is an exact copy of a pair of bronze altar candlestands in the church of San Stephano, Venice. One, made in 1577, is attributed to Alessandro Vittoria while the other is a replica cast in 1617.

PROV: Bequeathed by Henry Oxley, Spenfield House, Leeds 1948.   [13.22/48]

591 PAIR OF CANDLESTICKS
Probably late 19th century
Gilt softwood

The high domed bases of circular stepped design support ribbed and knopped baluster stems carved with leaf-clasps terminating in escalloped sockets.
H.71 (28); Diam.25·5 (10).

The lifeless carving and lack of wear indicate that these examples are modern copies of early eighteenth century Italian altar candlesticks.

PROV: Bought from Edgar Kennedy 1947.   [1. 1 & 2/47]

592 SET OF FOUR ARMCHAIRS
Late 19th century
Lime; walnut

The slightly shaped oval backs are fitted with detachable upholstered panels framed by carved and gilt surrounds outlined with fronds and having a pierced inner border of interlacing ribbons and husk chains, the cresting and shoulders are enriched with floral festoons; the loose, serpentine-fronted seat bases rest on moulded rails styled with an open interlacing system of ribbons and husk strings which travel down the cabriole legs, along the curved arm supports and below the arm pads; scroll elbows and toes. Upholstered beneath the modern damask covers in floral Genoa velvet.
H.99 (39); W.66 (26); D.51 (20).

The principal drawing room at Swinton Park was furnished with a large number of opulent Italian and gilt chairs, sofas and stools upholstered *en suite* (Cat. No.586) also lot nos. 81, and 84–93 (*q.v.*).

590

592

A photograph datable to *c*.1890 of the heavily furnished Victorian saloon at Wimborne House, London, shows an identical suite of armchairs (John Fowler and John Cornforth, *English Decoration in the 18th Century*, 1974, p.17, fig.1).

PROV: Lord Swinton, Swinton Park, Yorkshire; Swinton Park sale (Hollis & Webb, Leeds) 13 May 1947, lot 88; given by Lady Martin 1947.   [20.1/47]

593 BOX
Late 19th century
Fruitwood; walnut, various coloured woods

Rectangular, veneered in ebonized fruitwood on a walnut foundation, the top and base are decorated with intarsia bands, the sides and hinged lid are inset with figures of peasants in pairs and singly, executed in stained and natural woods; secured by a lock.
H.12 (4¾); W.11 (4¼); D.9 (3½).

PROV: Agnes and Norman Lupton Bequest 1952.   [5.527/52]

PORTUGUESE

594 SETTEE
c.1760
Mahogany; pine

The framework is composed of four separate chair backs having shaped top rails outlined with C-scrolls and conjoined at the shoulders by acanthus fronds; the pierced, vase-pattern splats are decorated with interlaced strapwork between volutes and headed by an open leafy cartouche in the Chippendale style; the bowed arms rest on curved supports; the front seat rail is of rhythmic design with serpentine sections alternating with blocks above the five keeled cabriole legs ending in claw and ball feet; splayed back legs; each chair unit is fitted with side, rear and an ogee shaped front stretcher; pine slip seat.
H.100 (39½); W.216 (85); D.56 (22).

LIT: *L.A.C.*, No.20 (1953) p.10, repr.

PROV: Purchased at a sale near Liverpool about 1916; given by Sir Adrian Boult 1952.   [36/52]

594

Part Three

COLONIAL AND ORIENTAL FURNITURE

CAPE COLONY

595 CHEST OF DRAWERS
*c.*1920
Light stinkwood; pine

Of folded front design with a moulded top, ogee end panels and canted forecorners, the lower edge has a shaped skirt; fitted with three graduated drawers, raised on low cabriole legs terminating in claw and ball feet. Silvered key escutcheons and loop handles with engraved plates. The crudely nailed drawer linings, pine backboards and inner structures are stained black.
H.69 (27); W.76 (30); D.43 (17).

595

Reproductions of eighteenth century Dutch colonial furniture were popular in South Africa during the early years of the present century. The Gascoigne collection formerly included a similarly styled side table in light stinkwood.

PROV: Recorded in the 1930s Lotherton inventory: '1 small chest of drawers, Light Stinkwood. Brought from the Cape in 1933'; the Gascoigne gift 1971.   [23.4/71]

596 COMMODE CABINET
*c.*1920
Redwood; pine, plywood

The upright rectangular cabinet has three graduated drawers with folded block fronts above a cupboard enclosed by double doors of shaped frame and panel design; raised on low cabriole legs having claw and ball feet at the front and pointed pads at the rear, flared ogee-shaped aprons, the forecorners faced with ebonized strips profiled to match the skirt. Pine carcase coated with dark stain, solid redwood top, drawer fronts and doors, plywood drawer bottoms, brass handle and key plates, steel door bolts. The veneered sides outlined at a later date with a beaded panel to protect the surface from scratches.
H.99 (39); W.69 (27); D.38 (15).

The Lotherton collection formerly contained a very similar folded front chest of drawers (see also Cat. No.595). Both are cheap products of the early twentieth century revival of interest in Cape Dutch furniture inspired by Sir Herbert Baker's restoration of old buildings.

PROV: Brought from the Cape to Lotherton Hall by Colonel F. R. T. Gascoigne about 1930; the Gascoigne gift 1968.
[7.171/68]

PERUVIAN

In 1955 Lady Margaret Ramsden of The Wheatleys, Gomersal, Yorkshire gave thirty-six items of Hispanic furniture to Leeds in memory of her husband. The collection had come to her from Dame Clarissa Reid (d.1933) whose husband James Guthrie Reid headed Duncan, Fox & Co's interests in South America between 1878 and 1909. He lived most of the time in Lima, the capital of Peru, and the colonial furniture which he brought back is certainly the most important holding of its kind in this country. It ranges from the rich seventeenth century Spanish-Peruvian baroque style, through rococo and empire fashions to late nineteenth century pieces reproducing earlier design types. Following James Reid's death in 1920 several pieces were lent to the V. & A., but the only time the collection has been displayed altogether was at an exhibition titled *Peruvian Furniture* held at Temple Newsam in 1975.

Spanish colonial furniture possesses its own special flavour derived from the mingling of European traditions with exotic aboriginal elements. The craftsmen of Cuzco in southern Peru, centre of the old Inca civilization, excelled in elaborate carving revealing the florid vitality of folk art (Cat. Nos. 613, 614): their creations are artistically no less valuable for being anonymous. Small cabinets known as *papelera* faced with engraved bone and tortoiseshell (Cat. Nos.619, 620) betray the influence of Philippine work, while many fall-front cabinets mounted on stands, termed *vargueño* (Cat. Nos.616, 618) provided on opportunity to display rich carving or fine inlay. Many of the chests are ornamented with elaborate wrought iron lock plates, hasps, hinges and other robust hardware; one *vargueño* is mounted with delicate silver drawer pulls, another displays intricate fretted brass escutcheons. Chairs upholstered in locally produced tooled leather were frequently decorated with fantastic stem systems inhabited by birds and beasts and often featured the double-headed Hapsburg eagle – the badge of Charles V, King of Spain and

Holy Roman Emperor which persisted as a motif on Hispanic furniture for more than two centuries after his reign ended in 1558. Leather chairs and trunks were also embellished with painted armorials and festive pictorial subjects (Cat. Nos.603, 604) usually bordered with handsome brass-headed nails.

Peruvian furniture possesses a number of interesting technical features: chair frames are invariably united by open wedged tenon joints, sometimes secured by pegs and the turned legs of Cat. No.604 have a distinctive bulbous knop of interlocking spliced construction alien to European traditions. Decorative turning, an important facet of Hispanic craftsmanship, is best represented by the massive splayed supports of Cat. No.630. Revealed dovetails provided another opportunity for decorative treatment, the end grain surfaces on Cat. No.613 being embellished with square rosettes while Cat. No.614 is jointed with dovetails of a special stepped profile common on the cedarwood furniture of Bermuda and some South American countries. The absence of veneers, dominance of simple chip-carved enrichment (notably a leaf-scale pattern) and frequent rough tool marks suggest the limitations of the craftsman's training and his tool chest, but it would be misleading to classify their products as primitive art. The most impressive woodwork was commissioned for churches (Cat. No.623). The group of lavish gilt pieces are nineteenth century reproductions.

I wish to thank Dr. Francisco Stastny of the Museo de la Universidad de San Marcos, Lima, Peru for his helpful interest; the British Leather Manufacturers Research Association for identifying samples of the leather as cattle hide and the Building Research Establishment for microscopic identification of timbers.

597 ARMCHAIR
Late 17th century
Cedar

597

597

Of rectangular design with squared uprights, the back posts and flat, undercut arms end in volutes and the front supports, faced with chip-carved leaf-scales, are connected by a deep valanced front stretcher bearing a fronded lunette design; plain side and rear stretchers. The leather back panel depicts a fashionable lady standing in a landscape with a church to the left and a garden balustrade, with columns and trees, on her right, the composition being framed by a scrolling arabesque trail; the seatboards are padded with vegetation and covered in leather richly decorated with a flowering stem system inhabited by pairs of pecking birds, squirrels and leopards outlined by interlace borders. One brass rosette headed nail remains; local repairs.
H.102 (40½); W.59 (23); D.42 (16½).

PROV. See p.463.   [33.12/55]

598 ARMCHAIR
Late 17th century
Cedar

Of rectangular design with squared uprights; the back posts and flat undercut arms end in simple scrolls, plain rear and side stretcher rails; the deep valanced front stretcher banded with leaf-scales, centres on a rosette. The leather back panel is decorated with a tall two-handled vase containing flower

598

stems and flanked by scrolling branches bearing exotic fruit and flowers, meander side borders. The seatboard is padded with hay and covered in leather centering on a geometric roundel amid fruiting stems inhabited by fantail birds. The leather, secured by circular brass nails, retains some original edge binding and displays trial cuts on the back. The left-hand back post is incised 'N'; local restorations.
H.106 (42); W.57 (22½); D.38 (15).

PROV: See p.463. [33.5/55]

598

599 ARMCHAIR
Early 18th century
Central American mahogany (aguano)

Of rectangular design, the slightly raked back posts and dipped arms end in scrolls; plain squared uprights and rails. The front supports are connected by a deep, elaborately pierced and profiled stretcher outlined with strapwork. The leather back and seat, bordered by a simple running fern pattern, are secured by circular brass nails. The top rail, both rear stretchers, the plank seat, front uprights and leather panels have been renewed, the ornamental stretcher is old but may not be original; cut down legs.
H.97 (38½); W.61 (24); D.43 (17).

PROV: See p.463. [33.1/55]

600 ARMCHAIR
Early 18th century
Central American mahogany (aguano)

The frame is constructed of heavily scrolled and moulded members united by open wedged tenon joints. The front uprights, supporting massive undulating arms, are connected to the shaped rear legs by paired scrolls bracing a similar medial stretcher; the inward-scrolling feet are carved with acanthus fronds and incised spirals. The rectangular raked back is covered with part of a wall-hanging embossed with gilt diapered patterns, palmettes and flowers on a blue ground, fragments of an earlier decorated leather survive

600

beneath the outer layer; the seat, stuffed with hay, is covered in hide. The backposts, cross bars and seat rails renewed, the top formerly supported finials and an ornamental cresting. H.99 (39); W.64 (25); D.54 (21½).

An armchair of similar character from the Convent of San Francisco Santiago de Chile is illustrated by G. H. Burr, *Hispanic Furniture*, 1964, p.110, fig.109.

PROV: See p.463.   [33.10/55]

601 ARMCHAIR
Early 18th century
Centrolobium

Of rectangular design with squared uprights, the back posts and flat arms ending in simple scroll profiles; the front supports carved with a leaf scale pattern are connected by a deep valanced stretcher faced with a similar foliate band centering on a floret. The back panel embellished with a double-headed eagle amid scrolling stems and pairs of birds and lions in each corner, is framed by a shuttle border; the seat-board, stuffed with hay, is covered by an identical enriched leather panel with scalloped fore edge; circular brass headed nails; arms renewed.
H.106 (42); W.59 (23); D.38 (15).

PROV: See p.463.   [33.3/55]

601

602 ARMCHAIR
Mid 18th century
Central American mahogany (aguano)

The curvilinear splat back supports a shaped top rail carved with leafy florets and crested by an open asymmetrical scroll; the seat rails are styled with a corner moulding and fronded

601

602

scrolls centering at the front on a pierced floral motif; the keeled cabriole forelegs are enriched on the knees and knurl feet with cabochon ornaments; the vigorously shaped outward-scrolling arms, which end in large volutes, rest on heavy moulded supports; leather covered slip seat. The back legs have new base blocks; side and turned rear stretchers missing; the pierced vase pattern splat may not be original.
H.122 (48); W.59 (23); D.48 (19).

PROV: See p.463.   [33.13/55]

603 ARMCHAIR
Late 18th century
Cedar

The squared backposts ending in simple scrolls support a profiled crest rail and are connected to the keeled cabriole forelegs by block-turned stretchers; the shaped seat rails centre at the front on a pierced floret and leaf-cluster between carved fonds; the undulating moulded arms with scroll terminals rest on curved supports, knurled 'Spanish' feet. The leather seat, reinforced underneath with hide webbing, is enriched with an interlacing stem system and stylized flowers. The lavishly tooled and painted back centres on a shield of arms surmounted by a plumed helm and inscribed below 'MARTINEZ ED PINILLOS'; the armorials are framed by

603

an elaborate cartouche composed of flamework scrolls, floral sprays and rococo foliage headed by a shell and with a mask at the base. The medial stretcher is missing, the crest rail has been renewed in walnut and a strip of plain leather has been sewn to the back.
H.121 (47½); W.60 (23½); D.40 (16).

Descendants of the Pinillos family still live in Trujillo, Peru. The quartered arms feature: a sheep and tree beside a tower; a pair of towers; a red cross; a tower being stormed with scaling ladders.

PROV: See p.463.   [33.8a/55]

604 PAIR OF ARMCHAIRS
Early 19th century
Cedar

The squared backposts ending in scroll finials support a profiled crest rail and the turned front legs are headed by a bulbous knop decorated with interlocking spliced cheeks; the shaped seat rails, outlined by a raised border, centre at the front on a carved foliate motif; low, block-turned side and medial stretchers, the moulded arms terminate in scrolls. The leather seats, reinforced underneath by interlaced hide webbing, centre on the embossed mongram 'M E R'; the backs are lavishly tooled and decorated in red, green, blue and gold with circus scenes of an acrobat on a horse accompanied by a man holding a whip framed by an elaborate rococo cartouche of paired cornucopiae, flamework scrolls and fronded shells; large rosette nails. One chair is inscribed underneath '6'.
H.107 (42¼); W.61 (24); D.40 (16).

The monogram may belong to the Martinez Es Pinillos family of Trujillo, Peru whose name and armorials figure on two similar painted leather chairs in the collection, Cat. Nos. 603, 605.

PROV: See p.463.   [33.6/55]

603

606

605

605 ARMCHAIR
Early 19th century
Cedar

The squared backposts headed by scrolls are united by a profiled crest rail and joined to the channelled cabriole legs by side stretchers formed of paired scrolls; the shaped seat rails centre at the front on a carved floret and leaf cluster between fronds; the moulded arms with volute terminals rest on curved supports. The tooled leather seat, reinforced underneath with hide webbing, bears an interlacing stem system with a later floral front border; the lavishly embossed and painted back panel centres on a coat of arms surmounted by a plumed helm above a ribbon emblazoned 'MARTZ EDPINLLS'; the heraldic shield is framed by a rococo cartouche of fronded scrolls, flamework and floral sprays; rosette pattern nails, traces of a nailing-ribbon remain. The cresting and upper part of the seat rails have been renewed; facing blocks on the knurled 'Spanish' front feet missing.
H.112 (44); W.61 (24); D.38 (15).

Descendants of the Pinillos family still live in Trujillo, Peru. A paper label on the underside records that Dame Clarissa Reid lent this chair to the V. & A. in 1922.

PROV: See p.463. [33.8b/55]

606 ARMCHAIR
Mainly early 19th century
Cedar

The rectangular frame, built of old and new members, has the original squared back posts ending in scrolls, plain front uprights, side and rear stretchers. The shaped front stretcher centering on a pierced wing motif, the profiled crest rail and rib-moulded arms are later additions. The plank seat is covered by a leather panel crudely incised with interlacing stems inhabited by a pair of lions rampant; the leather back is lavishly tooled and painted with an acrobat standing on a horse galloping in a landscape with trees and flowers, the circus scene being framed by an elaborate rococo cartouche composed of cornucopiae, flamework scrolls, foliage and shells; brass rosette headed nails.
H.112 (44); W.55 (21½); D.41 (16¼).

The basic chair frame was evidently 'upgraded' with a decorative front stretcher and moulded arms and the crest rail adapted to accommodate the lavishly styled pictorial leather panel, a rough attempt also being made to enrich the seat. Perhaps formerly owned by the family of Martinez Es Pinillos, Trujillo, Peru, see Cat. No.604.

PROV: See p.463. [33.9/55]

607

607 ARMCHAIR
Late 19th century
Central American mahogany (aguano)

The framework is of rectangular design with square section uprights each decorated on the outer face with chip-carved leaf scales; the back posts are surmounted by brass caps and finials. The valanced side and rear stretchers are banded with leaf scales while the deep front stretcher is carved with a stylized floral pattern; the flat slightly dipped arms have enriched scroll terminals. The leather-covered seatboard, padded with vegetation, and the back panel are secured by large fretted brass upholstery nails. A tear in the back has been patched with an ornamented leather panel inscribed 'SAN FRANCISCO / SOLANO / 1608'; the turned feet are later.
H.113 (44½); W.65 (25½); D.46 (18).

S. Francisco Solano was a Spanish saint who died in Peru in 1610. He was canonized in 1726. This chair presumably came from a church.

PROV: See p.463.   [33.11/55]

608 ARMCHAIR
Late 19th century, employing old work
Central American mahogany (aguano)

The shaped, heavily moulded arms with scroll terminals are supported on curvilinear front uprights styled with beak-like lugs and corner fillets; the upholstered seat and upright rectangular back stuffed with hay and covered in leather, is surmounted by an arched cresting bordered with pierced scrolls and flamework; spiral turned side and medial stretchers, chamfered rear legs, rounded block feet.
H.129 (51); W.66 (26); D.53 (21).

The frame has been created from several early eighteenth century Peruvian chairs. The arms, front uprights, cresting and stretchers are all married components.

PROV: See p.463.   [33.7/55]

609 PAIR OF ARMCHAIRS
19th century frames, earlier leather
Mahogany

Of rectangular design, the squared uprights, seat rails and arms built up with facing strips; the front supports and deep valanced stretcher are styled with traditional leaf-scale ornament while the flat arms and back posts end in scroll profiles, plain side and rear stretchers. The leather-covered seat boards padded with wood shavings and the back panels are embellished with an identical design of a double-headed eagle amid scrolling stems featuring pairs of birds and lions in each corner bordered by a shuttle-pattern surround; decorative brass nails.
H.106 (42); W.57 (22½); D.36 (14½).

The unorthodox construction and coarse carving betray the frames as nineteenth century copies of old colonial chairs. The leather backs and seats enriched with a traditional design appear to be reused eighteenth century panels.

PROV: See p.463.   [33.4/55]

610 ARMCHAIR
Late 19th century, made-up frame with old leather
Mahogany

Of rectangular design with block turned front uprights, squared back posts, flat moulded arms and a valanced front stretcher carved with leaf scales. The frame, which has been constructed mainly of old components with some new members, supports panels of much earlier chair leather. The back centres on a roundel enclosing a double-headed eagle with pairs of birds and lions in each corner amid scrolling stems. The seat, padded with vegetation, has a scalloped edge and centres on a bird medallion flanked by similar fan-tail birds beneath canopies; small rosette headed nails.

H.81 (32); W.56 (22); D.36 (14½).

PROV: See p.463. [33.2/55]

611 TRUNK
Late 17th century
Cedar; leather

Of shallow rectangular form; the carcase is covered with hide, stitched along the corners, seamed with thongs across the bottom, laced to the rim with twine and richly embellished with tooled, painted and gilt designs. The top centres on a fan-tailed bird, possibly an eagle, amid scrolling stems inhabited by lions; the border exhibits pairs of rabbits, dogs and birds among flowering plants with geometric corner roundels while the lid, edged with leafy scrolls inhabited by rabbits, has a scalloped frill. The front and ends are similarly enriched with scrolling stems and birds, the back is patterned with geometric roundels. Wrought iron strap-hinges, corner ties, spiral loop handles, hasp and a circular lock plate incised with radial lines. The painted decoration is executed in red, green and yellow.
H.18 (7); W.53 (21); D.28 (11).

From the Cuzco region of southern Peru. Four religious prints, the earliest dated 1794, and five texts in Spanish, one dated 1897, are pasted to the underside of the lid. They consist of hymns in praise of the Virgin Mary, prayers, carols and similar religious ephemera.

PROV: See p.463. [33.33/55]

611

612 TRUNK
Late 17th or early 18th century
Leather

Designed as an open rectangular box with a deep slip-over outer case; both parts are formed of thick folded layers of

612

cattle hide seamed with thongs, the inner case being braced square by hardwood slats concealed within the rim. The top is divided into four panels incised with a panther-like beast having two tails and a long tongue, enriched with stamped rosettes and fan motifs outlined by wave borders; the sides are decorated in the same manner. The outer case originally had circular metal lifting handles.
H.28 (11); W.69 (27); D.46 (18).

PROV: See p.463. [33.18/55]

613 CHEST
Early 18th century
Incense cedar

Of rectangular design with overall chip-carved decoration; the slightly domed top, fitted with scalloped end battens, centres on a vase of flowers with panels enclosing double-headed eagles on either side; the front is enriched with a similar pair of eagles while the end panels feature birds alighting on baskets of flowers; the backboard is styled with twin floral designs enclosed, like the other compositions, by a broad leafy frame incorporating rosettes outlined by narrow chiselled bands. The underside of the lid is similarly embellished with a crowned double-headed eagle between formalized baskets of flowers. The interior contains a small till with an enriched lid and a frond-carved frieze along the back and one side. The open wedged dovetails are decorated on the end-grain with rosettes at the front corners. The lock plate, incised with an octagonal pattern, hasp and internal strap-hinges are fixed with rivets. Modern corner blocks.
H.44 (17½); W.81 (32); D.46 (18).

A standard chest of urban quality for keeping household articles; the vigorous carving and in particular the flower vase motifs are typical of the Cuzco area.

LIT: *L.A.C.*, No.33 (1956), p.33, repr.

PROV: See p.463. [33.17/55]

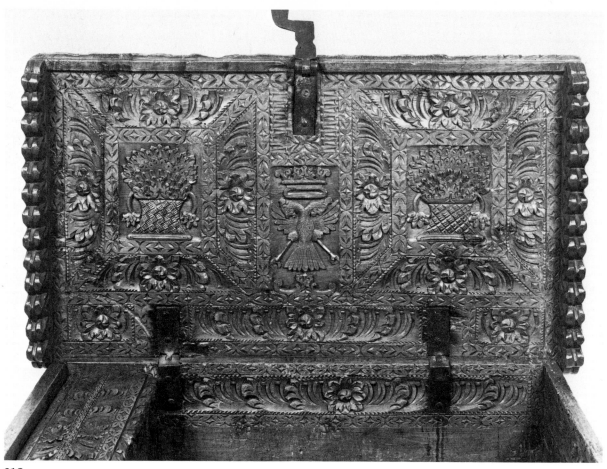

613

613

614

614

614 CHEST
Early 18th century
Incense cedar; parana pine

The slightly domed top and all four sides are elaborately decorated with incised, scored and chip-carved patterns forming panels and borders of stylized foliage; the underside of the lid and an inner frieze along the backboard and one end are enriched with similar geometric designs; the interior contains a lidded till on the left-hand side. The thick pine baseboard is hollowed underneath, thus raising the chest on a moulded foot rim; staple hinges. Local repairs include a strip of new wood around three sides of the top. The sides are united by open dovetails featuring a special stepped pattern, typical of Spanish colonial work, on the front corners. Probably from the Cuzco area of southern Peru.
H.31 (12¼; W.64 (25); D.33 (13).

PROV: See p.463.   [33.32/55]

615

615 CHEST
18th century
Peruvian walnut

Oblong with a canted lid; the sides and top are inlaid with an overall design of leafy scrolling tendrils bearing fruit and flowers executed in various coloured woods; the stem system on the front panel inhabited by pairs of birds and panthers centres on a circular domed lock plate backed by a rosette; the end panels are each ornamented by a vase and twin birds while the top is inset with a profile face flanked by two natives beating drums. The corners are outlined with thin applied strips of wood; silvered angle mounts, strap-hinges, hasp and lock plate.
H.25 (9¾); W.79 (31); D.43 (17).

PROV: See p.463.   [33.20/55]

616 VARGUEÑO
Late 17th century
Cedar

In the form of a compact rectangular chest with a slightly domed top and a fall-front backed by eight small drawers. The plain exterior is set with elaborately pierced and profiled wrought iron corner mounts, angle ties, strap-hinges and lifting handles, while the fall-flap bears a shield-shaped lock plate engaging an ornate hasp. The top, which opens to reveal a shallow partitioned tray and a lidded till, is carved on the underside with a crowned double-headed eagle amid a formal system of scrolling leafy stems and flowers with pearl shell insets, the internal backboard and till are similarly styled. The fall-flap is also carved inside with a low relief linear design representing two vases containing stylized floral

616

sprays, while the drawers, fronted by floral tendrils and chip-carved mouldings, centre on embossed silver medallions with shell drops. Constructed with revealed tenon and dovetailed joints; the drawer bottoms are pegged, lower rows lightly altered. The top edge of one drawer is inscribed in ink 'Berduras' – the Spanish word for vegetables. The chest rests on a low modern stand following the traditional pattern of two bars raised on end supports.
H.33 (13); W.53 (21); D.36 (14½).

The mother-of-pearl insets, silver fitments and somewhat coarse carving suggests this piece may be Indo-Portuguese rather than Peruvian in origin.

PROV: See p.463.   [33.34/55]

616

617

617 CHEST
Late 17th century
Cedar

Of rectangular design with two drawers in the base; the sides and slightly domed top are inlaid with an overall geometric pattern of lozenges, crosses, stars and triangles in light and dark woods, the lid is further enriched with lozenges on the underside; sliding pegs, operated from inside the trunk, lock into slots cut into the drawer fronts. Original staple hinges, faceted iron hasp and pierced shield-shaped lock plate backed by red leather. The low turned feet, drawer knobs, rear base moulding and corner facings renewed; internal lidded till missing.
H.38 (15); W.64 (25); D.33 (13½).

PROV: See p.463. [33.16/55]

618 VARGUEÑO
*c.*1700
Peruvian walnut

The exterior is enriched with linear designs executed in pale strings. The hinged lid, which opens to reveal a shallow compartment, is styled with a formal system of interlacing coils and opposed *fleurs-de-lis*, while the dummy drawer front is decorated with spiralling tendrils. Each end panel displays floral motifs and two crowned lions rampant bordered by scrolling arabesques. The cabinet accommodates six drawers inset with formal foliage outlined by pearl beading; the fall-front is missing. Elaborately pierced wrought iron corner ties, strap-hinges and ornamental hasp; the delicately fretted drawer pulls backed by traceried rosettes and the lifting handles are also original. Formerly supported on turned feet; the stand is modern.
H.48 (19); W.80 (31½); D.40 (16).

PROV: See p.463. [33.21/55]

618

619 PAPELERA
Late 17th century, with 19th century modifications
Alder; cedar, mahogany

The upright rectangular cabinet is formed of two almost identical units set one above the other, each accommodating one long and two short drawers. Plugged holes beneath the middle dustboard and on the underside show that, before their marriage, each section rested on low feet. The drawers

618

619

are faced with tortoiseshell tablets and bone borders engraved with gadroons and leaf scale patterns, surrounded by ripple mouldings. The cabinet is fronted with bands of crudely engraved bone; the ends are veneered with geometric panels executed in cedar and mahogany and the moulded cornice supports a rebuilt balustraded gallery fenced with pierced gilt-metal grilles. Locks and escutcheons missing, the keyhole openings masked by bone strips and turned pulls. The cabinet is raised on a modern stand.
H.56 (22); W.48 (19); D.29 (11½).

The two units would originally have resembled Cat. No. 620 and like that example reflects Philippine work. The Philippine Islands were for three centuries part of the Spanish Empire and their culture exerted a significant influence on Peruvian decorative art.

PROV: See p.463.   [33.25/55]

620 PAPELERA
Late 17th century with 19th century embellishments
Cedar and alder

In the form of a small rectangular cabinet containing two drawers. Later improvements to the original carcase include provision of a bone spindle gallery and ball finials, new cornice and base mouldings, facing the ends with geometric panels outlined with strings, veneering the front and adding decorative cast brass lifting handles and low turned feet; the new work has been coated with black stain. The two drawers are each fronted by a pair of panels centering on a tablet of red tortoiseshell banded with cedar and bordered by strips of bone engraved with an arabesque design framed in ripple mouldings. The original circular locks have cast brass escutcheons similar to the ornamental studs on the façade. Alder drawers.
H.43 (17); W. 43(17); D.24 (9½).

This type of cabinet is common in Peru; the decorative use of bone and tortoiseshell reflects the influence of Philippine work.

PROV: See p.463.   [33.29/55]

621 CHEST OF DRAWERS
Late 17th century
Cocobolo wood; walnut, parana pine

The top is secured to corbelled end bars by nails masked with lozenge insets; the square corner posts ending in turned legs support cross rails banded with walnut, framing fielded end panels carved with layered acanthus scales. The two deep drawers are fronted with sunk panels enclosing a low relief system of strapwork and scrolling arabesques; panelled pine back, dustboard and plank bottom. The keyholes are faced with oval bosses, locks missing, turned knobs renewed. The frame is united by open wedged tenon joints and the drawer linings constructed with revealed dovetails.
H.91 (36); W.132 (52); D.84 (33).

A good quality piece, probably made in Lima.

PROV: See p.463.   [33.23/55]

620

623

621

622 CUPBOARD
Late 19th century
Mahogany; satinwood, pine

Of upright rectangular design enclosed by double doors; the interior originally contained three shelves, but has been converted into a wardrobe with brass coat pegs. The façade is outlined with an intarsia band and the doors, each divided into two equal panels, are inlaid with the same border; the upper parts centre on satinwood insets depicting three roses tied with ribbons executed in green-stained and shaded elements; the lower panels are similarly styled with a putto seated on a cloud. The front cornice is of mahogany, stained pine sides, base and top, modern plywood back; brass lock and hinges renewed, frond-carved key escutcheon.
H.188 (74); W.116 (45½); D.40 (16).

The rough-hewn sides suggest this cupboard was originally built into a recess, the front may have been embellished when it was converted into a free-standing piece.

PROV: See p.463.   [33.19/55]

623 PAIR OF DOORS
17th century, second half
White cedar (tabebura)

Of framed panel construction united by pegs. Each door is faced with a geometric pattern of mouldings centering on a tablet carved with a baroque cartouche; the L-shaped corner segments enclose a low relief strapwork system of fronded scrolls enriched with circular stamps. Traces of the original reddish-brown paint on a gesso ground remain. The backs show scars of hinge, lock and bolt fixtures; local repairs on the façade. The two doors are mounted side by side on a modern frame.
H.81 (32); W.67 (26½).

Believed to come from a Peruvian church.

PROV: See p.463.   [33.28/55]

624

625

624 JUG
Perhaps 18th century
Oak

Bellied, with an open iron-rimmed neck and strap handle; of coopered construction hooped with four iron bands, plank bottom, lined with pitch.
H.41 (16¼); D.28 (11).

Owing to shrinkage of the staves few genuinely old coopered vessels survive; this example appears to be earlier than many. The use of oak suggests that, despite the Peruvian provenance, it was made in Spain – the label 'Hispanic' is a useful compromise.

PROV: See p.463.   [33.35/55]

625 LOOKING-GLASS
Late 19th century
Gilt pine and composition

The rectangular central plate is outlined by a pearl beading while the canted glass borders are contained within a cable-moulded frame; each corner is enriched with foliate clasps and flamework lugs; the cresting centres on an acanthus fan supporting open scrolls with floral cornucopiae at either side; rough pine backboards. The gilt composition decor is supported on a wire skeleton backed by an inner framework of wood.
H.137 (54); W.94 (37).

A richly styled reproduction of mid eighteenth century Spanish work in the rococo taste derived from Italian prototypes.

PROV: See p.463.   [33.27/55]

626 LOOKING-GLASS
Late 19th century
Gilt pine and composition

Of rectangular design, the central plate and canted glass borders are framed by gilt mouldings decorated with floral sprays in gilt composition; the open cresting of paired acanthus scrolls centering on a shell is executed in plaster backed by wood.
H.94 (37); W.59 (23).

The spandrel arch, which masks a damaged mirror plate, crude construction and liberal use of composition indicate that this looking-glass is a cheap colonial product imitating European prototypes.

PROV: See p.463.   [33.26/55]

627

628

627 SETTEE
Early 19th century
Mahogany; cedar, pine

The cedar backboard supports a shaped cresting composed of a central tablet inset with stylized leaf patterns in brass and surmounted by scrolling fronds with carved florets and acanthus plumes at either side; the scroll-over arms with boarded sides are enriched with ferns flanked by fruiting cornucopiae; the seat rail is faced with a cushion moulding and two brass-inlaid tablets set above the front supports conceived as hairy monster heads with lion's-paw feet, turned back legs; the plank seat, intended for a squab, is covered in leather.
H.114 (45); W.188 (74); D.53 (21).

The settee has been heavily restored with a view to enhancing its picturesque character: both arm rests rebuilt; one board renewed in plywood and carved cornucopiae wedded to the end supports; the upper cresting is not original and the shell finial has been added; the crouching monsters have new paw feet and base blocks suggesting they are re-used components, the rough-hewn backboard may also be reclaimed material. From the Cuzco region of south Peru.

PROV: See p.463.   [33.14/55]

628 SETTEE
Early 19th century
Mahogany; pine

The leather back panel is headed by a long profiled cresting carved with fronds terminating in volutes and centering on a tablet inlaid with stars and string borders executed in brass; the scroll-over arms with boarded sides are faced with long carved ferns and the front legs, decorated with eagle heads and wing brackets of layered foliage incorporating clusters of fruit, are capped by brass inlaid tablets and end in lion's-paw feet. The plank seat intended for a loose squab is covered in leather secured by brass headed nails. One arm facing and part of the crest rail renewed.
H.94 (37); W.162 (64); D.53 (21).

From the Cuzco region of south Peru.

PROV: See p.463.   [33.15/55]

629 CANDLESTAND
Late 19th century
Gilt pine

The dished hexagonal top, lined with canvas and bordered by a leaf moulding, is supported on an elaborately ornamented stem divided by an acanthus knop; the upper tier is profiled as two turned and gadrooned vases while the lower part, of triangular chamfered section, is faced with

629

scaled and floral diaper-work panels; raised on a scroll tripod carved with eagle heads emerging from leaf tongues; water-gilt finish.
H.130 (51½); D.40 (16).

A medium quality example of late nineteenth century furniture reflecting the taste of wealthy Peruvian families for showy reproductions of earlier European styles.

PROV: See p.463.   [33.22/55]

630 CENTRE TABLE
Early 18th century, modified at a later date
Amarillo and cedar

The rectangular top, edged with a plain leaf moulding, is secured to the end bars by nails masked with diamond insets;

630

the underframe is supported on splayed bulb and ring turned legs with head and foot blocks; valanced stretchers and frieze rail decorated with gouged fluting. Fitted with a single long drawer fronted by a fielded panel of chip-carved acanthus scales centering on a whorl motif; the two end and opposite frieze are similarly enriched. United by open wedged tenon joints. The top, rails and drawer are not original.
H.79 (31); W.155 (61); D.109 (43).

PROV: See p.463.   [33.24/55]

CHINESE

631 PAIR OF DOUBLE-CHESTS
Early 19th century
Spruce

Of rectangular design, in two stages divided by a shelf; the upper section, enclosed by double doors, contains four drawers while the lower cupboard fitted with six drawers has a shelf above, fronted by a shaped opening and with fretted side galleries. The exterior and drawers are surfaced with black lacquer decorated in gold, red and green with prunus blossom, irises and other floral sprays contained within angular scrollwork borders. Mounted with circular cloud-pattern escutcheons, fitted with oriental padlocks operated by sliding keys; shaped oval hinge plates and tab drawer-pulls. The drawer linings stained red.
H.99 (39); W.59 (23); D.33 (13).

Probably from Fukien province.

PROV: Bought in Peking from Major Fitz-Hugh by Colonel F. R. T. Gascoigne about 1925; the Gascoigne gift 1968.
[7.148/68]

632 HEAD-REST
Probably 18th century
Huang hua-li wood

The circular slab-end supports are raised on splayed bracket feet richly carved with oriental cloud-scrolls; the uprights are connected by an axle rod on which a cylindrical drum formed of flexible slats revolves. The axle, which is shaped by hand, not lathe-turned, has terminal tenons which fit into dovetail slots cut into the inner face of each slab end, so the

631

633

632

structure can be easily dismantled. One end support is a later replacement.
H.17 (6¾); L.34 (13¾); D.15 (6).

PROV: Acquired in Peru by James Reid and bequeathed by his widow to Lady Ramsden who gave it in memory of her husband 1955.   [33.31/55]

633 LANTERN
Late 19th century
Oriental hardwood

Of hexagonal design with two tiers of back-painted, slip-in glass panels; the framework is carved with pierced foliage, dragon 'gargoyle' finials and bird head terminals; the upper panes are decorated with oriental symbols and the lower row with scenes from a Chinese fable. The panels are united to the skeleton frame by interlocking grooves and lugs. Wired for electricity.
H.89 (35).

Hanging lanterns adorned with gaudy painting reflect the Chinese taste for decorative illumination.

PROV: Bought from a bazaar in Imperial China by Dr. G. S. Hughes, who bequeathed it to Leeds 1960.   [6/60]

634 'COROMANDEL' SCREEN
K'ang Hsi period (1662–1722)
Hardwood, possibly of the species *albizia*

The twelve leaves joined by iron pin and staple hinges are numbered from right to left in Chinese characters. The front, surfaced with polished dark brown and black lacquer, is

incised with a garden palace scene enhanced with soft distemper colours and gilt enrichment. The composition centres on a courtyard with a pavilion in which a dignitary sits receiving guests who carry gifts. Ladies playing musical instruments and games occupy pavilions set amongst trees while other buildings fly banners bearing the symbol of a general. Panel ten illustrates a scene from the *Dream of Red Chambers*, a classical Chinese novel. The border, which incorporates vases of flowers, utensils and traditional Taoist symbols, is guarded by an inner dragon pattern surround and an outer band of lotus motifs.
H.282 (111); W.572 (225).

Palace screens of this sort stood behind the master's seat.

EXH: Temple Newsam, *Chinese Art*, 1940 (189).

PROV: Bought from John Sparks Ltd 1940.   [21/40]

635 FOUR-FOLD SCREEN
Mid 19th century
Lacquer, padouk, soapstone

Constructed in two stages; each leaf is composed of a tall lower and square upper panel of black lacquer set in padouk frames, the short legs are united by shaped aprons. The upper tier of panels portray children at play while the main panels are decorated with Chinese ladies, mandarins and boys against a background of garden buildings. The figures have inlaid mother-of-pearl faces and hands, their clothes and the garden rockwork are represented in coloured soapstones; some of the facings restored in wax, the lapis lazuli represented by back-painted glass. Red, green and gilt painted details, the scenes outlined by diaper borders inset with pearl shell. Mounted with pierced brass hinges and corner clasps.
H.203 (80); W.264 (104).

Old scars on the framing show this screen has been made up from the doors of a combination set of four traditional Chinese cupboards – a pair for clothing below with two smaller hat cupboards above.

PROV: Recorded in the 1930s Lotherton inventory 'Chinese Lacquer Screen, inlaid Mother-of-Pearl (brought from Peking by Colonel and Mrs Gascoigne) 1924'; the Gascoigne gift 1968.   [7.219/68]

636 MINIATURE SCREEN
19th century
Padouk and stone

The eight leaves each frame four panels of semi-translucent Yunnan stone painted in red, green, blue and gold with figure scenes, legendary Chinese characters, utensils and poems about long life. The back is painted with craggy landscapes, lakes, trees and flowers.
H.65 (25½); W.101 (40).

635

636

Miniature screens were often placed on the table at banquets; this example was probably a birthday present.

PROV: Recorded in the 1930s Lotherton inventory as having been bought by Colonel F. R. T. Gascoigne in Peking; the Gascoigne gift 1968. [7.221/68]

637 SCREEN
19th century
Padouk and stone

The ten leaves each contain five panels of semi-translucent Yunnan stone set in hardwood frames pegged into the main structure; the two end leaves also feature panels of carved arabesque pattern fretwork. The tablets are painted in polychrome colours with crowd scenes, figure subjects, the circular 'shou' symbol of long life and inscriptions describing sweet scented blossoms, the autumn moon, flowers reflected in lakes and similar poetic sentiments; the seal of the author or calligrapher is also present. The back is painted with mountainous landscapes, lake scenes and further inscriptions. The ten leaves, originally united by iron pin and staple hinges, are styled with corner mouldings and end in short legs connected by shaped rails.
H.200 (78½); W.335 (132).

PROV: Recorded in the 1930s Lotherton inventory as bought in Peking by Colonel F. R. T. Gascoigne about 1925; the Gascoigne gift 1968. [7.222/68]

638 SETTLE
19th century, second half
Katsura wood (kokutan)

The elaborately carved and pierced back represents a dragon combat against a background of cloud scrolls; the arms are formed of clumps of iris rising from water and the double-serpentine-fronted seat is enriched with two coiling dragons

637

638

and pierced aprons composed of intertwining chrysanthemum and foliage; raised on six legs in the form of fish with scrolling tails, the corner supports styled with wings.
H.106 (42); W.144 (57); D.66 (26).

An example of what the Chinese call 'foreign antiques' made for the European export market. The dragons on the seat probably carved later.

PROV: The Hainsworth family, Claremont, Farsley; Mrs D. Gaunt, Hawksworth Hall, Otley; given by Mrs E. Gaunt 1955.   [18/55]

639 SHRINE
Early 19th century
Lacquered and gilt wood

Of architectural design with a platform base resting on crouching monsters. The temple-like shrine, fronted by corner balustrades, is constructed of elaborately carved and gilt panels representing Chinese rituals, dragons, birds amongst prunus blossom etc., framed by crushed pearl shell and red-stained borders. The interior features a screen of four hinged panels with a shelf behind and the backboard displays a gilt crane medallion. Many of the components are detachable; open wedged joints.
H.87 (34½); W.77 (30¼); D.44 (17½).

A domestic ancestral shrine, the internal shelf being intended for an 'ancestral' tablet; the façade centres on a panel depicting God surrounded by attendants sitting in judgment on a new soul. Said to come from Shensi province.

PROV: Brought from China by Colonel F. R. T. Gascoigne about 1925; the Gascoigne gift 1968.   [7.179/68]

639

640

640 STAND
Late 19th century
Hardwood

The rectangular top with canted corners rests on a narrow sill pierced by slits and the aprons centre on open panels enclosing paired fronds; the square cabriole legs of broken-scroll design with splayed feet are connected by cross stretchers supporting a fretwork platform. The upper part is richly carved with a system of arabesques, florets and angular scrolls in low relief enhanced with silver and gold on a red ground; the top is painted black and green.
H.85 (33½); W.40 (16); D.40 (16).

Stands of this type were normally made in pairs and used in domestic interiors for holding vases of flowers. Two of the legs are inscribed with the surname 'Wang' – a spelling characteristic of Peking.

PROV: The Gascoigne gift 1968.   [7.223/68]

641 TEA CADDY
19th century, second quarter
Lacquer; lead

Of rectangular design with rounded shoulders, canted corners and a bevelled base raised on four carved and gilt-wood paw feet. The hinged lid opens to reveal two fitted lead caddies, the tops and circular caps (concealing inner lids) are incised with floral sprays and ornamental borders. The top and sides of the black lacquer casket are decorated with Chinese figures in garden landscapes framed by borders of flowers and insects, executed in gilt with touches of red; brass lock and lozenge escutcheon.
H.17 (6½); W.28 (11); D.20 (8¼).

Almost certainly from Canton. A closely similar oriental export caddy in the Essex Institute, Salem, Massachusetts,

641

is illustrated by Carl Crossman, *The China Trade*, 1972, p.180, fig.150.

PROV: Given by Mrs Clive Behrens, Swinton Grange, Yorkshire 1940. [18.4/40]

642 TEA TABLE
Early 19th century
Softwood

The circular tip-up top is supported on a turned vase-shaped column headed by a 'bird-cage' and raised on a tripod base ending in gilt lion's-paw and ball feet. The top and stand are elaborately decorated in red and gold with Chinese compositions on a black lacquer ground, the stand being enriched with floral sprays, while the table top features a multiplicity of exotic scenes including a pagoda, sampans, islands, palaces, gardens, trees, figures and insects. The brass hinges are stamped 'C C & Co'.
H.65 (25½); Diam.94 (37).

The table was clearly made in the orient for export to Europe.

PROV: Given by Charles Roberts, Farfield Hall, Yorkshire 1941. [11.172/41]

JAPANESE

643 PAIR OF PICNIC-BOXES (Hokkai)
19th century (late Edo period)
Lacquered wood; copper

Each container is designed as a cylindrical box in the form of piled rings raised on four splayed wedge-shaped legs which buttress the sides to the height of the lid. The supports and domed top are ornamented with engraved copper mounts and studs; the lid is tied down by green silk tasselled cords.
H.43 (17); Diam.38 (15).

Used for holding gifts of rice or manjyu (Japanese cakes); similar boxes were made for ceremonial headgear.

PROV: The Gascoigne gift 1971. [23.22/71]

643

642

644

644 PAIR OF SCREENS
Late 17th or early 18th century (Edo period)
Softwood, paper, silk

Each six-fold screen is framed by a red lacquer fillet decorated with brass corner mounts, studs and clasps engraved with floriated ornament. The leaves, surfaced with stout paper, have borders of dark blue silk embroidered in light blue, pink and gold thread with floral repeats and an inner brown band worked in gold thread. When joined the screens form a unified composition centering on a large cherry tree viewed over a green garden fence; various oriental birds inhabit the branches, perch on the railings or strut on the ground against a background of gold sky and clouds. The back is lined with panels of black paper bearing dark red stencilled patterns.
H.173 (68); W.62 (24½) each leaf; L.747 (24ft. 6 in.) overall.

The back displays a label inscribed in Japanese with a number and a seal.

PROV: Purchased by Lady Gascoigne in 1950 from Nakaya Fine Art Curios, Tokyo; the Gascoigne gift 1971.
[23.20/71]

INDIAN

645 LOOKING-GLASS
Early 18th century
Indian rosewood; walnut, pearl shell, ivory, brass

The rectangular bevelled glass is contained within a broad, cushion-moulded frame veneered in rosewood and headed by a lunette cresting. The front is profusely inlaid with spiralling branches and foliage, worked in fine brass, bearing many different kinds of flowers (some resembling peonies, lilies and tulips) and fruit executed in engraved pearl shell and ivory. The interlacing stem system is inhabited by exotic birds, including cocks and quail, together with butterflies, moths and other insects executed in pearl. Each corner is ornamented with two ivory *fleurs-de-lis*; the sides centre on a tinctured shield charged with the Royal French coat of arms, suspending a ribbon bearing a six-pointed star and surmounted by a crown. The cresting features a large and two diminutive *fleurs-de-lis* beneath an ivory crown surrounded by floral stems, birds and insects, some of which are stained red.

645

The mirror plate and backboard are modern.
H.180 (71); W.109 (43).

The enrichment of this mirror is closely similar to the decorative ingredients – particularly border patterns – found on painted and dyed cotton palampores made on the Coromandel Coast for the European market. The design conforms to late seventeenth century European mirrors and the heraldic elements indicate that it was a French commission. Traces of pigment on the pearl marquetry suggest an attempt to reproduce the colourful effect of painted cotton. The walnut carcase implies a north Indian origin.

PROV: Bequeathed by Charles Brotherton, Kirkham Abbey, Yorkshire 1949.   [14.2/49]

646

646 JARDINIÈRS
*c.*1825
Indian rosewood or padouk

The trumpet-shaped bowls, embellished with a gadrooned border, formalized lotus flowers and overlapping leaves, are raised on turned scale pattern stems with foliate tops and bases; each stand is supported by three scrolled monopodia carved with stylized leaves, eagles' heads and claw feet; concave triangular platform bases with in-scrolled terminals; modern galvanized liners. A crescent mark and the letter 'T' are incised under the bowls.
H.85 (33½); Diam.34 (13½).

These stands display many Regency features – monopodia, triangular bases, eagle terminals, anthemion motifs, etc. – but the detailing and timber indicate a colonial origin – probably Ceylon or Java. The wood is either *Pterocarpus* or *Dalbergia* species. These are often very similar in structure and therefore hard to separate; *Dalbergia* includes the rosewoods and *Pterocarpus* the padouks.

Several jardinièrs of virtually identical design and ornamentation have been recorded: one, formerly in the Lady Lever Art Gallery (P. Macquoid, *The Leverhulme Art Collections*, III, 1928, No.135, pl.29) was sold at Christie's, 24 June 1965. lot 37; a pair from the Murray Adams Acton collection was illustrated in *Antique Collector*, Aug. 1936, p.207; Harrods Ltd., advertised a pair in *Connoisseur*, June 1953, p. xxxvii; a pair was sold at Christie's, 18 Feb. 1971, lot 103; the same same firm sold another pair on 8 July 1971, lot 63; in 1971 R. Morrison of York had a single stand in stock and H.M. the Queen Mother owns an example.

PROV: Purchased (Harding Fund) from Douglas R. Bird (Antiques) Bath 1937.   [20.1 & 2/37]

JAVANESE

647 CHAIR
*c.*1730
Chinese rosewood

Of bended-back design with angular shoulders and a curved, vase-shaped splat outlined by a raised border; the hooped uprights terminate in scrolls centred by a shell and pendant husk; the slip seat with shaped rails is raised on cabriole forelegs carved with shell and husk ornaments on hocked claw and ball feet, the rear cabrioles are plain with club feet. The back uprights are in two sections jointed at seat level by an interlocking pegged splice reinforced at the back with iron ties; the inner front corners are lined with curved wooden braces; later rear corner blocks and seat base. The back rail incised 'III'. For a note on the timber see Cat. No.646.
H.106 (42); W.54 (21½); D.46 (18).

The timber, construction and styling indicate an oriental origin; the undulating splat with a delicately scrolled border, light corner mouldings and vigorously carved paw feet invest this chair with a distinctive Chinese character: it was probably made in the East Indies for export to Europe (see Cat. No.648) or possibly originated in Ceylon.

LIT: *L.A.C.*, No.60 (1966), p.9, repr.

PROV: Bequeathed by Frank Savery 1966.   [1.24/66]

648 CHAIR
*c.*1740
Chinese rosewood; walnut, beech

The hooped uprights, bent vase-shaped splat and curvilinear seat rails are carved in low relief with a formal design of interlaced strapwork, arabesques, husk chains and flower heads; raised on hipped cabriole legs headed by stylized scallop shells and ending in pad feet featuring grotesque masks; the knees are enriched with ribbed acanthus fronds bordered by scrolls linked behind by husk collars, this pattern is abbreviated on the rear cabrioles; velvet covered slip seat. Chinese rosewood frame, walnut corner blocks (missing at the front), beech seat base; pegged construction, the back posts are united to the rear legs by an elaborately spliced joint.
H.106 (42); W.52 (20½); D.44 (17½).

The oriental timber, peculiarities of construction and highly enriched surfaces simulating carved gesso work on George I period chairs, indicate that this example was made in the East by Chinese craftsmen working under European supervision, either on the mainland or at a trading centre such as Manila or Batavia. Vilhelm Slomann, who discusses this class of furniture in *Burlington*, Nov. 1934, pp.201–14, illustrates on pl.3 a rosewood bureau made in 1741 at Canton for the European market carved with very similar low-relief designs. Chairs of this type were supplied in sets and the figure 12 crudely scratched inside the seat rails of this example suggests it formed part of a suite. Large sets are to be found at Hatfield House and Wilton; Christie's sold fifteen on 20 May 1971, lot 77 and Sotheby's auctioned two suites of identical pattern to this model on 7 May 1965, lot 95 and 26 Jan. 1968, lot 83, consisting of fourteen and twelve items respectively. Padouk, rosewood and walnut were the most popular woods; sometimes Chinese characters in indian ink are painted on the frames.

LIT: *Burlington*, July 1966, p.373, fig.55; *L.A.C.*, No.60 (1966), p.9, repr.

PROV: J. A. Lewis & Son; bequeathed by Frank Savery 1966.
          [1.11/66]

647

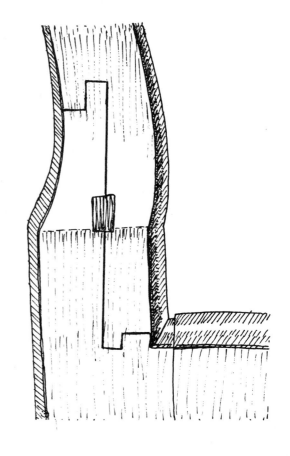

KOREAN

649 SEAL CHEST
Probably early 19th century
Huang hua-li wood

The rectangular cabinet with open dovetailed corner joints is enclosed by double doors and supported on a low stand with shaped side rails and bracket feet. The veneered flush-panel doors are backed by blue lining paper bearing a floral imprint and faced with a stylized cloud-pattern lock plate, corner mounts and bifurcated strap-hinges. The top is decorated with the engraved silhouette of two bats and the ends have bail handles. Reconstructed interior fitted with six drawers.
H.43 (17); W.56 (22); D.35 (14).

PROV: Bought in Seoul by Colonel F. R. T. Gascoigne in 1924; the Gascoigne gift 1968.   [7.162/68]

649

650

650 SEAL CHEST
Probably early 19th century
Huang hua-li wood

The cabinet is raised on a low ebonized stand with shaped rails and scroll bracket feet sheathed in brass united by modern runners. The veneered flush-panel doors, mounted with a circular cloud-motif escutcheon and bifurcated strap-hinges, enclose ten drawers of various sizes with fret-pattern pulls, the pegged linings varnished red. Revealed dovetail corners reinforced with angle clasps; loop lifting handles.
H.60 (23½); W.71 (28); D.40 (16).

PROV: Bought by Colonel F. R. T. Gascoigne in Seoul in 1924; the Gascoigne gift 1968.   [7.170/68]

651 SEAL CHEST
Probably early 19th century
Huang hua-li wood

The rectangular cabinet is fronted by double doors which open to reveal a varied arrangement of eight drawers with small ring pulls. The veneered, flush-panel doors are furnished with a circular brass lock plate, upright loop handles and ornamental strap-hinges; the sides support lifting handles and the case is set with corner and angle mounts; the low stand has scroll bracket feet sheathed in brass. The pegged drawer linings bear brush strokes to indicate correct placement.
H.48 (19); W.62 (24½); D.43 (17).

PROV: Bought in Seoul by Colonel F. R. T. Gascoigne in 1924; the Gascoigne gift 1968.   [7.161/68]

652 SEAL CHEST
Probably early 19th century
Huang hua-li wood

The cabinet, of upright rectangular design, is attached to a low stand with shaped rails and bracket feet; the flush-panel double doors, veneered in richly figured huang hua-li with ebonized borders, open to reveal an arrangement of ten drawers in four tiers bearing loop handles, the top pair fitted with engraved lock plates. The door junction is masked by a strip of brass finely engraved with pots of flowers while the circular elaborately lobed escutcheon, decorated with flowering trees and birds, bears six medallions featuring unidentified oriental characters. The door handles are backed by profiles of flying bats mounted on a brass band engraved with fishes; each door has six strap-hinges enriched with floral scrolls; the rear corners are set with dummy hinges. Revealed dovetailed corners reinforced with angle plates and clasps.
H.71 (28); W.76 (30); D.36 (14½).

PROV: Bought in Seoul by Colonel F. R. T. Gascoigne in 1924; the Gascoigne gift 1968.   [7.176/68]

652

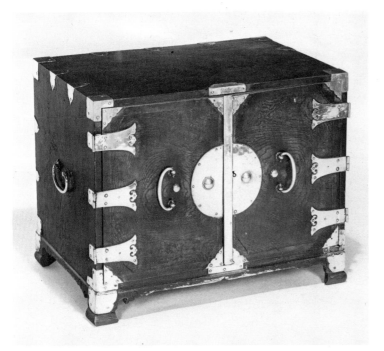

651

Part Four

DOCUMENTARY MATERIAL

MANUSCRIPT DESIGNS

Over the past ten years three groups of furniture designs have been acquired which, it is hoped, will eventually form the nucleus of a significant holding of graphic material in the field of decorative arts. Only the eighteenth century drawings merit full catalogue entries, the other two collections are briefly described.

SEVEN ROCOCO DESIGNS

PROV: Private collection in Dublin; Sotheby's Belgravia, 23 March 1976, lot 1; bought from C. Powney 1976.

Two are signed by Peter Glazier who contributed one plate to M. Lock's, *A New Book of Ornaments for Looking Glass Frames*, n.d., *c*.1750; published several small suites of metal-work designs for candelabra, snuff boxes, watch cases, etc. dated 1748 and 1754 (V. & A. Print Room, pressmark E0 20); and signed a drawing for a chair at the Henry Francis du Pont Winterthur Museum (69–193). The numbers, dates and prices jotted on the verso of each sheet indicate that they passed through the hands of a dealer in the 1780s.

653 OVERMANTEL AND CHIMNEYPIECE

the elaborate rococo overmantel frames a painting above a landscape mirror and supports two pairs of candle branches. Signed and inscribed 'P. Glazier. inv. delin.'
Pen, ink and wash with details in pencil, *c*.1750
Size: 19 (7½) × 13·4 (5¼).
Inscribed on the back: 'No.11856' and 'No.28 Mar 12 80, 1/6d'.   [35.7/76]

654 PIER TABLE

in the rococo style, with a marble top.
Signed and inscribed 'P. Glazier. Inv. Delin.'
Pen, ink and wash, *c*.1750.
Size: 14 (5½) × 18·5 (7¼).
Inscribed on the back: 'No.11857' and 'No.29 Mar 12 80, 2/-'.   [35.6/76]

655 PIER GLASS

the frame ornamented with palm branches and garlands.
Pen, ink and wash, *c*.1760.
Size: 30·7 (12) × 16·5 (6½).
Inscribed: 'The Palm approv'd' and on the back 'No 12014' and 'No.29 May 11 88, 2/-'.   [35.5/76]

656 PIER GLASS

the frame decorated with palms rising from rockwork.
Pen, ink and wash, *c*.1760.
Size: 15·3 (6) × 7 (2¾).
Inscribed on back: 'No 12011' and 'No 26 May 11 88, 2/6, lot 46'.   [35.1/76]

653

657 WALL SCHEME

showing an architectural chimneypiece between two door-ways flanked by festoons and brackets with alternative over-door paintings above, the ornament perhaps intended for execution in stucco.
Pen, ink and wash, *c*.1750.
Size: 10·2 (4) × 17·3 (6¾).
Inscribed in pencil above one overdoor 'this pannel' and on the back 'No. 11202' and 'No.22 Mar 26 83, 1/-'.
An alternative scheme to the following design.   [35.4/76]

658 WALL SCHEME

featuring a tabernacle frame, doorcases, decorative festoons and mural brackets etc., the ornament perhaps intended partly for execution in stucco.
Pen, ink and wash, *c*.1750.
Size: 10·2 (4) × 17·3 (6¾).
Inscribed in pencil: 'This dore Case' and on the back 'No 11203' and 'N 23 Mar 26 83, 1/-'.
An alternative proposal to the preceding design.   [35.3/76]

654

659 WALL SCHEME
showing an elaborate rococo pier glass between two windows with floral festoons on the side walls.
Pen, ink and wash, c.1750.
Size: 9 (3½) × 17·8 (7).
Inscribed on the back: 'No 11213' and 'N 31 Mar 26 83'.
By the same hand as the two previous drawings, but not necessarily associated with that project.   [35.2/76]

660 DOSSIER OF SKETCHES, SAMPLES AND ARCHIVE MATERIAL.
Messrs. D. Luff, 52 Elizabeth Street, Eaton Square, London c.1894–1907.

This miscellaneous working collection contains 56 items relating to the business of Messrs. D. Luff, decorators and furnishers. The material is housed in its original folder (17 × 10 in.) labelled 'Drawings & Sketches of Furniture Estimated' and on the evidence of dated documents ranges between 1894 and 1907. The collection includes rough pencil sketches and sophisticated watercolour designs for screens, mirrors, tables, upholstered chairs, cabinets etc., many of which are inscribed with measurements, prices, names and

notes about materials, or finishes. There are also tear sheets and clippings from furniture trade catalogues, price lists, samples of fabric and wallpapers, a few letters and similar commercial records.
Given by J. Peter W. Cochrane 1973.   [3/73]

661 PORTFOLIO OF DESIGNS FOR FURNITURE AND INTERIORS WITH RELATED MATERIAL
Hummerston Brothers, Leeds
c.1875–1913

In 1869 John Hummerston (1814–95) who, with his brother Joshua (1811–67), had carried on a decorating business at various addresses in Leeds since 1839, moved to new premises at 11, East Parade where the enterprise was extended to include the branches of cabinet-making and upholstery. When John Hummerston retired in 1886 the firm was divided between his sons: William (1852–1934) took over the furniture department while James (1849–1918) directed the decorating side. The portfolio of drawings contains over 100 items representing both branches of the business, many clearly pre-date the reorganization of 1886.

There are 23 neatly executed pencil sketches for cabinets, chairs (Cat. No.661), tables, clockcases and bedroom furniture in a style reflecting the influence of J. B. Talbert and a single sheet portraying tables and chairs inspired by E. W. Godwin's designs published in William Watt's *Art Furniture* trade catalogue of 1877. A clip of seven pen-and-ink and coloured wash drawings for a dining room suite bears, in addition to the firm's stamp, the inscription 'William Thorp, Architect, St Andrew's Chambers, Park Road, Leeds' indicating that William Hummerston executed architect-designed furniture before the cabinet-makers shop closed down in 1896.

The decorating branch managed by James Hummerston is well represented in the dossier by many coloured designs for chimneypieces, doorcases, panelled rooms, plaster ceilings mural ornaments and a particularly fine series of schemes for the decoration of St Silas' Church, Hunslet, dated 1892. There are also tear sheets from the *Builder*, 1891; the *Furniture Gazette*, 1875; a copy of Adin & Hassall's *Catalogue of Nursery and Sporting Wallpaper Friezes*, 1913 and numerous commercial documents. Five medals awarded to Hummerston Brothers at various Industrial and Fine Art Exhibitions accompany the archive material: London (1862); Wakefield (1865); Leeds (1875); York (1879) and Bradford (1882).

LIT: C. G. Gilbert, 'Hummerston Brothers of Leeds', *L.A.C.* No.68 (1971) pp.20–3.

PROV: Given by Miss E. Hummerston 1970.   [17/70]

662 PLASTER CASTS
forty-six casts of furniture ornaments
20th century, first quarter

Several of the large furniture makers in High Wycombe regularly sent plaster models to carvers working at home on a piece rate basis. They would farm out orders for chair legs, decorative tablets, masks and so forth. Clearly, better results were obtained if casts rather than drawings were supplied for the outworkers to copy. Parker-Knoll of Wycombe and the old established Edinburgh firm Whytock & Reid have retained large numbers of similar casts.

The present collection was purchased piece-meal during the 1930s and '40s by Mr. Ottrey who bought-up carvers' tool chests in the High Wycombe area and came across small groups of plaster models in domestic workshops; thus, the holding is not a coherent provenance group, but originated in the same locality. One cast, taken from the cabriole knee on the central leg of a Chippendale style settee, is inscribed 'more swell on knee too flat' and the crest rail of a chair '9 hrs top'; one component is incised 'WS' and two are signed 'F. A. Everett' – a free lance carver working privately from home. He also taught wood carving at the Wycombe Technical College, executed the coat of arms on the municipal offices and many local inn signs. Some of the casts were reputedly taken from his own work to show interested customers instead of keeping a photographic record.

656

Relatively few of the models reproduce genuinely old work, the majority appear to be casts of early twentieth century 'period' furniture. The models were made by encasing the original ornament in plasticine reinforced with small pieces of wood or hessian and then pouring plaster of paris into the hollow. A wire or cord loop was generally embedded in the cast since it was customary to hang them from nails on the workshop wall.

PROV: Part of a collection, originally numbering about 170 items, formed by F. A. Everett and others of High Wycombe and its environs; Ottrey Antiques, Dorchester-on-Thames; David Kenrick (Antiques); bought from the Lady Martin Bequest Fund with the aid of a government grant 1977. [31/77]

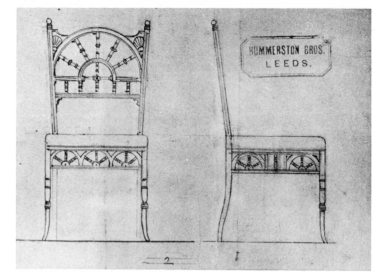

661

662

FURNITURE TRADE CATALOGUES AND EPHEMERA

The Pratt Collection

Christopher Pratt & Sons, Ltd of Bradford are the only old-established Yorkshire firm of cabinet-makers still in existence. Many of their nineteenth century ledgers, stock books, working drawings and other business records survive, which allow the history of this firm to be charted in some detail. An exhibition of their labelled furniture and related manuscript material was held at Bradford Art Gallery in 1969.

In 1972 a remarkable discovery was made during alterations to their premises in North Parade: while dismantling a staircase workmen found, walled up in a cavity, two packing cases containing an assortment of over three hundred Victorian and Edwardian furniture trade catalogues. This archive is of outstanding importance, for it preserves precisely the kind of ephemeral matter that was almost invariably destroyed when obsolete. Several of the catalogues and brochures were issued by Pratts themselves between *c.*1890 and 1920, but the bulk of the collection consists of copiously illustrated pattern books published by other furniture makers in England, Scotland, Germany, France, Austria and the United States. This 'working library' provides an invaluable survey of turn of the century furnishings.

Some catalogues are devoted entirely to wicker or bamboo wares, others illustrate ranges of bentwood, garden, invalid or office furniture, while several advertise only billiard tables, metalwork or leather goods. However, the majority portray (often with price lists) ordinary 'commercial' domestic furniture. Pratts did not stock elite or highly progressive work (although Liberty & Co. established a department within the store) hence this pictorial record is chiefly valuable as a profile of respectable upper-middle class provincial taste. By 1900 Pratts were offering a complete house furnishing and decorating service, the business being divided into fourteen separate departments. Inevitably, large amounts of ready-made furniture were purchased from wholesalers in London and the provinces for display in their showrooms.

It is likely that many of these catalogues are unique survivals; accordingly, a complete check-list of the collection is presented here together with an anthology of illustrations. The holding includes a few later items, such as Utility Furniture Guides, now surplus to the firm's needs. The schedule is sub-divided as follows:

DOMESTIC FURNITURE
  London firms
  Provincial firms (alphabetical by town)
OFFICE FURNITURE
CANE, WICKER & BAMBOO
GARDEN & SEASIDE FURNITURE
BILLIARD TABLES
INVALID FURNITURE

UTILITY FURNITURE SCHEME (1943–1953)
BENTWOOD & FOREIGN FURNITURE
METALWARES & CHIMNEY FURNITURE
NOVELTIES & MISCELLANEOUS
UNIDENTIFIED CATALOGUES BEARING INITIALS
ANONYMOUS CATALOGUES

Although it was not usual to date trade catalogues a number bear pencilled dates for internal reference; printed or inscribed dates are noted in the individual entries. All 'circa' dates are quoted from stray letters or invoices interleaved in the catalogues, the vast majority of which were issued between 1900 and 1915, a span which accords a useful but not infallible guide to the undated examples. Many firms only identified themselves by initials, most of which have been de-coded with the help of Pratts' old ledgers and Kelly's *Directory of Cabinet Makers*, 1903. However, some sets of initials remain to be traced and a few catalogues yield no clues to the identity of the manufacturer.

The whole collection, given by Christopher Pratt & Sons Ltd in 1972, is accessioned under 10.1/72 to 10.343/72; the second sequence of numbers only is cited in the check-list.

DOMESTIC FURNITURE

LONDON

1 Alesbury patent collapsoware (folding furniture) p.8, nd.
2 ALSTROM, C. *The 'Britsim' chest* (patent chest of drawers) p.11, nd.
3 ALSTROM, C. *Office, library and special furniture* (domestic and hospital) p.24, nd.
4 ANGUS, W. *Wood-seated chairs in oak* (Windsors, etc) single sheet, d.1900
5 ANGUS, W. *Chairs, couch and settee suites* (domestic) p.40, d.1906
6 ANGUS, W. *'Mollis' easy chairs and settees*, folded leaflet, nd.
9 ATKINS, E. *Seasonable specialities*, Cat. No.102 (music stools, coal boxes etc) p.36, nd.
10 ATKINS, E. *Seasonable specialities*, Cat. No.112 (fancy furniture) p.36, nd.
11 AYERS, J. AND SON. Frames for upholstered seat furniture, p.38, nd.

12 BAKER AND LUCAS. Upholstered seat furniture, folded sheet, nd.
13 BARR, J. AND SONS. *Furniture design book* (domestic) p.40, nd.
14 BERRISFORD AND HICKS. *Artistic upholstered furniture* (chairs, settees and couches) p.16, nd.
15 BERRISFORD AND HICKS. *Artistic designs in settees, chairs, etc* (mostly upholstered) p.24, d.1908 [2 copies]
16 BERRISFORD AND HICKS. *Smart designs in settees, easy chairs, etc* (upholstered) p.24, nd.
16a BERRISFORD AND HICKS. *The 'Uneedit' lounge spring bed* (patent convertible) single sheet, nd.
283 BOYS AND STURGE. *Catalogue of seats and seat standards* (music, hall, etc) p.24, nd.

17 CLEAVER, H. C. *The 'ideal' music cabinet* (patented) folded leaflet, nd.

18 DAVIS, L. Sheraton furniture (domestic) p.20, nd.
19 DRAGES. *Furniture of quality and distinction* (domestic) p.92, nd.

177 ERAD, C. *Original designs of artistic screens, pedestals and mirrors*, p.31, nd.
178 ERAD, C. *Original designs of artistic screens, pedestals and mirrors*, p.32, nd.

259   FINCH, J. *Mahogany inlaid trays*, single sheet, nd. [2 copies]

20   GILES AND WOOLLONS. *Stuffover chair frames*, p.8, nd.
21   GORDON, L. *Artistic upholstered furniture* (domestic) p.30, nd.

22   HABRA BROS. *Damascus furniture* (imported Turkish, Syrian and Eygptian, inc. metalwork and textiles) p.23, d.1909
23   HEMMINGS, G. P. *Mirrors, mantelpieces, bedroom and nursery furniture*, p.16, d.1907
24   HERMAN, H. Fitted wardrobes, four sheets and letter to Pratt & Sons, d.1914

290   JONES, C. A. Trade catalogue (folding furniture, ladders, chairs, etc) eight sheets, nd.

25   KAHN, E. Artistic furniture designs (domestic) p.68, nd.
26   KAHN, E. *Artistic period furniture* (domestic) p.8, nd.
27   KAHN, E. *Artistic period furniture* (occasional furniture) p.8, nd.
28   KAHN, E. *Latest designs* (domestic) p.12, nd.
29   KAHN, E. *English and French artistic furniture* (domestic and clocks, mirrors and screens) p.378, d.1914
30   KAHN, E. *Examples in artistic furniture* (domestic) p.16, nd.
31   KAHN, E. *Decorative furniture in noted styles* (drawing and dining room, also leather screens) p.12, nd.
32   KAHN, E. *French furniture* (drawing room and small items, screens and brass work) p.72, nd. [2 copies]
33   KAHN, E. *Inexpensive high class novelties* (small tables, cabinets, trays, etc) p.12, nd.
34   KAHN, E. *Latest designs in furniture and upholstery* (domestic) p.12, d.1916
35   KAHN, E. *Catalogue of furniture* (domestic and mirrors and screens) p.124, nd.
36   KAHN, E. *Novelties* (domestic) p.10, nd.
37   KAHN, E. *Reproductions of the antique* (domestic and screens, mirrors, etc) p.30, nd. [2 copies]
38   KAHN, E. *Reproduction 'Jacobean' dining hall* (domestic and upholstered) p.16, nd.
39   KAHN, E. *Reproduction 'Jacobean' dining hall* (domestic) p.8, d.1916
40   KAHN, E. *Special designs of dining room, drawing room and bedroom furniture*, p.8, d.1912
41   KAHN, E. Carved oak and Dutch marquetry furniture, etc. (domestic) p.16, nd.
42   KAHN, E. *Ye olde furniture and modern productions* (domestic) p.8, nd.
43   KAHN, E. *Ye olde furniture and modern productions* (domestic) p.16, d.1916 [2 copies]
45   KAHN, E. *The season's novelties* (domestic) p.4, nd.
46   KAHN, E. Untitled (domestic) two sheets, nd.
169   KAHN, E. *Screens* (supplementary cat.) p.8, nd. [2 copies]
171   KAHN, E. *Screens. Season 1905 and 1906*, p.36
172   KAHN, E. *Screens. Season 1907 and 1908*, p.36
173   KAHN, E. *Newest designs in decorative screens*, p.44, nd.

47   LAMB, W. *Period sideboards* (oak and mahogany) p.10, nd.
48   LAW BROS. Furniture catalogue (domestic) p.130, nd.
49   LEBUS, H. Artistic, durable and useful gifts (writing tables, cabinets, chairs, etc) p.14, nd.
50   LEBUS, H. Furniture catalogue (drawing room, hall and overmantels) p.60, d.1906
51   LEBUS, H. *Furniture designs* (domestic and office) p.445, d.1909
52   LEBUS, H. *Furniture designs* (domestic and office) p.511, d. *c.*1909
53   LEBUS, H. *The 'Lebus' sectional bookcase* (and bookstands) folded leaflet, nd. [2 copies]
54   LEBUS, H. *Nett price list* (domestic) p.74, d.1909
55   LEBUS, H. *Upholstery* (chairs, settees and couches) p.114, d.1906
56   LIBERTY. *Furniture by Liberty & Co.* (domestic) p.41, nd.
57   LIBERTY. *Solid oak panelling* (and friezes) p.40, nd.
58   LIBERTY. *Sketch suggestions for Tudor fitments and decorations* (interiors) p.14, nd.
59   LIBRACO. *Portable shelving* (commendations and explanations) single folded sheet, nd.

285   LIGHT, C AND R. *A selection of machine made bedroom suites, sideboards and hallstands*, p.16, nd.
286   LIGHT, C. AND R. *Overmantels* (various designs and styles) p.31, nd.
287   LIGHT, C. AND R. *Furniture – Special spring selection, 1912* (domestic) p.40
60   LOTINGA BROS. *High class upholstery* (chairs and settees) single folded sheet, nd.
309   LOWES, T. *Designs of cabinet furniture*, Ed. B (domestic) p.256, d.1907
310   LOWES, T. *Designs of cabinet furniture, upholstered goods, etc.* Ed. F. p.256, d. *c.*1908

61   MAPLE. Examples of a bureau, clock, chair and ottoman lounge, p.4, nd.
343   MAPLE. *Illustrations of furniture*, p.640, nd.

174   SINGLETON, BENDA AND CO. *Draught screens, season 1911–1912.* p.20
175   SINGLETON, BENDA AND CO. *Draught screens, season 1912–1913.* p.20

62   TRIER, S. *High class furniture* (occasional and novelty) p.27, nd.
63   TRIER, S. *Furniture novelties* (occasional) p.14, nd.
308   TRIER, S. *Refined stylish furniture* (domestic) p.146, nd.

64   WINDSOR, J. *Catalogue of furniture*, No.812 (domestic, fancy, etc) p.96, nd.

BANBURY

150   STONE, H. AND SON. *Cabinets for music, piano stools* ('Mozart' music cabinets) p.19, nd.
151   STONE, H. AND SON. *Furniture* (domestic and music cabinets and stools) p.80, d.1908
152   STONE, H. AND SON. *Furniture* (domestic and music cabinets and stools) p.104, d.1910
153   STONE, H. AND SON. *New designs in furniture* (bedroom) folder and 6 sheets, nd.
154   STONE, H. AND SON. *New designs in furniture* (sideboards, tables and bookshelves) folder and 7 sheets, nd.
155   STONE, H. AND SON. *Sideboards and dressers*, folder and 13 sheets, nd.
156   STONE, H. AND SON. *Revised prices* (price list) folded sheet, d.1916

BARNSTAPLE

139   SHAPLAND AND PETTER. *Bureaux and writing tables for boudoir or drawing rooms*, p.8, nd.
140   SHAPLAND AND PETTER. *General furniture* (domestic) p.262, nd.
141   SHAPLAND AND PETTER. *High class furniture* (domestic and fancy) p.161, d. *c.*1914
142   SHAPLAND AND PETTER. *High class furniture* (china cabinets and bookcases) p.21, nd.
143   SHAPLAND AND PETTER. *High class furniture* (hall, bedroom and cabinets) p.21, nd.
144   SHAPLAND AND PETTER. *Revolving boockases cabinet bookcases and magazine stands*, p.8, nd.
145   SHAPLAND AND PETTER. *Sideboards and buffets* (superior) p.14, nd.
146   SHAPLAND AND PETTER. *Tile top tables*, p.20, nd.
147   SHAPLAND AND PETTER. *Wall cabinets, smokers, cupboards, bookshelves*, p.9, nd.
148   SHAPLAND AND PETTER. Tables, bureaux and bookstands (various) four sheets, nd.
149   SHAPLAND AND PETTER. Tables, bedroom suites (various) 3 sheets, nd.

BATH

121   BATH CABINET MAKERS. Catalogue – sideboards, tables and chairs, p.48, nd.

138   POLLOCK, M. Price list for extending dining tables, 3 sheets, d. *c.*1913

BIRMINGHAM

125 HOSKINS AND SEWELL. *Metallic bedsteads, cots etc*, p.90, nd.

126a HOSKINS AND SEWELL. Metallic bedsteads and frames, 4 sheets, d.1912

126b HOSKINS AND SEWELL. *The 'Fordan-Lloyd' patent hospital bed*, single sheet, nd.

260 NEEDHAM, W. F. *The original patent musical resonating gongs*, p.10, d.1908

158 WALES LTD. *Couch beds* (convertible and folding) p.15, nd.
159 WALES LTD. *Folding card tables*, single sheet, nd.

BRADFORD

96 PRATT, C. AND SONS. *Patent compressible dining tables*, pamphlet, nd.
97 PRATT, C. AND SONS. *The Bradford desk* (patent writing bureau) folded leaflet, nd. [2 copies]
98 PRATT, C. AND SONS. *Illustrated catalogue of furniture and furnishings* (mainly domestic) p.301, d.1901
99 PRATT, C. AND SONS. *Illustrated catalogue of domestic furniture*, 2nd ed. p.86, nd.
100 PRATT, C. AND SONS. *Illustrated catalogue of furniture, upholstery, carpets. etc*, p.69, d.1905, [4 copies]
101 PRATT, C. AND SONS. *Attractive furniture* (domestic and fancy) p.24, nd. [2 copies]
102 PRATT, C. AND SONS. *Some suggestions for the house* (mainly fancy) p.35, nd.
103 PRATT, C. AND SONS. *Prices and details* (household and novelties) p.11, d.1912
104 PRATT, C. AND SONS. *The choice of floorcoverings* (carpets, linoleum and sundries) p.12, d. *c.*1923
105 PRATT, C. AND SONS. *'Tip-up' seating* (fixed or easily removable) p.16, d.1909 [2 copies]
106 PRATT, C. AND SONS. Loose pamphlets and sheets advertising novelties, presents, furniture etc, nd.
107 PRATT, C. AND SONS. *Grate ideas* (mantelpieces and fireplaces) p.10, d.1928
108 PRATT, C. AND SONS. *A critic on the hearth* (advice on fireplace schemes) p.8, nd.
109 PRATT, C. AND SONS. *An illustrated description of the capabilities of an experienced furnishing house* (Pratt's work) p.120, nd. [2 copies]
110 PRATT, C. AND SONS. *Interiors* (examples of Pratt's furnishings) p.158, nd.
111 PRATT, C. AND SONS. *Hints on furnishing* (guide to householders) p.85, d.1894
112 PRATT, C. AND SONS. *Photograph album* (room interiors) nd.
113 PRATT, C. AND SONS. Collection of photographs of household furniture, nd.
114a PRATT, C. AND SONS. *Artistic furniture* (photograph album) p.28, nd.
114b PRATT, C. AND SONS. Various postcards, blotters, advertisements and misc. ephemera
115 PRATT, C. AND SONS. Business letters and estimates received by Pratt, d.1909–15
116 PRATT, C. AND SONS. Folder containing articles on history of Pratts

BRISTOL

296 OSBORNE, J. *Chairs and settees* (upholstered) p.50, nd.
297 OSBORNE, J. *Designs in chairs* (and firecurbs) p.48, nd.

CHIPPING, Lancashire

122 BERRY, H. J. AND SONS. *Nett trade price list* (chairs inc. Windsor) pamphlet and single sheet, nd.

GLASGOW

298 MACFARLANE AND CO. *Furniture specialities* (household and invalid) p.77, nd.
299 MACFARLANE AND CO. *Furniture specialities* (domestic) p.102, nd.
300 MACFARLANE AND CO. *New art furniture specialities* (folding, revolving etc) p.30, nd.
132 MCPHUN, J. P. *Illustrated price list* (chairs, stools, tables and fancy etc) p.107, d.1911
133 MCPHUN, J. P. *Illustrated price list* (chairs, stools, tables and fancy etc) p.111, d.1913
134 MONTGOMERY BROS. AND MCLENNAN. Catalogue 'A' – chairs, babychairs, music stools etc., p.71, nd.
135 MONTGOMERY BROS. AND MCLENNAN. *Baby chairs, base rockers, music stools etc*, p.54 d.1911 [2 copies]

GLOUCESTER

120 BARTLETT, BEDWELL AND JONES. *Furniture for the home* (tables, chairs and bookcases) p.12, nd.

HALIFAX

119 ARCHER AND TEMPEST. *Occasional tables etc* (plant stands and music stools) p.24, nd.

HAYES

164 'X' CHAIR PATENTS CO. *The 'X' folding tables and sundry specialities* (chairs, swings etc) p.8, nd.
166 'X' CHAIR PATENTS CO. *Specialities* (folding, camping, garden and kitchen furniture) p.28, d.1912
167 'X' CHAIR PATENTS CO. *Catalogue of specialities* (folding, camping, garden and kitchen furniture) p.37, d.1911

HIGH WYCOMBE

65 BIRCH, W. *Chairs, settees and cabinet goods* (domestic) p.43, nd.
66 BIRCH, W. *Easy chairs* (upholstered) p.13, nd.
67 BIRCH, W. *Easy chairs and settees – booklet 21* (upholstered and tables and dining room suites) p.16, nd.
68 BIRCH, W. *Easy chairs and settees* (upholstered) p.16, nd. [2 copies]
70 BIRCH, W. AND SON. Dining room suites, folder, p.42, nd.
71 BIRCH, W. AND SON. *Furniture for the dining room* (and furnishing schemes) p.56, nd.
72 BIRCH, W. *Handsome presents* (chairs, stools, small tables, etc) p.8, nd.
73 BIRCH, W. *Inexpensive chairs and settees for the home and office* (and occasional tables) p.16, d.1911
74 BIRCH, W. AND SON. *Oak sideboards and dressers*, p.10, nd.
78 BIRCH, W. *Patent Reposo reclining chairs* (upholstered) p.11, nd.
79 BIRCH, W. *Settees, easy chairs and reclining chairs* (domestic upholstered) p.16, nd.
80 BIRCH, W. AND SON. Inlaid corner chairs and the Selbourne lounge, 2 sheets, nd.

81 COX, J. AND SON. *Antique chairs and settees from original examples*, p.16, nd.
82 COX, J. AND SON. *Chairs for public institutions* (wooden) folded sheet, nd.

83 GIBBONS, C. Plain and fancy chairs (40 designs) large illustrated sheet, nd. [2 copies]
84 GIBBONS, C. Plain and fancy chairs (56 designs) large illustrated sheet, nd. [2 copies]
85 GLENISTER, T. Catalogue – chairs, settees, stools etc (mainly domestic) p.87, nd.
86 GLENISTER, T. Drawing room chairs and music stools., p.16, nd.

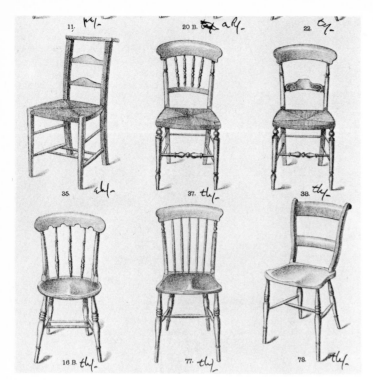

C. Gibbons, High Wycombe, *Plain and Fancy Chairs* [c.1910], detail from large trade sheet

87 HEARN BROS. *Illustrated catalogue of chairs* (and stools and settees) p.14, nd.

88 MEALING BROS. Wooden chairs and stools, single sheet, nd.

89 NORTH, B. AND SONS. *Catalogue of furniture* (mainly domestic) p.60, d.1915

90 SKULL, W. AND SON. *Catalogue of piano stools*, p.11, nd.
91 SKULL, W. AND SON. Catalogue of chairs, settees and stools, p.21, nd.

IPSWICH

162 WRINCH AND SONS. *The W & S folding card tables* (and chairs) folded sheet, d.1912–13 [2 copies]
176 WRINCH AND SONS. *Folding draught screens* (oak framed and wood panelled) folded sheet, d.1912–13 [2 copies]

KIRKCALDY

129 MCINTOSCH, A. H. *Artistic furniture* (domestic) p.85, nd.
130 MCINTOSCH, A. H. *Artistic bedroom suites of furniture*, p.16, nd.
131 MCINTOSCH, A. H. *Artistic bedroom suites in Sheraton, Chippendale and Jacobean styles*, p.8, d.1912.

LEEDS

92 DENBY AND SPINKS. *Beautiful homes* (carpets, linoleums, fabrics and furniture) p.32, nd.

93 LUPTON, J. *Sideboards, bedroom suites and bedsteads*, p.32, d.1913
94 LUPTON, J. General domestic furniture, p.30, d. *c*.1912

95 MARSH, JONES AND CRIBB. *Furniture and decorations* (domestic) p.16, d. *c*.1911

117 RAMSDEN, A. *Pianos, organs, harmoniums – Cat. A*, p.47, nd.

118 TOWLER, C. *The famous 'J' wood mantels*, p.16, nd.

LIVERPOOL

124 GRIFFITHS, J. D. *Sideboards and bedroom suites*, p.28, nd. [2 copies].

137 PLUMPTON, J. C. Illustrated chair advertisements, 3 sheets, d. *c*1912

LOCHWINNON, Renfrewshire

292 HAMILTON AND CRAWFORD. *Tea, club and boardroom chairs . . .* (and sofas) p.54, d.1901

293 JOHNSTONE, J. (Viewfield works) *Dining room chairs*, p.16, nd.
294 JOHNSTONE, J. *Catalogue* (various chairs and sofas) p.102, nd.

NOTTINGHAM
127 LACE WEB SPRING MATTRESS CO. *Marshalls Patent lace webb spring mattress*, folded sheet, d. 1915
128 LACE WEBB SPRING MATTRESS CO. *Frames* (and stuffover chairs, mattresses etc) p.28, d. *c*.1913

NEWCASTLE UPON TYNE

123 BOYD, J. J. AND SON. Catalogue of plain chairs, etc ('Ibex' brand) p.28, nd.

WOLVERHAMPTON

157 STROUD, R. AND SON. *List of restaurant and smoke room tables*, p.8, d. 1907

OFFICE FURNITURE

BRADFORD

221 PROBYN, H. *Perpetual ledgers and loose leaf account books* (loose-leaf box files) p.20, nd. [2 copies]

KIRKCALDY

237 MCINTOSCH, A. H. *Designs of office furniture* (chairs, tables, bookcases etc) p.20, nd.

LONDON

211 ALSTROM, C. *Britsim vertical letter filing cabinets*, folded pamphlet, nd.
212 ANGUS, W. *Roll-top and flat-top desks* (and boardroom tables etc) p.40, nd.
213 ANGUS, W. *'Gunn' sectional bookcase* (unit system) p.32, d.1907
214 ANGUS, W. *'Record letter and document filing cabinets*, p.32, nd.

75 BIRCH, W. *Office chairs* (and library and dining room) p.16, d.1913
76 BIRCH, W. *Office and library chairs* (including revolving) p.16, nd.
77 BIRCH, W. *Office and library chairs* (revolving, tilting etc) p.16, nd.

217 GLOBE–WERNICKE CO. *'Elastic' bookcases – Cat. No. 709* (unit system) p.32, d. 1912 [2 copies]

219 HOBBS, HART AND CO. *Patent bent steel body safes* (and doors, boxes, gates etc) p.23, nd.

220 MILNER'S SAFE CO. *Milner's safes* (and strong room equipment) p.68, nd.

222 RONEO LTD. *Modern methods of letter copying and letter filing* (copying machine) p.25, nd.

223 RONEO LTD. *Roneo Numeralpha filing system* (explanation system and equipment) p.16, nd.

224 RONEO LTD. *Price list of steel cabinets etc* (described in Cat. No. 796) folded sheet, d.1911

225 RONEO LTD. *Roneo cabinet supplies – price list no. 129* (stationery etc) p.7, nd.

226 SHANNON LTD. *Modern office furniture and fittings*, p.52, nd.

227 STANDARD DESK CO. *Standard desks* (mainly roll-top desks) p.33, d. 1911

228 STANDARD DESK CO. *Standard typewriter desks* (and cabinets and chairs) p.12, d.1910

229 STANDARD DESK CO. *Standard sectional bookcase* (unit system) large illustrated sheet, nd.

230 STANDARD DESK CO. *Trade price lists* (desks, chairs, cabinets etc) sheets, d.1911–13

231 STANDARD DESK CO. *Low priced desks*, large illustrated sheet, d.1912 [2 copies]

232 STOLZENBERG PATENT FILE CO. *Stolzenberg office specialities* (filing system and furniture etc) p.40, nd.

233 STOLZENBERG PATENT FILE CO. *Stolzenberg office furniture* (desks, tables and sundry) p.40, nd.

234 STOLZENBERG PATENT FILE CO. *Desks that really aid work* (and cabinets) p.12, nd.

235 STOLZENBERG PATENT FILE CO. *Stolzenberg filing system* (office equipment) p.8, nd.

236 STOLZENBERG PATENT FILE CO. *Office equipment* (filing system and desks etc) p.20, nd.

CANE, WICKER AND BAMBOO

BIRMINGHAM

136 NEEDHAM, W. F. *New designs in bamboo furniture* (domestic) p.44, d. *c*.1907

GRANTHAM, Lincolnshire

189 HARRISON, W. B. AND SONS. *Wicker and art cane furniture* (domestic and garden etc) p.107, nd.

LEICESTER

186 ELLMORE, W. T. AND SON. *'Aster' choice wicker and cane furniture* (cane, rush, upholstered etc) p.75, d. *c*.1912

187 ELLMORE, W. T. AND SON. *'Aster' furniture* (rush, wicker and misc.) p.16, nd.

188 ELLMORE, W. T. AND SON. Two photographs of upholstered cane chairs, nd.

183 PEACH, H. H. *'Dryad' cane furniture* (chairs, tables and stands) p.16, d.1913

184 PEACH, H. H. *'Dryad' cane furniture – new designs* (chairs and stands etc) folder, nd.

185 PEACH, H. H. *Presents bearing the Dryad mark . . .* (chairs, children's furniture and baskets) p.11, nd.

LONDON

192 SCOTT, G. W. AND SONS. *'Scotia' cane and wicker furniture* (garden etc) p.16, d. *c*.1912

291 BILL, H. *Designs of bamboo furniture* (domestic) p.32, nd.

NOTTINGHAM

193 ALBERT CANE WORKS. *'Stadium' cane furniture* (chairs) p.19, nd.

179 BALL, W. H. Rush, cane and wicker chairs and settees, p.25, nd.

180 DAY, E. A. *Newest designs in artistic cane and wicker furniture* (chairs and baskets) p.20, d.1908

181 DAY, E. A. *Cane and wicker furniture* (domestic and fancy) p.40, d.1911

182 DAY, E. A. *The Elite cane furniture* (chairs, settees and fancy) p.17, nd.

191a MORRIS, WILKINSON AND CO. *Art wicker furniture* (domestic) p.88, d.1913

191b MORRIS, WILKINSON AND CO. *The latest in up-to-date cane chairs*, large illustrated sheet, nd.

SOUTHPORT, Lancashire

190 MADEIRA CHAIR CO. *Madeira furniture* (chairs and tables) p.10, nd.

GARDEN AND SEASIDE

The New Safety Hammock Chair fitted with Patent Holdfast (with Canopy fitted).

E. Atkins, London, *Folding Garden Furniture*, 1912; 'Hammock chair fitted with the Patent Holdfast Clutch', price 8/4d.

HAYES

165   THE 'X' CHAIR PATENTS CO. *The 'X' superior garden furniture* (chairs, tents, tables, etc) p.8, d. *c.*1912

IPSWICH

160   WRINCH AND SONS. *Folding chair and tent list – no. 1150* (deckchairs, tables, seats etc) p.40, d. 1912
161   WRINCH AND SONS. Folding chair and tent list – *no. 132* (deckchairs, tables, seats etc) p.40, d.1913
163   WRINCH AND SONS. *Folding chair and tent list no. 138* (price list) folded sheet, d.1914

LONDON

7   ATKINS, E. *Folding garden furniture – no.98* (chairs, tents, beds etc) p.40, d.1911
8   ATKINS, E. *Folding garden furniture – no.108* (chairs, tents, beds etc) p.44, d.1912

BILLIARD TABLES

LONDON

198   BURROUGHES AND WATTS. *Price list 1889* (tables, accessories and sundries) p.74
199   BURROUGHES AND WATTS. *Revised catalogue 1905* (room designs and tables, and accessories) p.92
200   BURROUGHES AND WATTS. *Sundries list* (billiard accessories) p.74, d.1905
201   BURROUGHES AND WATTS. *Section I. Billiard tables, full size* (room designs, description and prices) p.40, d.1906
202   BURROUGHES AND WATTS. *Section III. Billiard table cushions and pockets*, p.8, d.1906
203   BURROUGHES AND WATTS. *Section V. Seats, surrounds and covers: portable billiard rooms etc.*, p.16, d.1906
204   BURROUGHES AND WATTS. *Section IV. Lighting* (gas and electric pendants etc) p.16, d.1906
205   BURROUGHES AND WATTS. Billiard cabinets, spirit cabinets, parquet flooring and panellings, p.6, nd.
206   BURROUGHES AND WATTS. *The game beautiful* (history of billiards and price list of equipment) p.32, nd.
207   BUSSEY, C. G. *Billiard tables, bagatelle tables and indoor games*, p.32, nd.

208   EDWARDS, G. *Billiard and bagatelle tables* (and accessories) p.72, d. *c.*1906

MANCHESTER

209   ORME AND SONS. Undersized and semi-billiard tables (and bagatelle board) p.8, nd.
210   ORME AND SONS, Billiard tables – different period designs, 3 sheets, nd.

INVALID

ILKLEY, Yorkshire

241   ROBINSON AND SONS. *Patent invalid couches* (and chairs, rests, supports etc) p.48, d.1897

LONDON

238   CARTER, J. AND A. *Invalid and surgical furniture and appliances*, p.208, d.1910

239   FOOT, J. AND SON. *Foot's rests for rest and other comforts* (adjustable chairs and reading stands) p.16, nd.
240   FOOT, J. AND SON. *Foot's wheel chairs* (self-propelling, adjustable and reclining) p.15, d.1905

253   THONET BROS. *Invalid appliances* (chairs, walking sticks and sofa) single sheet, nd. [2 copies]

UTILITY

194   BOARD OF TRADE CATALOGUE. *Utility furniture* (domestic) p.48, d.1947

195   *The Cabinet Maker – Utility furniture guide, 3rd edition* (British manufacturers and products) p.328, d.1948
196   NORTHERN FURNITURE TRADES FEDERATION. *Buyer's guide to utility furniture, 2nd edition*, p.96, d.1947
197   NORTHERN FURNITURE TRADES FEDERATION. *Buyer's guide to utility furniture, 3rd edition*, p.96, d.1947

BENTWOOD AND FOREIGN

AUSTRIA

245   KOHN, J. AND J. *Kohn's A1 Austrian bentwood furniture* (chairs) large illustrated sheet, nd. [2 copies]
246   KOHN, J. AND J. Bentwood furniture (chairs and hat stands) 5 sheets, nd.
247   KOHN, J. AND J. *Wholesale nett price list* (domestic) folded sheet, d.1911

248   'MUNDUS' UNITED AUSTRIAN BENTWOOD FURNITURE MANUFACTURERS. *'Mundus' bentwood furniture, 5th edition*, p.12, nd.

249   THONET BROS. Bentwood furniture (export catalogue in six languages and price list) p.156, d.1904
250   THONET BROS. *Nett wholesale trade price list* (bentwood furniture) leaflet, 4 pages, d.1908
251   THONET BROS. Catalogue – bentwood chairs, stools and novelties, p.18. d.1908 [3 copies]
252   THONET BROS. *Wholesale nett price list of stock patterns*, folded page, d.1911
254a   THONET BROS. *Reproductions of old English styles* (bentwood chairs) single sheet, nd.
254b   THONET BROS. Bentwood chairs and stools (including rockers) single illustrated sheet, nd.

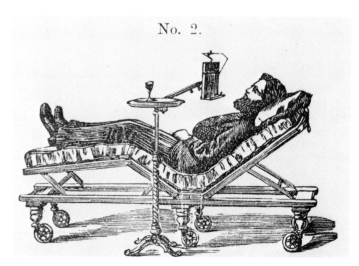

Robinson & Son, Ilkley, *Invalid Couches*, 1897; the catalogue quotes many testimonials from doctors and clergymen

GERMANY

242 FRITSCHE, H. *Feine holzwaren und luxusmöbel* (domestic) p.48, d. *c.*1904
243a FRITSCHE, H. *Feine holzwaren und luxusmöbel* (domestic and clocks etc) p.48, d. *c.*1908
243b FRITSCHE, H. *Price list 1908* (domestic) p.13, d.1908
244a FRITCHE, H. Fancy furniture (sculpture stands and bookcases) large illustrated sheets, nd.

LONDON

244b BENTWOOD FURNITURE CO. Bentwood furniture (chairs, settees and stands) single sheet, nd.

SWEDEN

215 ATVIDABERGS SNICKERIFABRIK. *Baltic office furniture* (mainly desks and cabinets) p.48, d.1910
216 ATVIDABERGS SNICKERIFABRIK. *Baltic office furniture requisits* (bookcases, cabinets etc) p.21, nd.

USA

270 BERLIN MACHINE WORKS, WISCONSIN. *Berlin quality* (trade journal, Jan–Feb., 1916) p.16
272 FRIGIDAIRE LTD. *Frigidaire* (illustrated booklet advertising refrigeration) p.14, nd.

CHIMNEY FURNITURE AND METALWARES

BANBURY

265 STONE, H. AND SON. *Art Brass work* (mirrors, plate stands, coalboxes etc) p.137, d.1910
307 STONE, H. AND SON. *Artistic novelties in metal* (pots, boxes, ashtrays, vases etc) p.46, nd.

LONDON

255 CHAPMAN, G. H. *Heraldic armour for decorative purposes* (swords, daggers etc) display card, nd.

278 MELHUISH, R. *Catalogue of ironmongery, sanitary fittings etc*, p.256, d.1903

MANCHESTER

279 MORRISON, INGRAM AND CO. *Discount sheet for no.7 catalogue* (baths, sinks etc) single sheet, d.1914

PAISLEY

281 SHANKS AND CO. *Shank's plunge, spray and shower bath* (patent 'Perfecto' cast-iron bath) 2 sheets, nd.

STIRLING

271 CARRON CO. *Architect's catalogue* (grates and chimney furniture) p.276, d. *c.*1903
284 CHRISTIE AND MILLER. *Spark guards and fire screens*, single illustrated sheet, nd.

NOVELTIES AND MISCELLANEOUS

BIRMINGHAM

257 CRACKNELLS. *Smart and unique lines in slipper boxes* (wood and metal) single sheet, nd.

275 HALESOWEN CYCLE AND PERAMBULATOR CO. Catalogue of perambulators, toys, carriages etc. p.52, d.1913

GLOUCESTER

277 LISTER, R. A. *Lister's tubs for palms and shrubs* (and stands, garden seats and tables) p.47, d. *c.*1912

KEIGHLEY

280 MURTON AND VARLEY. *Anchor brand washers, mangles etc*, p.95, d.1909

LONDON

266 ATKINS, E. *Atcars – the worlds most famous baby carriages – no.96* (and accessories) p.40, d.1911
267 ATKINS, E. *Atcars – the best all round folding baby carriage on the market, no.104* p.48, d.1912
268 ATKINS, E. *The 'Bethneena' car* (steel folding pushchair) p.16, nd.

168 BATSFORD, B. *English decoration and furniture* (by F. Lenygon and M. Jourdain) illustrated prospectus, p.16, d.1922

256 CHAPMAN, SON AND CO. Catalogue novelties (suitcases, bags, picnic baskets etc) p.72, d.1903

258 FAUDELS LTD. *Xmas and winter wares* (novelties, jewellery, workboxes etc) p.152, d.1912

276 KENT, G. B. AND SONS. *Best British brushes*, p.126, nd.

261 LESSER, S. AND SONS. *Art jewellery, gold, silver and diamond goods – list B* (toilet sets, cutlery etc) p.219, nd.
262 LESSER, S. AND SONS. *Leather goods, perfumery, picture albums etc – list E*, p.96, nd.
263 LESSER, S. AND SONS. Novelties (mainly silver and metalwork) 8 sheets, nd. [2 copies]
264a LESSER, S. AND SONS. *Special lines in our musical instrument department* (gramaphones) large illustrated sheet, nd.
264b LESSER, S. AND SONS. 19 sheets of designs for a variety of fancy goods, nd.

282 UNDERWOOD, J. AND SON. *Monumental and ecclesiastical art* (cemetery and church memorials) p.75, nd.

SOWERBY BRIDGE

273 ELGIN, W. P. *Special lines 1912–13* (suitcases and trunks) large folded illustrated sheet.
274 ELGIN, W. P. *'Globe' trunks 1912–13* (coloured designs – trunks, bins and boxes) large folded sheet

UNIDENTIFIED

288 C. V. AND S. Chair and table designs (novelty sheets – domestic) p.38 d.1900

289 G. P. C. AND CO. L., *'Selbat' dining tables* (various styles) p.15, d.1905

295 J. AND J. G. B. *Modern dining room and drawing room suites*, p.40, nd.

301 M. AND A. L. *Catalogue of inexpensive household furniture*, p.48, d.1907
302 M. AND A. L. *Catalogue of inexpensive furniture* (domestic) p.95, nd.
303 M. G. AND CO. *Novelties in artistic furnishing* (household and invalid) p.70, nd.
304 M. S. Novelty – rocking and armchairs, 11 sheets, nd.

305 O. A. B. F. W. CO LTD. *Oak furniture* (domestic and panelling) p.64, nd

306 S. C. AND CO. F. *New designs of oak furniture* (domestic) p.23, nd.

313 W. T. AND S. *The 'Resta' table* (patent adjustable bed and library table) pamphlet, nd. [5 copies]
314 W. T. AND S. *Modern metalwork – season 1911–12* (chimney furniture) p.71, d.1911
315 W. T. AND S. *Table gongs, bracket gongs, floor gongs* (sectional catalogue) p.15, d.1909
316 W. T. AND S. *Plate stands, trivets and afternoon tea stands* (sectional catalogue) p.7, d.1909

ANONYMOUS

311 WHITE ENAMEL. *Bedroom furniture in white enamel – no 12*, p.40, nd.
312 WHITE ENAMEL. Untitled catalogue – bedroom furniture, p.34, nd.
335 WHITE ENAMEL. White enamel bedroom suites, 4 sheets, nd.

317 UNKNOWN. *Drawing room, dining room and library chairs*, p.20, d.1908
318 UNKNOWN. *Furniture, mirrors, mantelpieces etc* (domestic) p.40, d.1910 [2 copies]
319 UNKNOWN. *Hall furniture* (stands, benches and chairs) p.45, nd.
320 UNKNOWN. *New designs of bedsteads in Sheraton and other styles*, p.50, nd.
321 UNKNOWN. *Overmantels, cabinets, fancy tables, etc – no.4*, p.28, d.1905
322 UNKNOWN. *Overmantels, looking glasses, etc*, p.13, nd.
323 UNKNOWN. *Oxford oak* (tables, desks and bookcases, etc) p.19, nd.
324 UNKNOWN. Designs for bedroom suites, sideboards, hall furniture etc, p.16, nd.
325 UNKNOWN. Catalogue of dining room chairs, p.31, nd.
326 UNKNOWN. Designs for bedroom and kitchen furniture, p.12, nd.
327 UNKNOWN. General domestic household furniture, p.32, nd.
329 UNKNOWN. *Bent oak chairs*, single page, nd.
330 UNKNOWN. *The 'Cadenza' gongs*, single sheet, nd.
331 UNKNOWN. Various chairs. 5 sheets, nd.
332 UNKNOWN. *Furniture in Jacobean style*, single sheet, nd.
333 UNKNOWN. *The 'Overland' folding trouser press* (Watts's patent) 3 sheets, nd.
334 UNKNOWN. *Savonarola chair* (reproduction of Florentine original) single sheet, nd.
336 UNKNOWN. Bedroom furniture, 6 sheets, d.1912
337 UNKNOWN. Office chairs and stools, 2 pages, nd.
338 UNKNOWN. Chairs, tables and stools, folded sheet, nd.
339 UNKNOWN. *Pillow back chair, the 'Kelmscott' lounge, and pillow back settee*, 3 sheets, nd.
340 UNKNOWN. Set of 6 booklets illustrating carpets in a folder, d.1914
341 UNKNOWN. Designs for carved chests, folded sheet, nd.
342 UNKNOWN. 2 display cards – coloured designs for carpets and curtains, nd. (French)

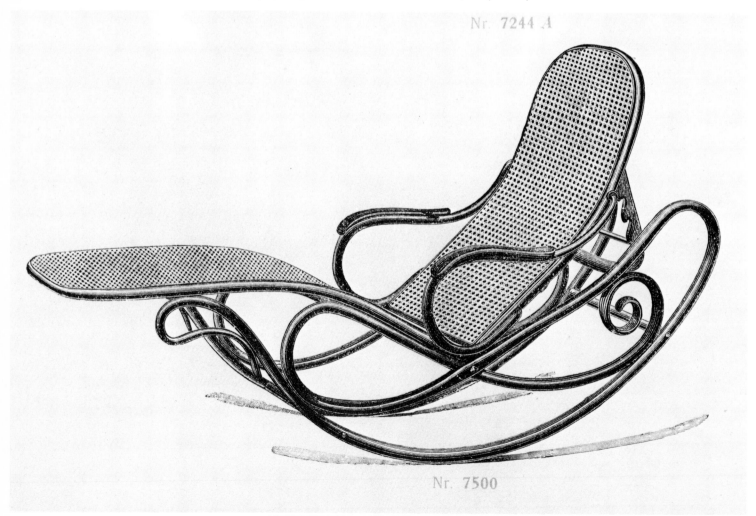

Nr. 7244 A

Nr. 7500

Thonet Bros, Austria, *Bentwood Furniture Catalogue*, 1904 (in six languages); rocker, price 65/–

INDEX

The index is principally of names, but does not include the firms represented in the Pratt collection of furniture trade catalogues since they are listed alphabetically on pp. 503–10. The term 'cabinet maker' is employed to describe general furnishers; workmen who signed items are identified as 'journeymen'; the names occurring on clock movements are assumed to belong to repairers and those found on pianos are recorded as 'piano maker(?)' unless clearly belonging to the manufacturer or a tuner. Page numbers are given in italics, all other numbers refer to catalogue entries.

Abbot Hall, Cumbria 125
Aberford Almshouses, Yorks *414–5*
Acomb House, York 28
Adam, Robert, architect/designer 452
Adams Acton, Murray 646
Adlin & Hassall, wallpaper makers 661
Airedale, Lord 104
Aldby Hall, Yorks 4
Allard, J., *ébéniste* 570
Allen, Richard 397
Allerton Park, Yorks 561
Alnwick Castle, Northumberland 447, 521a
Alstrom, C., cabinet maker 243
Althorp, Northants 429
Ambler, John 248, 338
Amedros, metal engraver 213
Ams, A., clock repairer 209
Antes, John, inventor 349
Antoinette, Marie 209, 564
Arbuthnot, Mrs J. E. 378
Arlington Street, No.19, London 46
Armley House, Leeds 32, 89, 285, 349, 431
Armorials and heraldic devices
    Bellot 37
    Berchere 462
    Boissier 462
    Connock 69
    Conyers 47
    Cooper 236
    Crewe (Marquess) 419
    Dronsfield 3, 6, 231
    Fitzwilliam 231
    France 178, 566, 645
    Gascoigne 1
    Hapsburg 571
    Irwin (Viscount) 93
    Jackson 100
    Jenkins 246
    Leeds, (Duke) 322–3
    Mann 236
    Mills 464
    Pinillos 603, 605
    Pitfield 464
    Popeley 6
    Unidentified 15, 261
    Wentworth 3, 231
Armour Trust 260
Arniston House, Scotland 545
Arondeaux, medalist 545
Arundale, Richard 561
Ashmolean, Oxford 426, 429
Aske Hall, Yorks 46, 453
Aspinall, John 96, 511

Astley Hall, Lancs 233
Astor, The Hon. Michael 353
Athelhampton Hall, Dorset 564
Atkinson, Henry, cabinet maker *414*
Auckland Museum, New Zealand 59
Audubon, John James, artist 295

Bachen, architect 574–5
Baert, I., tapestry weaver 45
Baildon Lodge, Yorks *394*, 521a–n
Baily & Jackson, silk weavers 483
Baker, Sir Herbert, architect 596
Baldock, Edward H., cabinet maker/ dealer 395
Balfour, Earl of 545
Balgownie House, Aberdeen 271
Ballinclea, Ireland 213
Bamford, Francis 271
Barber, Cattle & North, clock retailers 220
Barbon Church, Yorks 232
Barclay-Harvey, Lady Muriel *13*, 156, 276, 336, 357, 587
Barker, A., cabinet maker *414*
Barker, David 209
Barnard, Lord 39
Barraclough, John, clock maker 216
Barrow, journeyman 497
Bassetsbury Manor, Bucks 359
Barstow, Mrs N. 378
Barton, Humphrey, Tunbridge ware mfr 477
Barton, Thomas, Tunbridge ware mfr 480
Bealing, Richard, chair maker 23
Beckett, Sir Gervase 433
Behrens, The Hon. Mrs Clive 438
Belfast Children's Hospital 350
Bell, J., snr., journeyman 521g
Bellaigue, Geoffrey de 395, 561
Bellot family 37
Beloudy, Joseph, organ builder 39
Beningbrough Hall, Yorks *13*, 12
Bennett, John, globe maker 245
Bentall, Ruth 423
Benton, W. J., piano maker(?) 295
Bequests of furniture to Leeds, see also Gifts
    Burniston, Walter H. 202
    Brotherton, Charles 333, 645
    Gott, Mrs Frank 14, 32, 62, 89, 147, 153, 285, 349, 428, 431, 458, 482
    Holland Child, Dr C. 162
    Hughes, Dr G. S. 633
    Jackson, Wilfred 100
    Kitson Clark, Mrs Ina 209
    Lupton, Agnes and Norman 22, 31, 44, 86, 90–2, 110, 154, 208, 247, 252, 254–5, 273, 278, 286, 303, 307, 335, 385, 388, 417, 425, 434, 441, 455, 481, 488, 593
    Martin, Sir George 28, 30, 65–7, 85, 95, 97, 119, 219, 234, 238, 272, 318, 362, 393, 401, 404, 415, 439, 549
    McGrigor Phillips, Mrs D. U. 293, 320, 568–9
    Murphy, Mrs Dorothy 155
    Oxley, Henry 590
    Read, Miss Emma 145, 232
    Savery, Frank 60, 63–4, 70, 81, 83, 88, 113, 257–8, 284, 315, 360–1, 373, 403, 459, 647–8

Schofield, David Dunstan 274, 356, 358–9, 384, 387, 406, 429, 475, 490, 493
    Tolson, Roger W. 205
    Wilson, Sam *11*, 42, 84, 226–9, 329, 344–5, 365–8, 386, 391–2, 435, 456–7
Bérain, Jean, designer 209
Best & Rloyd, founders 138
Beurdeley, A. E. L., *ébéniste* 570
Bevan, Charles, designer 40, 297, *394*, 521a–n
Beverley, Yorks 18
Bidder, George Parker 209
Bing, S., retailer, Paris 378
Birch, William & Co., cabinet makers 111, 116, 378
Bircklé, Jacques, *ébéniste* 563
Birmingham Museums and Art Galleries 209, 398, 510
Bisseker, Henry, founder 139
Blake, G. E. 349
Boconnoc House, Cornwall 223a
Bodley, G. F., architect *408*, 484, 522–34
Boissier family 462
Bolton Percy Church, Yorks 18
Borthwick-Norton family 222
Bosse, Abraham, engraver 19
Boston, G. S. 326
Boughton House, Northants 324
Boulle, André-Charles, *ébéniste* 548
Boulton, Matthew, ormolu maker 209, 510–13
Bowhill House, Scotland 395
Boynton Hall, Yorks 270, 300, 337, 347, 444
Bradford Art Galleries 58
Brahan Castle, Scotland
Bramhope Chapel, Yorks 18
Bramshill, Hants 69, 451
Brechin Castle, Scotland 271
Bretton Hall, Yorks 3, 6, 15, 146, 231, 235
Brew & Co., cabinet makers 105
Bridge House, Bury 198
Bridgens, Richard 395
Brighton Art Gallery 125, 172
Brinkburn Priory, Northumberland 268
British Museum 378
Britism Desk 243
Broadwood, John & Son, piano makers 295
Brooking, Miss Blanche 38
Brooks, J., piano maker (?) 297
Brooks, The Hon. Marshall 150
Brotherton, Lord 13
Broughton Hall, Yorks *376*, 418, 501, 502
Brown, Richard, inventor 412
Brudenell, J. R. 586
Bruern House, Oxon 353
Buccleuch, 5th Duke of 395
Buckingham, Dukes of 209
Buckingham Palace 96
Buckley, J. W. 125–6, 172, 400
Bucknell, Alfred, metal worker 41
Building Research Establishment *464*
Bull, Arthur 222
Bullock, clock maker 213
Bulmer, J. E. 374
Burges, William, architect/designer 398
Burghley House, Lincs 46
Burke & Co., marble merchants 398
Burlington, Lord 300
Burns, T. G. 47

Burrell, Sir William *13*, 47
Burton Constable, Yorks 18, 306
Burton, Lord 224
Burton Park, Sussex 29
Bute, Lord 398

Cadogan, Earls of 348
Callot, Jacques, artist 395
Cambray, France 45
Cannon Hall, Yorks 327
Canons Ashby 363
Carley, Jonathan, clock maker 219
Carlisle Cathedral 231
Carlo Maratta frame *246*
Carlton House Terrace, London 580
Carlton Towers, Yorkshire 395
Carr Manor, Leeds 85, 401, 493
Carron Co. founders 165, 189–90
Carteret, Lady Sophia 426
Casteels, P., artist 300
Catherine the Great 571
Castle Howard, Yorks *13*
Castletown, Ireland 29, 209
Castlewellan, Ireland 29
Cave Brown Cave collection 37
Chadwick, Dr 335
Chalut, A., clock repairer 209
Chamberlain, Digby 261
Chambers, Sir William, architect 275
Chane, Ricardo a Armando 511
Channon, John 79, 222
Charlecote Park, Warwiks 395
Cheetham, Joseph, clock maker 217
Cheltenham Art Gallery 41
Cheltenham Parish Church 117
Chesterfield, Earl and Countess of 12
Chiddingstone Castle, Kent 336
Chippendale, Thomas *12*, 9–10, 69, 72, 74, 76, 222, 239, 355, 427, 433, 452
Cholmeley, Sir Hugh 71
Cholmondeley, Marquess of 57
Christ Church, Oxford 49
Chrysler, Walter P., junr 353
Cipriani G. B., artist 467
Claremont Nursing Home, Leeds 287
Clark, Commander 69
Clark, James & Eaton, glass merchants 408
Clay, Charles, clock maker 209
Cleland & Patterson, cabinet makers 340
Cliff, W. H. 65
Clifton Castle, Yorks 5, 330
Cluny, Hotel de 533
Cobb, John, cabinet maker 337, 347
Cobham, Viscount 353
Collier, cabinet maker 237
Collins, William & Son, cabinet makers 97
Collinson & Lock, cabinet makers 104
Collinson, G. F., piano maker (?) 521a
Colman, Sir Jeremiah 560
Cologne Cathedral 144
Colt, Sir Thomas 35
Colville, Colonel Norman 348, 383
Conisbrough Church, Yorks 18
Connock, Nicholas 69
Connock-Marshall, William 69
Constantine & Co., cabinet makers 287
Conyers, Lady Anne 47
Conyers, Sir William 47
Cooper, H. W., journeyman (?) 84

Cooper Union Museum 239
Copland, Henry, designer 265
Coppinger Prichard collection 73
Corsham Court, Wilts 250
Cossow, piano maker (?) 295
Courcy, The Hon Mrs J. de 79
Court, J. P., carver 343
Courtice, piano maker (?) 297
Coventry, Earl of 46, 452
Cowtan & Sons, fabric retailers 487
Crewe, Marquess of 419
Crichton, David 571
Crockett, metal gilder 213
Croome Court 46, 452
Crossley, Catherine, *394*, 521a–p
Crowbank, Leicester 41
Crozier family 566
Crucifix, John, clock maker 202a
Culford Hall, Suffolk 348
Culver, metalwork engraver 213
Cunard, Lady 363
Cuxhaven, Germany *413*

Dagenham Park, Essex 375
Dalkeith Palace, Scotland 395
Damson, A., clockmaker 565
Daneway workshop, Sapperton 41
Darcy family 47
Darley, Colonel G. 4
Darnley, Earl of 297
Darrington Hall, Essex 197
Dasson, Henri, *bronzier/ébéniste* 567, 570
David, *ébéniste* (?) 298
Davidson How, Mrs 40
Davis, journeyman 521k
Dawson, F., clock repairer 210
Day, marble worker 213
Dealers in Furniture
Adams, Norman 38
Afia, S. 352
Amor, Albert 74
Austins of Peckham 390
Beevers & Shaw 382
Bell, John 66, 224
Biggs of Maidenhead 37, 454
Bird, Douglas R. 646
Blairman, H. & Sons 25, 41, 53, 56, 58, 61, 69, 78, 96, 204, 237, 395, 427, 442, 512–14, 544, 571
Bulmer, G. L. 492
Butler, Market Deeping 586
Carey, Charles 33
Castro, Signor Ernesto di 586
Cook, A. 448, 451
Cooper & Launder 17
Cutter, W. D. 16
Dower House Antiques 372
Dowling & Bray 453
Edwards of Regent Street 448
Edwards, Thomas & Son *156*
Field, G. E. 442
Foot, H. C. 27, 75, 151, 311
Fowler, John 353
French & Co 61
Gibbs, Christopher 376
Gill & Reigate 579
Gillingham, P. H. 370, 469
Goldstone, M. & Son 18, 233
Gosling, Wilfred 299
Greenwood, F. W. & Sons 12, 261, 321, 381, 572

Hamilton, J. B. 481
Harrington, R. L. 325, 442, 586
Harris, M. & Sons 16, 223, 363, 416, 430
Harris, Solomon Myers 436
Harrods 646
Head, Sylvia 377, 396
Hill, Burgess 329
Holgate, Milton 471
Hotspur 37, 39, 59, 213, 299, 326, 374, 442, 445, 511, 565
Hus, Ole Haslund 204
Hutchinson, G. 290
Jellinek & Sampson 94
Jetley, G. 57, 336
Kelso 277
Kenrick, David 662
Knight, Leonard 39, 52, 88, 324, 353
Langdale, Mrs., Market Weighton 410
Lawson, George 333
Lee, R. A. 37, 309, 375, 445, 454
Lenygon & Morant 317
Lewis, J. A. & Son 256, 325, 571, 648
Litchfield & Co. 345
London Curio Club 392, 456
Loewi, Adolph 61
Lumb, Charles & Sons 118, 354, 546
Mallet & Son 69, 291–2, 336, 353, 359, 446–7
Marcussen, M. 264
Millar, Cecil 59, 326
Morrison, Robert 646
Nakaya Fine Art Curios 644
Needham, New York 353
Nyman Bros 37, 571
Ottrey, Dorchester-on-Thames 662
Parker, John 432
Partridge, F. & Sons 69, 213, 265, 322–3, 348, 364, 383, 447, 452, 462, 560, 561
Pelham Galleries 39, 61, 204, 565
Phillips & Harris 398
Phillips of Hitchin 48, 49, 57, 383
Powney, Christopher 653–9
Pratt & Sons *156*, 177, 197
Pratt, J. C. 180–1, 187, 189
Pratt, Stanley J. 442
Pratt & Burgess 117
Quality Wood Antiques *388*, 515–21
Ramus, L. 391
Rice & Christy 266, 325
Richards, W. T. 443
Sangiorgi, Galerie, Rome 589
Sellick Antiques, Exeter 69
Shrubsole, S. J. 426
Smith, Paul 374
Spanish Art Gallery 61
Sparks, John 634
Spero, 448
Spink & Son 69
Stair & Co 53, 59, 359
Stamford Properties, Ltd 586
Stokes, William 33, 52
Sutton, Thomas 365, 386, 457
Temple Williams 222
Thornton, Charles 119, 313, 450, 545, 550
Tweed, J. & W. 316
Waddingham, Walter 289, 314, 351, 353, 356, 359, 419, 426, 450
Walker, Frederick 570

Waters, William 101, 111, 346
Webster, Percy 214
West, A. J. 101
Wheeler, Herbert, E. 344
Wolff, J. J. 60, 284, 315, 360
Wolsey, S. W. 47, 50, 54, 152, 370
Woolstin 364
Young, William 58, 268, 271

Decoration, Subjects of, see also Armorials
Adam and Eve 536
Africa 514
Annunciation 536
Apollo 557
Ariadne 21
Arts 298
Asia 514
Astronomy 298
Atlas 529
Bacchus 543
Blackamoor 588
Britannia 217
Canephorae 586
Ceres 543
Charles II 19
Chinese fable (unidentified) 395
Christ the Good Shepherd 540
Circus acrobat 604, 606
Comedia dell' Arte 587
Crucifixion 212, 577
Daffodil pattern 489
David and Goliath 3
Diana and Apollo 209
Dove, emblem of peace 269
Dramatic poetry 298
Dream of Red Chambers 634
Drinking 208
Eagle 357
Espagnolette head 561, 586
Europe 514
Freemasonry 471
Friendship 71
Hagar and Ishmael 78
Harlequin 587
Hebe 186
Hercules 446
Hercules and Iole 167
Isaac, sacrifice of 536
Jester 24
Justice 188
Kirkstall Abbey 519
Learning 298
Love 567
Lyric poetry 298
Mary Magdalene 540
Mathematics 298
Mercy 188
Mercury 559
Muses, the Seven 209
Music 213, 453
Nativity 536
North wind 237
Playing cards 555
Prince of Wales feathers 89, 114, 431, 572
Resurrection 536
St George and the dragon 3
Samson with the jawbone 3
Sculpture 224
Serpent 357
Singeries 560

South wind 237
Spring 237, 321
Summer 237
Vigilance 186
William and Mary 545
Winter 551
Delafosse, J. C., ornamentalist 511
De Lorme, clock maker 559
Denston Hall, Suffolk 364
Denton Hall, Yorks *394*, 521a–p
Deramore, Lord and Lady 223, 416
Design Centre, The 409
Design Workshops, Ltd 408
Detroit, Art Institute of 511
Devonshire House, London 324
Dickenson, Major F. B. N. 299
Dieppe bonework 566
Digby, Lord 512
Dillon, Viscounts 446
Ditchley House, Oxon 446
Dixon, Miss D. M. 125–6, 172, 400
Dixon, J., journeyman 500
Dixey, G. &. C., barometer makers 2
Dobson, George & Son, furniture dealers 252
Doddington Hall, Lincs 269
Doe, Robert, statuary *154*
Downe, Viscount 69
Downes, Mr 558
Dropmore House, Bucks 223a
Drumlanrig Castle, Scotland 372, 395
Duesbury, William porcelain maker 213
Dumfries, Earl of 490
Duncan, clock maker 220
Duncan, Fox & Co. *463*
Duncombe, Sir George 223, 416
Dundas, Sir Lawrence 46, 459
Dundas, Thomas 46
Dunham Massey Hall, Cheshire 545
Dunn Gardner, A. C. W. 364
Dunns of Bromley, retailers 409
Duppa & Co, fabric retailers 487
Dutton, Sir John 324

East, Peter, clock maker 201
Eastlake, C. L., designer 101
Easton Hall, Lincs 71
Easton Neston Hall 426
Eaton Hall, Cheshire 419
Eborall, John, clock repairer 209
Ebury, Lord 372
Eddison, Harold T. 549
Edmonds, J., cabinet maker 440
Edwards & Roberts, cabinet makers 102
225, 395, 420, 555
Egerton, Admiral H. J. 433
Egerton, T. W. 508
Egter, Pieter, clock maker 549
Elliott, John C., clock maker 221
Ellis, John A. 346
Elsley, Thomas, founder 122–3, 125–6,
172, 182–5, 187, 189, 191, 343
Emsley, Miss E. K. 72
Enkhuizen, Mayor of, 551
Erad, Charles, cabinet maker 281
Erard, piano maker 297–8, 521a
Erard, Sebastian and Pierre, harp makers 294, 296
Escare, Burt, electric light mfr 133
Eskilsfunci, Sweden 204
Essex Institute, Salem 641

Euston Hall 336, 365
Evans, B., cabinet maker 5, 330
Everett, F. A., carver 662

Fairfax, The Hon. Mrs 28
Fardon, John 33
Farfield Hall, Yorks 157, 463, 466, 491,
554, 556, 567, 642
Farley, Major 326
Farmer, Edward 572
Farnborough Barn, Banbury 409
Farnley Hall, Yorks *13*
Farrington Hurst, Hants 26
Fauconberg, Earls of 275
Fauconberg, Lord 47
Fell, William, cabinet maker 46
Fenwick, Captain 268
Fernfield House, Bingley 144
Ferrand, Guy 48, 49
Ferrand, H. W. J. 48, 49
Ferrand, Thomas, cabinet maker 263
Ferry, Walter A. 548
Finch, John & Co, cabinet makers 482
Finel, piano maker (?) 298
Firle Place, Sussex 69
Fisher, Richard, carver 23, *154*
Fitz-Hugh, Major 631
Fitzwilliam, Earl 447
Fitzwilliam Museum, Cambridge 222
Flitcroft, Henry, architect/designer 446–7
Forbes, Duncan 271
Forbes, Colonel Ian 271
Fortescue family 223a
Foster, W. 260
Fothergill, John, ormolu maker 209,
510–13
Fountains Hall, Yorks 18
Fox, Duke 553
Framlingham church, Suffolk 31
Freeman-Smith, Ralph, decorator *155*,
379
Frick collection 224
Fulford, Frank H. 318
Furdezer, Z. clock repairer 209

Gainsborough, Thomas, painter 363
Galliers-Pratt, A. M. G. 275
Galloway, John, clock maker 218
Galton, Sir Douglas 114, 563
Galway, Viscounts 561
Garrowby, Yorks 45
Gascoigne, Sir Alvary *14–15*
Gascoigne, Sir Edward 45
Gascoigne, Elizabeth 296
Gascoigne, Gwendolen 144, 241
Gascoigne, Lady Lorna P. 51, 102–3, 225,
413–4, 555
Gascoigne, Mary Isabella 296
Gascoigne, Richard Oliver I, 296,
494–509
Gatehouse, John, cabinet maker 26
Gaudreau, Antoine, *ébéniste* 570
Gaunt, Mrs D. 638
George IV 96, 376
George, Mrs H. 151
Gersh, Martin 38, 365
Gibbons, Grinling, carver 299, 381
Gibbs, Matilda 237
Gibbs of Stavely, cabinet maker 20

Gifts of furniture to Leeds, see also Bequests

Abram, G. T. 221
Allendale, Viscount *13*, 3, 6, 15, 146, 231, 235
Andrews, C. A. 98–9
Askham, Mr. and Mrs. E. 207, 212
Beardsmore, Rev. John 421
Behrens, Mrs. Clive 465, 468–9, 472–4, 476–8, 480, 641
Bird, Mrs Florence 82
Blairman, Philip 58
Boult, Sir Adrian 594
Brotherton, Charles 45, 328
Burkett, Mrs A. H. 201
Burrell, Sir William 440, 460
Burton, Arnold 78
Burton, Sir Montague 45
Burton, Raymond 78
Burton, Stanley 78, 290
Carlton, Mrs E. C. 216
Cochrane, J. Peter W. 660
Cooke, Mrs Alfred and family 77, 308
Cooper-Abbs, Miss K. E. M. 467
Cresswell, Mrs M. B. 312
Curzon-Herrick, Mrs J. H. 5, 330
D'Arcy Hann, Dr 340
Farmery, Mrs R. 394
Fox Hunter, Miss M. 553
Fulford, Frank H. *12*, 20–1, 214, 224, 230, 242, 277, 318, 430, 470, 572
Garrett, Mrs H. 261
Gascoigne, Sir Alvary and Lady *14–15*, 1, 2, 8, 10, 43, 51, 68, 87, 102, 103, 106, 112, 114, 116, 127–30, 132–43, 161, 163–6, 173–4, 185, 188, 190–3, 195–6, 202a, 211, 220, 225, 240–1, 243, 249, 296, 319, 327, 334, 410, 412–14, 437, 461, 487, 494–509, 541, 547, 552, 555, 563, 576, 595–6, 631, 635–7, 639–40, 643–4, 649–52
Gaunt, Mrs E. 638
Goodricke, Rev. G. A. 9
Gorton, Mrs Olive Mary 521a–521p
Government, H. M. 26, 223a
Grey, Colonel 543
Halifax, Earl of (the Rt Hon E. F. Lindley Wood) xiii–xiv, 23–4, 36, 93, 108, 115, 122–3, 167, 182–4, 194, 200, 203, 215, 217, 245, 250, 279–80, 294–5, 301–2, 310, 379, 380, 522–34, 542, 551, 573, 577
Hamwee, Mr and Mrs Neville 61
Harvey, Edmund T. 559
Hawkyard, the Misses 104, 339
Hawkyard, Miss H. M. 199
Hobbins, Colonel and Mrs J. 244, 246
Hummerston, Miss E. 661
Jackson, Miss M. E. 420, 479
Karmel, Barbara 78
Kenworthy, Mrs A. 148
Kitson, Robert 582, 585, 589
Kyte, C. J. S. 297
Learmouth, Mrs Ivy, 105
Leigh, Mrs Blanche, 149, 331
Lumb, Charles & Sons, 510, 583
Martin, Lady 206, 248, 265, 269, 281, 283, 321, 338, 448, 451, 556, 560
Martin, Sir George 72, 282, 452, 561
Mexborough, Earl of 159, 176
Mlada, Miss Ludmila 19, 389

Myddleton, Mrs A. 13
Newton, Mrs Margaret 382
Nickols, Mrs M. 564
Parkinson, Frank 45
Peacock, H. P. 158
Pepper, E. and H. 148
Phaidon Press 574–5
Pratt, Christopher & Sons *503*
Pratt, Mrs Christopher 422
Price, Sir Henry 45, 322–3
Ramsden, Lady Margaret *463*, 597–630, 632
Rhodes, F. E. 454
Rishworth, Miss Amy 144
Roberts, Charles 157, 463, 466, 491, 554, 567, 642
Smith's, John, Brewery Co. 218
Smith, Samuel 405
Stokes, William 55
Symmonds, Alderman and Mrs S. 124
Taylor, Mrs K. 148
Tetley, F. E. 121, 450
Tugwell, Mrs Frank 29
Turberville, Mrs K. 350
Uttley, W. 210
Watson, the Hon Richard Mark 557
Gilbert, Sir Alfred, sculptor *154*, 368
Gilbert Barney, Mrs Joan 397
Giles, John, brass founder 117
Gillows of Lancaster, cabinet makers 5, 16–17, 29, 37, 42, *156*, 198, 226–9, 307, 331, 337, 366, *375–6*, 396, 435, 494–509,
Gimson, Ernest, cabinet maker 41
Glamis, Lady 47
Glasgow Art Gallery 47, 50
Glazier, Peter, designer 653–4
Gobelins, Musée des 46
Gobelins tapestry 46
Godwin, E. W., designer 661
Goodchild, John, clock maker 212
Goodison, Benjamin, cabinet maker 309
Goodricke, C. A. 9
Gori, F. A. 513
Gorton, Mrs Olive Mary 521a–p
Gott, Elizabeth 349
Gravelot, Hubert, designer 303, 310
Gray, Thomas, poet 32
Grendey, Giles, cabinet maker 61, 326
Grenville, William Wyndham, Bt 223a
Greuzav, L., clock repairer 204
Griffiths, Percival 58
Grimsthorpe Castle, Lincs 309
Gubbay, Mrs Hannah 322–3
Guibert, Philip, upholder 322–3
Guildford, Earl of 325
Guilsborough Grange, Northants 171
Gurk, Jos, clock repairer 209

Haas, brass worker 213
Hadley chests 233
Hadzor House, Worcs 563
Hagley Hall, Worcs 355
Hainsworth family 638
Halifax, Old Assembly Rooms 205
Hall Barn, Kent 209
Hallett, William cabinet maker *12*, 60
Hallifax, Joseph, clock maker 207
Hamilton Palace, Scotland 446, 546
Hamilton, W. G. 'Single-Speech' 426
Hamilton, Walter Kerr 426
Hampton Court Palace 351

Hampton Court, Herefordshire 283
Hanson, L., journeyman (?) 521b
Harding Fund 73, 94, 332, 375, 545–6, 646
Harding Rolls, Colonel J. C. E. 117
Hardware, maker's marks on Castors:
Auto Castor & Wheel Co Ltd 7
C B & ? 398
C & C Patent 390, 521e–f
Cope & Collinson 297
Cope's Patent 100, 479, 519, 521n
Loach & Clarke's Patent 412
Yates & Hamper 394
Hinges:
Baldwin 319
C C & Co 642
Hornes Patent 521k–n
Huxley & Ching 235
Rodgers Patent 534
Tibats, H. 386
Locks:
Barrons Patent 518
Bramah(s), I. 44, 235, 421
Chance Son & Co 422
Chubb & Co 41
Chubb & Son 534
Cope & Collinson 521d, f, k
F E (French) 562
J.D.B. & Co Ltd 433
Needs, J. T. 241, 421
Mordan, S. & Co 241
V R beneath a crown 516
Various fitments:
Copes 521d
Cope & Austin Patent 287, 517, 521f
Croft & Assinders Patent 421
F T (French handle) 560
Hinde's Patent 534
Taylors Patent 250
Walters Patent 421
Harewood, Earl of 427
Harewood House, Yorks *376*, 418, 427
Hardwick Hall, Derbys *115*, 372
Hardy, John, cabinet maker *15*, 408
Harris, H., cabinet maker 436
Harrison, A., cabinet maker 423
Harrowby, Earl of 38
Hasley Court, Oxon 375
Hassall, Samuel, cabinet maker 263
Hasius, Jacob, clock maker 549
Hawkyard, Dr Arthur 339
Heal, Ambrose, designer 346
Heal & Son, cabinet makers 8, 112, 346, 408–9
Heathcote, Ilkely 421
Heath Lodge, Hampstead 142, 188, 195
Heckmondwike Grammar School 297
Hedingham Castle, Essex 259
Henderson, piano tuner 295
Hendre, The, Wales 117
Henry VIII 231
Henry, Dr I. 423
Henry, J. S., cabinet maker 111
Henry, Thourenel, hurdy-gurdy maker 290
Hendy, Philip *12*
Hepplewhite, George, designer 89, 224, 248, 348
Herriard Park, Hants 26
Herron, piano maker 293

Hertford, Lady 279, 295
Hertford, Lord 570
Hesketh, Major Fermor 447
Heslington Hall, York 223, 416
Hickleton Hall, Yorks 119, 120, 260, 353, 450
Higgins, Cecil, Art Gallery 172
Higgs, Robert, clock maker 206
High Wycombe Museum 111
Hill, Mrs A. 171
Hill End, Bingley 144
Himbleton Manor, Worcs 114
Hindley, Henry, clock maker 200
Hirst, journeyman 521c
Hoare, Sir Richard 45
Hoare, Thos., journeyman 96
Hodges, John, clock maker 204
Hodgson, William, glass merchant 285
Hoguet, *horloger* 565
Holborn (pseudonym) 46
Holden, Mrs Alfred 205
Holland & Sons, cabinet makers 432
Holm Lacy, Herefordshire 12
Hooch, Pieter de, artist 542
Hoole, Henry, E. & Co, founders 181
Hooton Pagnell Hall, Yorks 30
Hope, Thomas, designer 569
Hopkinson family 148
Hornblotton House, Somerset 37
Hornby Castle, Yorks 47, 50, 160, 322–3
Horner, Albert, cabinet maker 407
Horovitz, Dr Bella 474–5
Horowitz, Mark 513
Horrocks, Mrs Leonora H. D. 284
Houghton Hall, Norfolk 57, 324
Howsham Hall, Yorks 269, 543
Hoyt collection 61
Hughes, H. B. L. 387
Huguenin, brass worker 213
Hummerston Bros, cabinet makers/ decorators 661
Hunt, Holman, artist 304
Hunt, John 363
Hunter, Joseph, antiquarian 6, 231
Hunzinger, A., clock repairer 209
Hutton Castle, Scotland 440, 460
Hutton, Timothy 5, 330

Ilkley church, Yorks 100
Ince & Mayhew, cabinet makers 250
Infantado, Duke of 16
Ingham & Sons, Wortley 185
Inscribed (maker's) initials, see also **Hardware marks**
    BR under a crown 326
    BVRB (French) 561
    EA 61
    EM 148
    EW 33
    FH 52
    FL (French) 561
    GJ IT 95
    HW 61
    IC 52
    IM 144
    IT 61
    IW 81, 92
    J.M.S. & Co (Textile) 487
    MW 61
    RB 54
    RP 53, 293

    SC under a crown (Grate) 185
    TT 326
    WK (1747) 108
    WP 151
    WvL 430
Irish furniture 29, 37, 213, 350, 449, 571
Irwin, Frances, Dowager Viscountess 93
Irwin, Henry, 7th Viscount 45, 310, 353

Jackson, journeyman 521h, 1
Jackson family of Leeds 100
Jackson & Graham, cabinet makers 101
Jacques, Maurice, tapestry designer 46
Jamaica 349
Jansen, *ébéniste* 298
Janz, B., clock repairer 209
Jenks & Holt, cabinet makers, 390
Jennens & Bettridge, papier-mâché makers, 320, *388*, 515–21
Jersey, Earl of 510
Jervoise family 26
Johnson, Thomas, carver/designer 268, 272, 355
Johnstone & Aitchison, restorers 224
Joiners' Company 71
Jones Collection 226–7
Jones, General 500
Jones, George Fowler, architect *415*
Joseph, Maxwell 53, 371, 424
Joubert, carver/smith 107, 249
Jowett, Alfred 34, 76, 118, 262, 283, 314, 546

Kahn, E. H. & Co, cabinet makers 321, 333
Keene, Henry, designer 426
Keene, Stephen, spinet maker 289
Keiller, Alexander 351
Kelwoolds Grove, Yorks 100
Kempe, C. E., designer 108, 123, 182, 343, 533
Kendell, John & Co, cabinet makers 418
Kennedy, Edgar 591
Kensington Palace, London 209, 322–3, 324
Kent, H.R.H., Duke of 265
Kent, William, architect/designer *154*, 300, 309, 324, 353, 363
Kenwood House, London 452
Kirkby Lonsdale Church, Yorks 232
Kirkdale Manor, Yorks 433
Kirkham Abbey, Yorks 13, 328, 333, 645
Kerridge, cabinet maker/restorer 239
Kiveton Hall, Yorks 322–3
Knole Park, Kent 156
Knowsley Hall, Lancs 570
Kohen, J. & J., bentwood furniture mfr *413*

Lady Lever Art Gallery 144, 276, 365, 646
Ladymead, Sussex 557
Lafontaine, Alfred de 564
Lamerie, Paul de, silversmith 462
Lamport Hall, Northants 447
Lancaster, Mrs C. G. 375
Lancaster Priory church 56
Langford, John, silversmith 464
Langley, Batty, architect/designer 37
Langlois, Pierre, cabinet maker 453
Langstaff 373

Lascelles, Edwin 427
Laverton & Co, cabinet makers 237
Lawson, Jon, journeyman 500
Lazcano, Castle, Spain 61
Leader, Mrs H. C. 364
Leandri, Pierre 27
Leatham, Edmund 51, 102–3, 225, 413–14, 555
Leathly church, Yorks 52
Leathly Hall, Yorks 239
Lebesgue, François, *ébéniste* 561
Lebus, H., cabinet makers 230
Ledston Hall, Yorks 168–9
Leeds Art Collections Fund *11*, 38, 46, 248, 290, 338, 348, 436, 443, 452, 556, 561, 570, 578–9, 581–2, 585, 589
Leeds Art Gallery *11*
Leeds, Dukes of 47, 50, 322–3
Leeds Fireplace Co. 192
Leeds Invalids' Kitchen 31
Leeds Museum 186
Leeds Town Hall 115
Leighton, Lord, artist 305
Lennox, Miss Jessie 350
Lennox-Boyd, A. T. 560
Le Noir, Etienne, *horloger* 565
Lenygon & Morant, cabinet makers/ decorators 107, 194, 379–80, 402
Lepaute, Jean-Baptiste, *horloger* 565
Levy, George 61
Liberty & Co, furnishers 334, 378
Lichfield, Earls of 446–7
Light, Edward, organist 291–2
Lindsey, Earls of 156, 276, 336, 357, 587
Linke, François, *ébéniste* 570
Linnell, John cabinet maker *12*
Linstrum, Derek 495
Little Rushwood, Yorks 95, 282
Liverpool, Lord 13
Llangattock, Lords 117
Lock, Matthias, carver/designer 265, 281, 310, 446
London, Museum of 209
Long & Dew, dial makers 213
Longman, John, piano maker 293
Lonsdale, Earls of 580
Lotherton Hall, ancestral furniture 7, 43, 68, 112, 116, 127–41, 143, 163–6, 173–4, 185, 190–3, 196, 202, 211, 220, 243, 249, 327, 334, 410, 461, 541, 552, 563, 567, 595–6, 631, 635–7, 639–40, 649–52
Lotherton chapel furnishings *413*
Lotherton, development as a museum *14–15*
Lotherton Endowment Fund 101, 111, 125–6, 172, 346, 400, 408–9
Loudon, J. C., designer 331, 341, 394
Louvet, Pierre, musical instrument maker 290
Lowther Castle 580
Lucy, George 395
Luff, Messrs D., furnishers 660
Lupton, Mrs 31
Lutyens, Edwin, architect/designer 421
Lyttelton, Lord 355

MacBraire, C. A. 89, 349
Madeley Manor, Staffs 419
Maine, Jonathan, carver 299
Makepeace, John, cabinet maker *15*, 409

Malahide Castle, Ireland 213
Malahide, Lord Talbot De 213
Malton, Thomas, designer 429
Manby family 201
Mango, Mr and Mrs 223
Mansfield, Earl of 452, 566
Manton, Lady F. C., 557
Marley Hall, Yorks 144
Marot, Daniel, designer 322–3, 546, 548
Marsh & Jones, cabinet makers 40, 297, *394*, 418, 521a–p
Marsh, Jones & Cribb, cabinet makers 84, 205, 365, 368, 421, 521p
Marshall, journeyman 297
Marshall, Mrs F. D. 282
Mason & Bandin, organ builders *414*
Mason & Hamlin, organ builders *414*
Martin, Benjamin, globe maker 245
Martin, C., piano maker (?) 297, 521a
Martin, Fred, French polisher 13
Martin, Lady, Bequest Fund 223, 383, 416, 544, 662
Martin, Paul, Ltd 281
Mawley Hall 275
McCallum & Hodson, papier-mâché mfrs *388*
McCreery & Son, spinning wheel makers 350
McGregor family 340
McGrigor Phillips, Mrs D. U. 19, 389
McKenzie-Clark, K. 557
Mekan Patent 196
Melbourne Art Gallery, Australia 57, 337
Mentmore Towers 229, 545, 565
Mereworth Hall 586
Merton Abbey 489
Metcalf, H., journeyman 442
Methley Hall, Yorks *13, 156*, 159, 175–6
Metropolitan Museum of Art, New York 46, 57, 61, 309, 446
Meynell, Hugo Charles 294
Meynell Ingram, The Hon Mrs E. C., 7, 24, 108, 122–3, 170, 182–4, 343, 399, *408*, 522–34, 540, 542, 551, 573, 576–7
Mexborough, Earl of 175
Mildenhall Manor, Suffolk 406
Miller, Sanderson, architect/designer 426
Mills, Thomas, cabinet maker 98–9
Milner Field, Yorks *394,* 521a–p
Milnes-Coates, Lady Celia 572
Minshall, Colonel T. H. 398
Mirecourt, France 290
Mitchell, John, cabinet maker 154
Molin, J. A., clock repairer 204
Moor Park, Harrogate 79, 354, 558
Moor Park, Herts 46, 372
Moor Crag, Cumbria 125–6, 172, 400
Moore, James, the Younger, cabinet maker 324
Mopherson, Robert 376
Moravians 349
Mordant Cope, Sir John 451
Morel & Seddon, cabinet makers 96, 376
Morgan, J. Pierpont 309
Morland Hall, Hants 48–9
Morpurgo, Joseph 551
Morris, Robert, architect 37
Morris, William, designer 489
Moscow 439
Mount Grace Priory, Yorks 467
Moyr Smith, J., decorator/designer 237

Moynihan, Lord 85, 401, 493
Mulliner, H. 239
Myers, Thos, journeyman 500
Naples, Royal Palace of 209
Nash, Joseph, artist 376
National Art-Collections Fund 45, 46, 398, 427, 452, 561
Neave, Sir Richard 375
Neilson, Jacques, tapestry weaver 46
Neville Holt, Leics 363
Newburgh Priory, Yorks *13*, 275, 510
Newby Hall, Yorks 46, 336
Newdigate, Sir Roger 426
Newman, Edward, cabinet maker 71
Newton Bros, carvers/decorators 280
Newton Hall, Cambs *388*, 515–21
New York 391
Nichols, Edwin, cabinet maker 114
Nicholson, P. and M. A. 5
Nightingale, Florence 241
Norfolk, Duke of 395
Norman & Burt, wood carvers, 123, 182, 343
Norris, Edward, clock maker 199
North, B. & Sons, cabinet makers 378
Northumberland, Duke of 521a
Norton, Claude 272
Norton Conyers, Yorks 47
Nostell Priory, Yorks 9, 148, 436
Nussey, Lady Theda, 95, 282
Nye, Edmund, Tunbridge ware mfr 480

Oakley, George, cabinet maker 389
Ogden, Thomas, clock-maker 205
Osborne House, Isle of Wight 432
Osler, F. & C., glass merchants 121
Oudry, J. B., artist 310
Over Wyresdale church, Lancs 233
Oxley Bequest Fund, 371, 424

Page, John, upholsterer 330
Palagonia, Villa of 586
Paris, Exhibition of 1900 298
Parker-Knoll, cabinet makers 662
Parker, Robert 144
Parker, Lady *388*, 515–21
Parlington Hall, Yorks 1, 2, 10, 106–7, 161, 296, 319, 412, *415*, 437, 494–509
Partridge, Claude A. 348
Pascall, James, carver 45, 353, 450
Patent Office 181, 378, 390, 487
Patent Silvering Co. 285
Pattison, journeyman 521e
Peach, Harry H. 41
Pearson, Alfred 46
Pelletier, John, cabinet maker 351
Penheale Manor, Cornwall 348, 383
Pergolesi, M., ornamentalist 454, 467
Perry & Co, light fitting mfr 120, 132–5
Peruvian furniture *463*
Peter, Alexander, cabinet maker 490
Peto, Sir Morton 209
Philadelphia Museum of Art 46, 355
Phillips, Hugh 60
Pigou, Mrs Georgiana 294
Pilkington, Dr H. O. 233
Pilgrim Trust 452, 561
Pinillos family 603, 605
Pitts, William, silversmith 475
Planta, John, cabinet maker 349
Plender, Lord 78

Plucknett, James, cabinet maker 237
Pole, Cardinal 231
Pomfret Castle, London 426
Pomfret, Earl and Countess of 426
Portsmouth, Earl of 277
Pother, Mrs G. 289
Powderham Castle, Devon 222
Powell, H. B. 26
Pratt, Christopher & Sons, cabinet makers 422
Pratt collection of furniture trade catalogues *503–10*
Price, Richard, chair maker 53
Priestley, Henry 288
Prior Park, Bath, 571
Puddleston Court, Herefordshire 35
Pugin, A. W. N. 96, 100, 376
Punnett, E. G., designer 111
Pyke, George, organ/clock maker 209

Rakusen, Philip 124
Ramsden, Lady Margaret *463*
Rapkin, G. H., piano maker (?) 521a
Ratcliffe, D. U., see McGrigor Phillips, Mrs D. U.
Ratee & Kett, cabinet makers *408*, 522–7
Rawlins, J. E., 299
Raynham Hall, Norfolk 324
Redcliff Hall, Scotland 545
Reid, Dame Clarissa *463*
Reid, Mrs Emma 558
Reid, James Guthrie *463*, 632
Reid, Robert 79, 354
Reid, William, journeyman 427
Rennison, C., clock factor 202a
Rhodes, Mrs William 891, 349
Richards, James, carver 309
Richardson, William, cabinet maker 243, *413*
Riesener, J. A., *ébéniste* 298
Rijksmuseum, Amsterdam 557
Risenburgh, Bernard II Van, *ébéniste 14*, 561
Rishworth, Thomas 144
Risso, John, barometer maker 1
Roade, James, cabinet maker 571
Robbins & Co, founders 195
Roberts, Charles 157, 556
Robins, John, silversmith 514
Robinson, Dr Arthur 312
Rockingham, Marquess of 447
Rogers, W. G., carver 381
Roland, clock repairer 210
Rollison, Dollif, clock maker 210
Rolls, John E. W. 117
Rosen Foundation, New York 61
Rosier, journeyman 96
Ross, J. 71
Ross, Sir David 46
Rotherhithe church 117
Rothiemay Castle, Scotland 271
Rous Lench Court, Worcs 47
Rousham Hall, Oxon 363
Royal Horological Institute 213
Royal Institute of British Architects 125–6, 172, 398, 548, 561
Rubin, Henry 213
Rufford Old Hall, Lancs 233
Russell Collection, Edinburgh 295
Russell, Gordon, cabinet maker 423
Rysbrack, John, sculptor 209

Saddlers' Company 33
St Clement Dane's Vicarage 259
St Dionis, Backchurch 117
St Pancras Ironworks 182
St Silas' Church, Leeds 661
St Vincent, Earl 339
St William's College, York 231
Salisbury Cathedral School 426
Salkeld screen 231
Salt, Gordon Locksley *394*, 521a–p
Salt, John *394*, 521a–p
Salt, The Misses N. K. and S. M. I. *394*
Salt, Titus, Jnr. *394*, 521a–p
Saltram House, Devon 35
Sanderson, K. W. 158, 160, 168–9
Sassoon, Philip 322–3
Savage, J., journeyman 495
Savery, Frank 253, 256, 259, 263, 266
Scafe, William, clock maker 208
Scotland 27, 59, 214, 271, 340
Seacroft Hall, Leeds *156*
Seaman, journeyman 521j
Sebille, John, silversmith 464
Seddon, cabinetmaker – see Morel & Seddon
Semple, J. and A., cabinet makers 442
Senex, Johan, cartographer 245
Serlby Hall, Notts 561
Shadbolt family 442
Shannon Ltd, cabinet makers 116
Shearer, Thomas, designer 338, 429–30
Sheppard, T., journeyman 96
Sheraton, Thomas, designer 31, 39, 44, 93, 284, 342, 348, 440, 442, 460, 572
Sherborne House, Glous 324
Sheriff Hutton Park 433
Shugborough Hall, Staffs 446
Simpson, A. W., cabinet maker 400
Simpson, H., joiner 5
Simpson, Roger, designer *15*
Sinclair–Wemyss, Major Robert 378
Skull, Fred 359
Slag, E., clock repairer 204
Slodtz brothers, *ébénistes* 570
Slomann, Vilhelm 648
Smedly Aston, W. 143
Smith, Benjamin, journeyman 40
Smith, Edmund, surgeon 117
Smith, George, designer 44, 341
Smith, Hamilton 370
Smith, The Hon H. A. 46
Smith, James, piano tuner 295
Smith, Lancelot Hugh 46
Soames, Mrs 69
Southampton, Earl of 231
Southport Museum 390
Southwark, London 144
Southwick Park, Hants 222
Sowerby Manor, Cumbria 293
Speer, George, cabinet maker 429
Speller, Mrs H. I. L. 125–6, 172, 400
Spenfield House, Leeds 590
Spofforth Hall, Yorks 564
Stair, Earl of 395
Stanmer House 336
Stastny, Dr Francisco *464*
Staveleys, carvers 306
Steele, Mrs, Valley Drive 272
Stevenson, journeyman 521b
Stewart, Dr B 566
Stewart family 397

Stewart, James, clock-maker 214
Stewart-Mackenzie family 59
Stiftung, Palladio 462
Stockhom, French Embassy 570
Stodart, Robertus, piano maker 454
Stolzenberg Patent File Co *415*
Stolzl, Gunta, fabric designer 574
Stoneleigh Abbey 483
Stourhead House 326
Stowe House 209
Street, G. E., architect 533
Strickland, Sir George 337, 347
Strickland, The Hon Mrs I. M. H. 269, 543
Strickland, The Rev. J. E. 270, 300, 337, 347, 444
Strickland, Sir William 270, 300, 444
Stroganoff, Comte 511
Stuart and Revett 512
Sudbourne Hall, Suffolk 557
Sunderland family 144
Sutcliffe-Smith, Sir Henry 449
Swann, Abraham, architect 37
Swindon-Barber, W., architect 205
Swinton Grange, Yorks 438, 465, 468–9, 472–4, 476–8, 480, 641
Swinton, Lord 562, 584, 592
Swinton Park, Yorks 562, 584, 592
Symonds, R. W. 58, 326
Syston Court, Glos 299

Talbert, B. J., designer 521p, 661
Tassie, James, seal cutter 186, 571
Tatham, C. H., designer 375
Tatton Park, Cheshire *376*, 501, 508
Taylor, Kathleen 37
Teale, J. R. & Son, cabinet maker 115
Tell, L., 574–5
Temple Newsam, ancestral furniture *12*, 7, 23–4, 36, 45, 93, 108–9, 115, 122–3, 167, 170, 182–4, 194, 200, 203, 215, 217, 245, 250–1, 279–80, 294, 301–2, 310, 312, 334, 341–3, 353, 379–80, 399, 402, 450, 483–6, 522–34, 540, 573, 576–7
Temple Newsam chapel furniture *408*, 522–34
Temple Newsam Gallery furniture *11–12*, 45, 310, 353, 450
Temple Newsam, development as a museum *11–14*
Tessier, Louis, tapestry designer 46
Testolini Freres, fabric mfrs 485–6
Tetley, F. E. 464
Thistlethwayte, Lt.-Col. E. 222
Thomas, T., clock repairer 209
Thomas, William 322–3
Thompson, journeyman 96
Thornley, John 283
Thorp, John, statuary *154*
Thorpe Underwood Hall, Yorks 454
Thorpe, William, architect/designer 661
Thwaites, clock maker 220
Thwaites House, Keighley 144
Times Veneer Co 408
Topino, Charles, *ébéniste* 229
Tortman family 299
Tower, E. W., architect 343
Towneley Hall, Lancs 233
Townend Hall, Cumbria 232
Townley Balfour family 571
Townley Hall, Ireland 571

Tree, Lady Anne 586
Tree, Ronald 446
Treworgey Manor, Cornwall 69
Trianon, Château de 564
Trondheim Museum 378
Tuileries, Palais des 209, 564
Tunbridge Wells 477, 480
Turner, Edgar, cabinet maker 423
Turton, Lawrence, cabinet maker 46
Turton Towers, Lancs 233
Tweed, Harold 460
Tyntesfield, Bristol 237

Upton Scudamore, Wilts 535
Uffington House, Lincs 156, 276, 336, 357, 587

Vandercruse, Roger, *ébéniste* 224
Vardy, John, designer 324, 561
Versailles, Palace of 561, 570
Vert, marquetry worker *394*, 521a–n
Victoria and Albert Museum 35, 57, 61, 69, 94, 102, 222, 223a, 225–7, 265, 297, 307, 310, 355, 355, 365, 375, 432, 446, 488, 545, 548, 574–5, 586, 605
Victoria, National Gallery 61
Victoria, Queen 350, 432
Vile and Cobb, cabinet makers 223a, 452
Vincenti et Cie, *horlogers* 567
Vine, W., joiner 343
Visscher, Nicholas 78
Voysey, C. F. A., architect/designer 125–6, 172, 400
Vries, P. Vredeman de, designer 377, 540–1
Vulliamy, Benjamin, clock maker 213

Waals, P. Van Der, cabinet maker 41
Waddilove, Stanley 421
Wainwright, Clive 521a
Walden, cabinet maker 398
Walker & Hughes, clock factors 219
Wall, A. C. J. 510
Wallace, Sir Richard 557
Walpole, Horace 426
Walpole, Sir Robert 57
Walsh, Mrs A. 436
Walston, Lord *388*, 515–21
Ward, Sir John 325
Ward, K. R. 35
Warde-Aldham, Colonel 30
Ware, Isaac 300
Waterford glass 475
Wateridge, John, designer 133
Watson, Sir Francis 564
Watts & Co, art furnishers, 484
Watts, William, cabinet makers 661
Waverley Abbey, Surrey 241
Weale, John, publisher 281
Webster, E. A., restorer 224
Webster, Henry, clock maker 202
Weddell, William 46
Wedderburn Castle, Scotland 378
Wedgwood, Josiah & Sons, potters 365, 377
Weeks' Museum, London 39
Weetwood Garth, Leeds 14, 32, 62, 89, 147, 153, 285, 428, 431, 458, 482
Wentbridge House, Yorks 51, 102–3, 413–14, 555
Wentworth family 3, 6, 15, 146, 231, 235

Wentworth Woodhouse, Yorks 209, 225, 446–7
Westminster, Duke of 419
Weston Hall, Yorks 220
Wetherell, piano maker (?) 293
Wheatleys, The, Yorks *463*
Whiteley Wood, J. 205
Whytock & Reid, cabinet makers 662
Wildsmith, John, marble merchant 452
William III 322–3
William and Mary 545
Williams, Robert 30
Wilson, Alderman Sir Charles *11*
Wilton, Earl of 322–3, 446–7
Wimbledon House 322–3
Wimborne House, London 592
Windsor Castle 96, 223a, 322–3, 376, 432
Winkworth, Stephen 239
Winterthur Museum 653
Wittkower, R. 357
Wombwell, Captain V. M. 275, 510
Wood, Frederick 122
Wood Hall, Herts 223, 416
Wood, J. Jnr, journeyman 418
Wood, John, Snr, organ builder 534
Wood, Peter, organ builder 209
Woodhouse, J., journeyman 495
Woodlands, Harrogate 288
Wordsworth's Cottage, Cumbria 47
Wordsworth & Maskell, organ builders 534
Wrangham, G. W. 239
Wraxall, Baron 237
Wright, journeyman 521p
Wright, B. & Co, clock factors 202a
Wright & Elwick, cabinet makers 37
Wright, J., journeyman 378
Wrigley, Thomas & Son, Bury 198
Wroxton Abbey, Oxon 325
Wyatt, James, architect/designer 571
Wycombe Technical College 662
Wykeham Abbey, Yorks 69
Wynn-Penny, G. W. 38

Yeoman's table 460

Zetland, Marquess of 46